Innocence destroyed

D0076288

How common is child sexual abuse? How do we recognize it? Who are the abusers? How can we treat victims and what can be done to prevent abusers from abusing again? *Innocence Destroyed* investigates these difficult questions. It shows that too many people still believe that such abuse is rare and cannot bring themselves to accept that perhaps as many as one-third of women and one-fifth of men experience as children some form of abusive sexual attention, ranging from exposure to intercourse.

Jean Renvoize has studied child abuse for many years and is the author of well-known studies in the field, including *Children in Danger*, *Web of Violence* and *Incest*. She has travelled extensively in Britain, the United States and Australia, meeting professionals in the field such as social workers, paediatricians, psychiatrists, police officers, lawyers, doctors and researchers, as well as victims and abusers themselves. Survivors of abuse talked openly to her about their years of pain and their efforts to overcome the effects of their abuse, and their 'first person' histories illustrate vividly the reality of child sexual abuse. In addition, *Innocence Destroyed* builds up a comprehensive picture of the most recent research and professional practice.

This book shows that, although considerable advances have been made in the treatment of victims, a great increase in resources needs to be devoted to improvements in the understanding and treatment of abusers, particularly of juvenile offenders, to prevent the continuation of this problem from one generation to the next.

Jean Renvoize was a Research Associate at Wolfson College, Oxford, during the writing of this book. Her previous books – *Children in Danger*, *Web of Violence* and *Incest* – have been widely acclaimed by professionals working with abused children.

'The tragedy of child sexual abuse is graphically portrayed in this excellent book by Jean Renvoize. The powerful and moving case histories bring home the devastating consequences for the victims of abuse and the challenge for the helping professions. Jean Renvoize's overview of research and practice in the UK, Australia and America, so clearly written and researched, provides a rich source of up-to-date information for all those who seek to help. This book is a testimony both to the suffering of many victims and the dedication and skill of those who strive to bring humane help to both victims and perpetrators.'

John Pickett OBE, *Director of Inspection Services,*
National Society for the Prevention of Cruelty to Children

'Ten years ago Jean Renvoize published a pioneering book on the subject of incest. Her new book, *Innocence Destroyed*, substantially complements her earlier work. Richly informative, it is clearly and unpretentiously written.'

Dr Henry Giarretto, *Director of the Giarretto Institute*
International Child Abuse Treatment and Training Programs,
California, USA

'As public awareness of child sexual abuse has greatly increased since the author's brilliant book *Incest: A Family Pattern* was published in 1982, so also has a spate of much-needed research developed in the English-speaking world. Jean Renvoize has provided a signal service in another brilliant book, *Innocence Destroyed*, by pulling together the findings of scores of books and journal articles on child sexual abuse researched on three continents – America, Australia and Europe, including Britain. This is a most readable and informative book suitable for the general public as well as busy professionals needing an accurate overview of a grave social problem. The case studies alone make the book enormously valuable, and in the rest of the volume the essential statistics and exploration of their meanings provide a unique summary. No one working with and for young children should miss its message. It is an enlightening and unparalleled contribution to the understanding of the continuing sexual dangers to which children are exposed.'

Dr Juliette Goldman and Professor Emeritus Ronald Goldman,
Griffith University, Queensland, Australia

Innocence destroyed

A study of child sexual abuse

Jean Renvoize

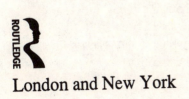

London and New York

First published in 1993
by Routledge
11 New Fetter Lane, London EC4P 4EE

Simultaneously published in the USA and Canada
by Routledge
29 West 35th Street, New York, NY 10001

Typeset in Times by
NWL Editorial Services, Langport, Somerset
Printed and bound in Great Britain by
TJ Press (Padstow) Ltd, Padstow, Cornwall

A Tavistock/Routledge Publication

British Library Cataloguing in Publication Data
A catalogue record for this book is available from the British
Library

Library of Congress Cataloging in Publication Data
Renvoize, Jean.
  Innocence destroyed: a study of child sexual abuse / by Jean
  Renvoize
  p.   cm.
  Includes bibliographical references and index.
  1. Sexually abused children.   2. Child molesting.   I. Title.
  [DNLM: 1. Child Abuse, Sexual.   WA 320 R424i]
  RJ507.S49R46   1993
  616.85'836 – dc20
  DNLM/DLC   92–49994
  for Library of Congress   CIP

ISBN 0–415–06283–7 (hbk)
      0–415–06284–5

RJ
507
S49
R46
1993

To Pat Thomas in gratitude

Contents

Acknowledgements

It is impossible to thank individually all those who have freely given me their time and shared with me their thoughts and the results of years of study and work on child sexual abuse. In particular I want to thank those survivors of abuse who have talked openly to me about their years of pain and their efforts to overcome the effects of their abuse. Their bravery and courage continues to astound me, and bears witness to the extraordinary resilience of human beings in the face of adversity. Barbara's, Peter's and Jane's stories vividly illustrate between them almost all the various aspects of child sexual abuse that I look at in this book, but obviously I cannot publish their real names – they know who they are and are already aware of my gratitude. To the many other victims I have spoken to but whose stories I have not written about separately I also express my debt.

For this new book I travelled to Australia where I met a host of professionals who helped me, but first I would like to thank those I originally met on previous research visits to America such as Hank Giarretto and his wife Anna Einfield, Lucy Berliner, Gene Abel and especially David Finkelhor, all of whose work is repeatedly referred to here. Ann Burgess and Barbara Bonner were also kind enough to share with me some of their many papers on child abuse.

In Australia I was given unlimited hospitality, but I would especially like to thank Don Edgar, Director of the Australian Institute of Family Studies, and his colleagues, through whose aid I was able to meet so many of the professionals spread across the vast continent of Australia. Ronald and Juliette Goldman, Elizabeth DeLacy, Helen Winefield and Jan Carter I want particularly to thank for generously taking me into their homes or arranging accommodation as well as allowing me to interview them and meet their colleagues, and I am also indebted to Sally Castel-McGregor, Margaret Dunlop, Liz Drew, Jennifer Wiltshire, David Jefferies, Alan Fugler, Delys Sargeant, Jennifer Harvey, Dorothy Scott, Chris Goddard,

David Wells, Juliet Harper, Tony Vinson, Jan Breckenridge, Kim Oates, Adrian Ford, Cath Laws, Gordon Charteris, Alexandra Bates, Brenda Kuhr, Joan Thompson and Susan Tattersall, with whom I spent many hours discussing their innovative and influential work.

In Britain many people concerned professionally with every aspect of child care work have given me considerable assistance and I would like in particular to thank – again in no special order – Lewis Anderson, Dave Compton, Danya Glaser, Ray Wyre, Trevor Price, Graham Davies, Tony Heal, Linda Jones, Judith Trowell, Chris Lyne, Suzanne Hood, Clare Huffington, Judith Kettle, Helen Armstrong, Tilman Furniss, Eileen Vizard, Jane Wynne, Helge Hanks, Chris Hobbs, Tony Morrison, John Pickett, Marcus Erooga, Paul Clark, Mai Bentley, Dorothy Jessop, Libby Reed, Bob Taylor, Clint Brannigan, Leslie Vasey, Janet Whincup and especially Anne Bannister of the NSPCC who has given me a great deal of her time and advice.

I carried out my research while I was a research associate at the Centre for Socio-Legal Studies, Wolfson College, Oxford, and I would like to acknowledge the support and advice of Mavis Maclean, John Eekelaar and Robert Dingwall (now at the University of Nottingham), whose expertise in this field has been invaluable. Finally, I owe a debt of gratitude to Pat Thomas and especially to the Nuffield Foundation whose travel grants have enabled me in the past to travel to America and recently to Australia, but in particular for the Foundation's generous project grant without which it would have been impossible for me to spend three years researching and writing this book.

Introduction

When, ten years ago, I published the first British book on incest (Renvoize 1982) many booksellers at first refused to stock a work on such an unpleasant subject. Now the situation has changed so dramatically there scarcely seems to be a day when some report or article is not published somewhere about child sexual abuse. Recently a newspaper article detailed a list of American celebrities, including Michael Jackson's sister LaToya Jackson, Roseanne Barr and Oprah Winfrey, who admitted having endured various 'bizarre' and 'grotesque' forms of sexual abuse as children. The article continued, 'Incorporating incest support groups [and] co-dependency workshops . . . the rapidly growing "recovery" movement is founded on a basic belief that America is one big, traumatised, dysfunctional family' (*Independent* 2 December 1991).

An exaggeration, certainly, but the suspected numbers of sexually abused children indicate a problem grossly exceeding anything imagined even a decade ago. David Finkelhor writes, 'In a society that encourages predatory male sexuality, that sexualises all intimacy, and that fosters male irresponsibility towards children, it will be hard to prevent sexual abuse' (Oates 1990). Abuse is not committed only by men, however; female abuse is now considered by many to be considerably more frequent than previously thought, but even more worrying is the growing concern about young offenders who may be so confirmed in their behaviour that by the age of 10 it can already be too late to redeem them.

Not all is gloom, however. The Cleveland affair meant the welcome end of any possibility of sweeping child sexual abuse under the carpet. A great deal has been written, internationally as well as in Britain, about what happened at Cleveland (UK) when in 1987 a rising awareness in the community of the prevalence of child sexual abuse resulted in paediatricians Drs Marietta Higgs and Geoffrey Wyatt, working at Middlesbrough General Hospital, reporting a far higher number of sexual abuse cases than would normally have been expected in the period. Contrary to media reports, most of these children had in fact been referred to the hospital by social services etc. for investigation into some kind of child abuse – physical, sexual or other. Because of the unprecedented rush of c.s.a. cases and a lack of clear government guidelines to follow, insufficient investigation was undertaken; when most of the suspected victims were removed from their parents there was such a public outcry that eventually a judicial enquiry was held by Lord Justice Butler-Sloss. The two doctors were suspended (Higgs was not reinstated and is now practising in another area) and virtually everyone connected with the affair was criticized at the inquiry. However, after the publication of the Butler-Sloss report many fellow paediatricians complained it had not made its central finding, that the majority of the doctors' diagnoses were justified, sufficiently clear (earlier, legal experts had put this figure at between 70 and 90 per cent), and called for the reinstatement of Higgs and Wyatt (*Independent* 20 February 1989). An unfortunate side-effect of all the publicity has been a reluctance on the part of many doctors to diagnose child sexual abuse.

Nevertheless, there is a far greater awareness than there used to be of the effects of sexual abuse on children and on adults with an abusive past who present with personality disorders, behaviour problems and depression, although the sad fact is that if every case of sexual abuse were discovered and reported the protective and treatment systems would be overwhelmed. The scarcity of reliable empirical data in general adds to the difficulties of developing programmes and policies, but in spite of this, the lack of funds and a shortage everywhere of properly trained staff even in the richest countries, there is a clear movement forward. In Britain the new Code of Practice for Joint Interviews to be issued by the Home Office, for example, insists that the video-taping of interviews is essential: too many offenders have escaped prosecution and treatment in the past for lack of evidence, and have consequently been free to re-offend.

At the moment even when an abuser *is* convicted the chances of his being given effective treatment during imprisonment, with proper therapy and follow-up care after release, are derisory. The legal system of pre-trial diversion, as followed in some American states where an offender is mandated to follow a lengthy period of treatment in exchange for a brief or no period at all in jail, does not yet exist in Britain or Australia, although first-time offenders admitting responsibility and already responding well to treatment may be received with some sympathy by the judge. The real problem is that the crime of child sexual abuse is so loathed that few people even want to think about it, let alone consider ways of treating the offenders. But incarcerating for a brief period those who are caught achieves nothing: sexual abuse will have been part of their lifestyle for many years, perhaps from their own childhood, and within a short time of leaving jail they will almost inevitably set about finding another victim. Where is the progress or the hope in allowing that to happen?

One very important innovation would be to provide more residential accommodation for newly arrested abusers, where initial treatment could begin, which would allow them instead of the children to leave home. This is particularly useful if the offender is still denying; an admission of guilt considerably smooths the victim's path, helping avoid the secondary trauma not only of their having to appear in court but also of possible scapegoating by the rest of the family. The future emotional, physical and mental health of the child must lie at the heart of the care and treatment of victims.

I have tried in the following pages to present the subject of child sexual abuse with sufficient 'live' case histories of victims and their families in their own words, along with interviews with professionals, to help newcomers grasp the essence of the effects of child sexual abuse, and to give those already working in the field an interesting overview of the findings of other professionals in other places.

Chapter 1

A victim's story

I had intended to start this book with two separate case histories – one male, one female – illustrating very different aspects of child sexual abuse, but having spent most of a whole day with Barbara (not her real name) I felt that to do justice to her remarkably honest account I would need to devote the entire chapter to her alone. It makes painful, difficult reading. What happened to her should happen to no child but, as she herself remarks, in comparison with what might have happened, and what does happen to millions of other children around the world, it could have been much worse.

A second reason for producing a chapter of such length devoted to one person's own words is that most of the subjects to be covered later in this book appear one way or another in Barbara's account. I hope that illustrations from a life which has been so painfully lived will bring vividness to material that might otherwise seem a little laboured. Professionals reading Barbara's story will find their heads nodding in recognition, but for those who are less familiar with this type of abuse it might be helpful to suggest in advance a few pointers to look out for.

To start with, multi-generational abuse is unfortunately common; Barbara's mother, Sarah, was sexually abused by her own grandfather, Barbara herself by a friend of the family and her 4-year-old daughter by her husband. A further common factor is that victims often love their abusers deeply, and the betrayal of such love can be one of the most painful aspects of the abuse: all three victims in this chapter have been grossly hurt by their love. We can also see from the physical and moral squalor of the early part of Barbara's upbringing how her mother's emotional problems were passed on from one generation to the next. Sarah's own upbringing, as described by her daughter Barbara who lived for a year with her grandmother (Sarah's mother), was over-strict and riddled with middle-class parsimony of the kind which suggests at the very least some inherent emotional difficulties in the family as a whole.

This question of what kind of problems cause which kind of abuse is finally unanswerable, as so many unrelated factors necessarily affect each individual case. We don't know much about Peter, Barbara's abuser: what was it in his upbringing as the illegitimate son of a prostitute that made him enjoy degradation and physical pain at the hands of his child victims? Barbara is no collusive mother, but how is it that this woman, who is intelligent, loving and sensitive, allowed her own child to continue to be abused, blocking out of her mind what was going on until she was finally able to acknowledge the truth openly to herself and thus act on that knowledge?

We are given, too, some insight into how abusers deliberately choose to move into families where there are young children, by marrying the mother or befriending the family. Often charming, friendly, loving and persuasive, they are rarely the monsters popularly imagined but instead are frequently people with their own deep problems whose own inner suffering gives them fatal access to the emotions of others. This muddying of the emotions involves everyone dealing with child sexual abuse, professional helpers as well as those personally involved. Barbara's doctor does not pick up the abuse of her daughter partly because the Cleveland affair has taught him and many like him to be ultra-cautious and partly because Barbara herself encourages him to believe that her husband, Ted, is innocent. Later, Ted also persuades his own therapist he is not guilty, causing Barbara distress and self-doubt.

Finally, and most important of all, this story is on its way to a 'happy ending'. As Barbara says, at last she is in control. She sees her path ahead, and she is standing at the beginning of it with her feet firmly on the ground, encouraged by a host of helpers whom she gratefully acknowledges. There is a great deal of pain in this story, and as it is fact and not fiction many ends are not yet tied up – but yes, there is hope, and for Barbara and her children the strong chance of success.

THE UNSPOKEN SECRET: THE STORY OF BARBARA

There've been three generations of it. My mum. Me. My daughter. Perhaps further back as well – who knows? But no, it wasn't all in the family, blood to blood, like you were talking about. Each case was different. But that's going to be the end of it, if I have my way. It stops here.

Sarah, the grandmother

My mum was abused by her grandfather, her father's father, when she was about 10 or 12. That was dealt with by her parents, my grandparents – they were very middle class, very strait-laced – they went to him and had it out with him. From then on her grandfather, the abuser, blamed her for all the argument and wouldn't talk to her any more, and that was very painful to her because she'd loved him dearly. He never touched her again. No, it had only happened on one occasion. Well, that's what was said, but the way my mum came across to me, I think he'd done things she wasn't sure of, like on occasions he asked her to hold his penis, and she did that, but when *he* did something to *her* she felt something was wrong, and she told.

I think it wasn't the abuse that affected her so badly, it was his behaviour towards her afterwards. All the time she was doing what he wanted she was his favourite girl, but then when she stopped and when she told on him he rejected her completely. She said she felt terrible, it was like she'd lost her grandad, and she really loved him. That, I think, is what affected her most.

I didn't know anything about all that until in therapy at the age of 26 I relived my own experiences: that was when my mum told me about herself. My childhood had been very unhappy – the house was filthy, my mum very . . . aggressive. She'd had her first child at 17 and had four by the time she was 23. She was pregnant when she married, and had had her first and was already carrying another when her husband – he was doing his National Service – was killed: he trod on a mortar bomb and died instantly. His best friend looked after my mum and they ended up married with two children.

It was all very quick; a year after the second child by her first husband was born she had her third child, and then I came two and a half years later. At 24 Dad had the responsibility for four children, only two of them his. As for Mum, I think she'd stopped growing when she fell pregnant at 17 with the first one. As I said, she'd come from a middle-class family, but my father's family is very stereotyped working class. They believe in going to school because it's the law, and then you leave as soon as you can and get a job: you know, *education – what do you want it for?!* My dad's not very educated, he can't even write a cheque out. I forced him by all sorts of nagging to go to night-school and he got as far as managing to write paragraphs, but when I was a kid all he knew was to drive a long-distance lorry and he did that very well. That's his world still, and nothing else around him really exists.

My mum's first husband, Jack, couldn't read or write at all. My mum had done O' levels at school, and then went straight into dancing school and for a while did what they called nude dancing at the Windmill – you know, with fans and things like you did in those days. She was lovely to look at, really slender with a 19-inch waist – she's huge now but there was nothing of her then. At 52 she's still a lovely woman. She was supposed to have been going abroad with a dancing group but the bloke at the Windmill wouldn't put her name forward because she refused to sleep with him. She was disgusted by that. She was already courting Jack, so when she got pregnant she married him and put all her energies into that. Her parents had wanted her to go away somewhere, have the baby and get it adopted, they didn't want her to marry Jack. He wasn't at all what they wanted for their daughter, though they liked him.

Why did she pick that kind of man? I get the feeling that she just didn't realize her own worth. She needed to feel . . . superior in a way to those around her, she couldn't bear ever to feel inferior. She'd helped her first husband, mothered him, taught him to read and write, and it was exactly the same with my father.

Our first years of childhood she'd been very clean, very fussy, the way she'd been brought up. But gradually it all changed. Things got worse and worse at home, really awful, the nurturing and the caring all stopped. When I was about 6 she had a breakdown and we were looked after by my dad and my mum's mum. When she came out of hospital the place was kept good for a while, cleaned and decorated and all that, but then slowly things got worse again. My mum would shout at us kids, 'Do you want to put me back into hospital? Do you want me to have another breakdown?'

One of the problems was I had an enlarged kidney, and what with that and the unhappy situation at home I wet the bed every night, and my sister who was two and a half years older than me did as well. Four kids and two of us wetting the bed every night, it was too much for her to handle. Instead of stripping beds and accepting it she'd get mad and hit me across my backside and my legs and across my vagina with this black plastic fish slice thing from the kitchen. She'd hit me all over and say, 'That's where the piss comes from and I'll beat it out of you.' My sister didn't wet the bed so much, so she got much less.

My mum took me for tests and they explained it was a medical reason why I was wetting – I'd never been dry from a baby. But she couldn't accept that and whenever I tried to stop her hitting me she'd just beat me worse. So I just took what she gave me, and so did my brothers and sister. One day when the second boy, Harry, was rude to her she punched him and he hit her back. She just grabbed at his eyes with her nails and gouged his eyes like this, and the skin was all split and she punched him again and he actually blacked out. I think he fainted out of fear. We were petrified of my mum, we were frightened because we never knew what would set her off. She'd be up in her bathroom doing her hair and she'd come thudding down the stairs – she was really big by this time – her hair all up on end because she was backcombing it, then she'd go for us all and scream and shout and jump up and down and throw things. She'd yell 'You want to put me back in the hospital!' and we used to sit there and feel it was our fault, all of us did.

When we were very young she'd been very loving, and she'd played with us, took us to parks. But by the time I was 8 I was doing her housework and her washing for her, to try and make up for being there, and I'd say sorry to her – for being her child. The house always looked like a tip, but when we were young we'd be out in the park. But as we got older the house got worse. It was disgusting, she never changed the beds. I was sleeping on a mattress that had been wet so many times it was just black, and the blanket would have dried by itself, never washed, and it all stank. You'd find plates under the settee with mould growing all over them, I couldn't ever take friends back.

But that wasn't the worst thing. Ordinary times when my dad got back from work they'd both go to the pub for the evening, but sometimes, especially when he'd been away on one of his three-week driving trips, she'd tell him to hit us all for all the bad things she'd say we'd done. So my dad would take his belt to the boys, buckle and all, and take out the cane for me and my sister. But he didn't hit us in temper; he was like my mum's puppet, really, and he'd do whatever she said. He'd threaten to use the belt on us girls but he never did – sometimes, but rarely, he did use the cane, but mostly it was just his hand or a slipper. It was very controlled, like going to a headmaster to be caned. I don't think he really understood what was going on, he doesn't seem to have a mind of his own.

Barbara, the mother

So life at home was abusive, yes, but not sexually – it was all physical abuse, emotional abuse. Michael, the oldest boy, and my sister would go to pubs very young, and I'd stay at home alone with Harry, or go to Peter's.

Peter? That's the man who abused me. And Harry, my brother.

I was saying earlier that when I was 7 or 8 I was beginning to do housework and look after the home, and so was my sister. Then my mum started to work full-time and we were left on our own, coming home to an empty house, sometimes sitting on the door-step, that sort of thing. No, we didn't have our own key, if she was in she was in, if she wasn't she wasn't. She'd started as a veg cook in school kitchens, and worked her way up to Catering Officer, so usually she was home an hour or so after school came out. It was a bit after this that my brother Harry met Peter, at the swimming baths I think it was. Harry was about 11 or 12 then, so I'd have been 8 or 9. Peter had a Bedford van, the old-fashioned type with a sink and all that, and he used to take Harry out fishing and he'd come home full of the wonderful times he'd had. Peter always had a lot of kids around him and he'd take them down to Catford dogs and let them smoke and give them beer, and let them do all the sort of things your parents said no to.

Harry introduced Peter to our family and my parents liked him. My sister never did, she was always very wary of him though she never knew why, but he was always really nice to me, really fatherly. He took me swimming and taught me how to swim, he taught me how to fish and to ice-skate. He was everything I wanted my dad to be. He drove too, for a delivery firm, but he was intelligent, he had things to say – not like my dad who just sat there quiet not saying anything. I looked up to him, he was fun to be with.

It feels like it was forever before he introduced me to any abuse, because I have this memory of a long time of getting to really love him and looking on him as my dad – and as my mum too, because by then I wasn't getting any nurturing from her at all. He was everything to me. When my mum and dad went to the pub they didn't have to bother to find babysitters for me if the others were out, that responsibility was lifted off them by Peter. They liked him, never suspected anything.

Not that there was anything to suspect, for a long time. He used to give us a fag and whisper, 'Don't tell your mum', and he'd give us alcohol and say the same; when we stayed over at his flat watching horror films on telly he'd always buy some big sausages and make us sandwiches for a midnight feast. That was great. Yeah, I was allowed to stay overnight because I was there with my brother, at that time I never stayed there without him. I suppose they assumed if Harry was there everything must be all right.

The first time anything happened was when Peter walked into the main room with just his Y-fronts on. I'm not sure if he was exposing himself as well, I think he might have, because later I told my sister I saw Peter's willy, giggle, giggle. She asked Harry about it, but he just said, 'Oh,

Peter's not used to Barbara being there and he probably didn't think about it.' But afterwards Harry grabbed me, put his fist up against me and threatened me that we'd get taken away from Mum and that Pete would go to prison if I told anyone else. I was petrified after that. He must have told Peter I'd tried to tell on him, because when I saw Peter next I felt as though I'd disappointed him terribly and let him down – all I wanted to do was to make that up to him because he'd given me all those wonderful things and been such a nice friend to us.

My brother Harry had a close friend his own age, another Harry – little Harry we used to call him because he was smaller than my brother – he and I had been sort of childhood sweethearts for ages. He'd be there at Peter's as well, and very soon after that incident I found out they all had this regular thing, where Peter would sit in a chair and the two Harrys would get boot polish, black or brown, and polish his penis, all round his testicles and all round his backside, all over. I remember Peter had this big stomach, he was a stout man going bald – he was 47 at the time – with sort of wiry, curly hair, big blue eyes, and he wore a massive brown belt so that the top of his trousers came above it, like this, and he had an overhanging chest sort of over this tight round belly. Now, when I think of him sitting there, he reminds me of a Buddha, that was his sort of shape; but he wasn't fat, if that makes sense.

Then the boys would get a shaving brush and soap, and soap him all around all over where the polish was, and then, with a cut-throat razor which my brother would sharpen on a strap first, they'd shave all his hair off where the polish was, shave and clean it all completely away, rinse it all off. That would really excite Peter and he'd be all erect and excited. The worst thing was that Peter had false teeth, they were all perfectly white and straight and he had a very, very thin top lip. He suffered from angina, so he breathed very heavily anyway, and when this was happening he'd be breathing through his mouth, then he'd close his mouth and try to breathe through his nose and it would make his nostrils really inflated, then he'd breathe through his mouth again. It all sounded such a strain I was frightened he'd have a heart attack.

When he was all clean again he'd get into his bed with one of the boys and I was never included in that, so I never saw what happened. I suppose it was like a foreplay for him. No, the bed was in the same room, a big old-fashioned room with a double bed right at the back behind the chair. I'd look over, but they'd be under the blankets and I never knew what they were doing. I do now, of course, but I didn't then.

Peter used to ask me if I wanted to put the polish on as well, and to begin with I wouldn't because I was frightened of cutting him with that razor, but I wanted to be part of it, I didn't want to be left out – he was always so pleased with the boys and he'd smile at them as though it was very special. So he got one of those razors you unscrew from the bottom and I used that instead.

You see, I was really frightened of hurting him, I loved him. I knew what we were doing was wrong because it had to be kept secret, but it was something he liked us to do for him and it would always be after he'd done something for us or taken us out for a treat. Sometimes he'd ask me to touch him and play with his penis, and I remember he'd be soft when that started, and very heavy. In therapy I get flashbacks that I took him in my mouth, and then I think – but did I do that, or was it knowledge from adult sex? All I know is that in my first adult experience when I was nearly 18 and very much in love with my first proper boyfriend I remember not being able to bring myself to do it, though I worshipped him and he wanted it.

No, I'm pretty sure Peter never ejaculated in my presence, I've tried and tried, but I can't remember that happening.

Another thing, Peter was into pain, his own pain. He used to lie face-down on the bed and get us to tie him to the bed-posts by his wrists and his feet, and he'd say to me, 'Don't hit me when I'm looking, hit me when I'm relaxed, and as hard as you can.' Then I'd have to hit him with his belt. It had heavy studs in it, and a buckle on the end. I remember liking hitting him with it, wanting to hurt him, and feeling sick at the same time. Sometimes in therapy I think I remember there being blood, but that might have been what I was frightened of seeing.

He had a great big battery as well, connected with wires to this transformer type thing, and the wires off that were connected to two metal prongs. To begin with he'd put the prongs onto his penis and then he'd ask me to stand with my back to him so he couldn't see me connecting the wires, to give him more of a shock when it happened. One time I was talking to my brother and holding the wires and I forgot what I was doing. When I looked round at Peter he was writhing on the bed, his knees all drawn up, looking at me with his face like this, but not saying a word! I laugh now and wish I'd kept the wires on him and exploded him – burn! you bastard, I think – but at the time it was awful that I'd inflicted that sort of pain on him, it was awful. I see the funny side of it now, but as that child I felt so disturbed inside myself that I'd not been concentrating and caused him so much pain.

What I find difficult to talk about even now is the things that he asked me if he could do to me. He used to touch me and caress me and kiss me and hold me, which I didn't like. Even thinking about it now makes me want to . . . writhe. The thought of his touching me, his breathing; he was always sweaty and hot and heavy. He used to lick me all round my vagina and inside. It makes me think when people talk about evidence, there wouldn't have been an ounce of evidence, he was very careful. That was the thing I hated, I hated his tongue in me, it was a real intrusion on me. I'd be there on my hands and knees over him the way he wanted and while he was doing that Harry, little Harry, not my brother, would be sitting on the bed kissing me.

Before Peter was on the scene Harry and I used to kiss and cuddle anyway, we were only kids but we were 'in love', and I always liked what we did, but this was different. Peter . . . Peter tried to make us have intercourse, and because he was fed up with me wetting in his house he used to put nappies on me and put Harry and me in bed together and watch while Harry would try to have intercourse with me, though he never managed it, of course. He was only about 11 then. Afterwards Peter'd get into bed with Harry, without me, and they'd shuffle around under the blankets for a while. I remember too Peter lying behind me in bed and putting his penis between my thighs, but that was all.

No, I don't feel guilty now at what I let him do, *now* I feel angry that I was used, but I've only got that far through therapy. I feel anger now, and I feel the unfairness of it, and how I was let down by everybody; whereas when I first went to Great Ormond Street for my little girl over *her* abuse with my husband and they asked me how I felt about my own abuse I said I felt grateful to my abuser because as an adult I was aware of the physical damage he could have caused and the things he could have done to me.

When I was nearly 10 my mum had had another breakdown. That one lasted three months and then for nine months she was an out-patient. While that was going on I went to stay with my grandmother for over a year. I remember falling asleep thinking my mum was going to die and I'd lose her. We spoke to her once on the phone, but after that Gran wouldn't let us talk to her because she was so ill and saying horrible things and Gran didn't want us to be hurt. So I thought she'd died and Gran wasn't telling us. I think I was wetting the bed worse because of all that.

The house was very disciplined: you weren't allowed to run up and down the stairs because you'd wear the carpet out, you had to wash the bath out so you didn't leave a ring round it, you had to use a small amount of toothpaste because you mustn't waste things, you had to have clean clothes on every day. I couldn't wait to get back and do as I pleased, go to school when I wanted, stay at home when I wanted. There was such a lot there I didn't like. Gran wouldn't let me stay at Peter's, she disliked him and didn't think a little girl should be on her own with a man, anyway. So I hardly ever saw him, and I hated my Gran for that, I really hated her.

When finally I did go back to Peter's after I was back home again he'd moved to a new job as caretaker of this estate, and he had a bigger flat on the ground floor now, two bedrooms, so I had a bedroom of my own whenever I stayed.

I was surprised to find that Harry, little Harry, was living there and sleeping with Peter in his bedroom in the same old double bed. Harry's mum had let him leave home and move in with Peter – as a father/son relationship, so his mum thought, or pretended to, at least. His own dad wasn't at home. I remember trying to get to sleep and I couldn't, because I could hear Harry crying. It was a sort of 'no'-crying, 'don't'-crying, if you know what I mean. I could hear Peter's voice angry, and then persuading.

This was one of the things I asked my brother about after I'd had some therapy last year and we spoke about the unspoken secret that had been between us for those eighteen or nineteen years. My brother confirmed all the things I said and he also shared with me things that I didn't remember. It was very strange talking about it after all those years with someone who'd been there and done the same things. Peter had never tried to penetrate me in any way, and I asked my brother if Peter had ever tried to penetrate him. He didn't say anything for a few seconds, and then he said, 'Well, he tried to, but I didn't let him. I fought him off.'

So that confirmed to me what had been going on with Peter and the other Harry. I remember lying there trying to sleep, thinking why is he crying? It was nice to be held by Peter sometimes, and he had this clean well-kept home and Harry was looked after really well by Peter, so what did he have to cry for? He ought to try living with me and the shit I had to put up with!

The thing is, Peter never once physically forced me to let him lick me, never once forced me to hold him, but if we wouldn't do what he wanted he'd be angry and wouldn't give us a cigarette or wouldn't buy us sweets or take us anywhere; or if he did he wouldn't talk to us properly, it would be yes, no, type of thing. But no, he never hit us, he did it purely by power of manipulation.

We'd see Peter every weekend and school holidays, and he used to take us away on holiday. We'd drive around, and I'd sleep in the Bedford and the boys in the tent. My grandparents would lend us their chalet down in the Isle of Sheppey, and sometimes if we were going down there on holiday Pete would come as well and then my parents could get on with whatever they wanted to do, while I'd opt to sleep in the Bedford rather than the chalet.

Until I was 26 the only thing I could remember about what had happened was the fact that I had been abused. I remembered Peter, of course; I could picture the first place I had been abused in, could smell that room and see the furniture in it – the double bed, the heavy blankets – then I'd shut my mind to the memory. That was all there was for me, nothing else, all other memories had completely gone. I remembered too that at the age of 11 I was told that Peter had died. He'd had a heart attack and was found down by the bins with all the rubbish.

That pleases me now, but it didn't at the time. It broke my heart, I couldn't believe that he'd left me. I loved him so much, he was always there for me. He really cared; he used to say, 'You shouldn't let your mum hit you.' But I suppose he thought he'd better not risk saying anything, he'd come in for a cuppa and a fag and then he'd take us off.

When he died my mum wouldn't let me go to the funeral, I never forgave her for that. She said I was too young and in too much of a state; you only had to mention his name and I'd be in floods of tears. It took me a long time to get over it, there was nothing anyone could do.

And that was it. Well, almost. That time I spoke to my brother, when I was having therapy, he said to me, 'It does screw you up, what Peter did to us.' I asked him what he meant and he told me that after Peter died he used to ask me to touch his penis, and I think I did, though I don't remember anything about it. I honour him for telling me that, because I'd forgotten all about it. He didn't have to tell me. No, Peter had never encouraged my brother and me to do things together when he was alive – not to each other, that is, only to him.

There are several other interestings things I've discovered recently that perhaps explain something about Peter. One was that it turns out his mother was a prostitute, an awful woman by all accounts, and he was one of three illegitimate sons, all the result of soldiers. Another was that he'd told my mum his wife and son were killed in a car accident, but he'd told me he had a wife and two daughters and that he was divorced and his wife wouldn't let him see the two kids.

When I was 14 my mum remarried – she'd told my dad to go and we didn't mind really, he hadn't had much to do with us except hitting us when she told him to – but before she married again she lived life to the full, had lots of men in and out. She didn't have any morals or anything.

We had lodgers living there, street boys that were taking drugs who'd been kicked out of where they were living, so there were thirteen people living in a four-bedroom house and only five of those were family. My bedroom was next to my mum's and some of the plaster was broken down so I could see her through holes in the wall having it off with different men. Some of the boys were the same sort of age as my older brother – but she was still only 34 herself at that time.

By then I was keeping my bedroom clean, I kept it spotless, and my brother who'd been screwing around since he was 14 would take his girlfriends into my bed because it was the cleanest room, and when I got into bed at night I'd smell them and find used Durex. I used to go mad, but my mum would say, 'Don't be silly.' I remember really wanting my mum to be all organized – to have underwear in my drawer, and clothes to wear, instead of her having her own wardrobe full of all the clothes she'd buy for herself. I remember my sister washing out her one pair of knickers every day.

After I was about 14 instead of wanting to explore and being curious about sex I felt it was dirty, and I was totally unable to cope with any sex-talk. When I was 9 or 10 I'd had a couple of boyfriends, little Harry and another one, and they'd fight to be the one to take me out. I used to let them look at me and so on, and I suppose they liked that, because none of the other girls would let them do it. Another thing, as a child I recognized the opportunities that were put to me by other adults and took those opportunities up. Like a bloke that was lodging at our house used to give me a piggy-back and while I was on his back he used to try and put his thumb up my backside, and I didn't used to keep away from it, I'd spend more time with him. I just followed being like that until I got to a certain age, I suppose. Then I turned all tomboyish, dressing as a boy, wearing shorts and ties, short hair.

When girls at school talked of living with their boyfriends and the things the boys did to them, I was disgusted. They were very modern, had dressy clothes, big busts, plucked their eyebrows, and I just kept away from them. I was a real tomboy at that time. With a girlfriend I used to go upstairs and chuck raw eggs out of the window at people, and there was a boy up the street I hated, a real cretin he was, and we used to go down the road, smash a window then knock on the door and pretend we'd seen him doing it.

And there was the youth club. I was in the football team, and one of the girls said to me when I was about 14, 'Barbara, if you're going to run round like that, don't you think you should wear a bra now?' Up to then I didn't realize I had tits. My body just didn't belong to me. I don't think

I wanted my body to become mature, I wanted to be a kid, and that's how my family all treated me, as though I was still a baby.

Things changed when my mum married my step-dad. He began to decorate the house and they bought it off my gran. They started putting walls back and a roof on and building in a proper bathroom and that. And all of a sudden my mum became this parent that you had to be in at a certain time, and you had to go to school. From being almost *her* parent, doing her housework, giving her money I'd earned from babysitting and working in local shops, I had to become this good child.

My step-dad, John, works in oil-rigs abroad, so he's away for three months then home for four weeks. I loved him. I was so close to him. . . . There's something that's quite difficult, really, which I'd forgotten. I only got in touch with it about three months ago in therapy. Whenever he came home I followed him around everywhere, he brought me little presents and I thought he was really wonderful, because with him in the family it meant our lives had improved. What happened was that . . . only on one occasion, it must have been not long after he moved in . . . I went into their bedroom and he was busy putting things away, and I sat down on the bed and then lay down on it. I remembered lying there playing with the elastic on my knickers, thinking I shouldn't touch myself in front of him, but I did it, masturbating myself really. He looked, and frowned, not at me but sort of at himself, and walked out the room.

When the memory of that came back to me three months ago I found it so difficult to go round to my mum's. I kept thinking, oh, *no*, if he remembers that! I understand now what it was I was doing, and why, but it's so embarrassing, even to remember.

Yes, after I'd had therapy for a while I told all the family, and they all shouted, 'Who was it, who was it!' When I told them my mum went mad. She went, *'The bastard, I didn't know! Oh! and I was letting you stay there, Oh! I went up the pub while he was there!'* And it turned out she'd been warned by the police to keep us away from Peter because he was seen letting kids smoke and drink alcohol, and they'd told her he wasn't a good influence on us, but she hadn't taken any notice. To be fair, if she'd asked us if he let us smoke and drink alcohol we wouldn't have said yes, would we?

It's thanks to Jane, my therapist, I've been enabled to reach down to all these memories and get in touch with myself. When I first started talking to her I couldn't even bring myself to say the word 'willy'. I kept saying, 'his It' and 'the thing', and she'd say, 'his penis, his willy, his prick', and she allowed me. . . . I've been with her for a year, she's a clinical psychologist at the local hospital, and she's been wonderful.

When I was just 16 I went out on a foursome with a schoolfriend and met Mike. I thought he was far too good-looking and grown-up to fancy me, but he did. I went out with him for a year and in that time he only ever kissed me. He was very gentle, very kind and he really gave me confidence because he thought I was wonderful. There was one time I was staying over at his house and because I'd said I'd stay he really thought I was going to let him have sex with me. He was lying on top of me on the bed, and I could feel he was hard – we were both fully clothed – and I pushed him off. He couldn't believe it, but I just felt it was wrong, I was repulsed by the thought of it. I just felt sex was for marriage and sex before marriage was all wrong.

We got engaged but I broke it off in the end. Later he married someone else and had a baby and found out he was gay; I wasn't surprised, I'd wondered if he was. Then for a while I had a crush on a boy I'd known from childhood but I had an experience where there was some foreplay involved and it really upset me, I just ran out of the house.

Then I met Geoffrey and he was my first full sexual experience. I was 18. It was awful at first, very painful. Neither of us really knew what we were doing – I just bled a lot and I felt so unclean, though I really loved him. After the first time it was all right for him, so I just let him bang away. I knew what I needed but there was no way I could have told him what turned me on. I just went on feeling hurt inside myself that I wasn't enjoying it.

It was very difficult to break that relationship, but then there was another bloke I had an affair with and he awakened my sexuality for the first time. I wasn't in love with him, but he just seemed to know what to do and I really enjoyed it for the first time. When that broke off I met Bill. That was a real on and off affair. He'd been married, they split up and we'd got together, but after a while his wife wanted him back because of the children, and I encouraged him to go back. It seemed the right thing to do, though I didn't want to let him go.

That was when I met Steve. After a while I found myself pregnant by him, but life with Steve was very difficult – he was very secretive and he'd come and go without any explanation, and eventually we split up, even though I was going to have his baby.

As it happened Bill left his wife not long after the baby was born, and as I was alone I let him come back into my life again. At that time I was in the throes of getting a council maisonette for myself and the baby, and it seemed a good idea to share with Bill. But it didn't last long, his wife decided after all she wanted him back again, and so he went back. Yes, that was very painful, because we had a lot going for us.

But after a bit – the story unfolds! – Bill was accused of abusing his oldest child, his little girl of 3, who said Daddy had done things to her. There wasn't enough evidence for court, but the social workers were sure he'd done it and so Bill and his wife separated and got a divorce. When this was all happening he wanted to come back to me, but I wouldn't have it. No, my own abuse was still very unclear in my head, but I just knew I didn't want to be with him any more.

After that Steve came back on the scene, and the sexual relationship between us was so powerful I'd never experienced any sexual delight like that before in my life. But he was still being very secretive, and I felt there was a lot about him I didn't know. I began to realize that if we had a lot of sex, good as it was, he'd disappear for a while, so I tried for several months not having any sex with him at all. At that point he was helping me move into my new flat – he was very loving and said we should buy the flat and stay together. We had all these plans and of course we began a sexual relationship again. It was as good as it had always been and I fell for the second child. But then he started coming and going again, always without any explanation or excuse. Now I was pregnant I felt I had a right to find out the truth, so I went up to St. Katherine's House to check out the records and it was as I suspected, he was married. He had a wife and two daughters. That hurt me so much.

I suppose I thought that that was all I was worth, all I deserved, but I decided not to put up with the way he'd been behaving any longer. So I confronted him with what I'd found out and he was furious with me for checking up on him. But as far as I was concerned I was going to have two children by him, and that was a very serious matter. So I gave him an ultimatum, that he came and lived with me properly – I didn't insist he married me but I couldn't stand the coming and going any more – and he chose to leave. And that was it, really, that was the end of Steve.

Towards the end of that second pregnancy I was really lonely and I filled in a form for a dating agency called something like 'Mamas 'n' Papas'. I wasn't looking for a husband, I had a daughter nearly 3 and was about to have another baby, and I was looking for a friend, really. I'd just come out of hospital with the new baby when the phone rang and it was Ted. I wouldn't actually meet him for a while because I said I hadn't got anything to talk about except nappies and babies and breast-feeding, but he just laughed and said, 'I love it all, I've got nieces and nephews and I know just what you're on about.' He was so in touch with women's needs, he was just really there for me from the beginning. No, he'd not been married before, but he'd lived with women who had children. It's true, he'd met a couple of them through dating agencies. Yes, they all had daughters, all of them.

He wasn't good-looking, he wasn't my Mr Universe, but there was something about him, it was as though I'd known him forever. I felt so comfortable with him and he was so gentle and so lovely. He was a good friend, he was my mate: he took me around to meet everyone he knew after I told him how secretive Steve had been, and he really supported me. No, I didn't tell him about my abuse, it wasn't on my mind. Five months later we bought a house together and within a couple more we were married. We hadn't had sex together until we moved into the house, but we'd got engaged. It was me, I was still a bit sore from the baby and I wanted to wait. A year and a bit after we were married I gave birth to Susan.

But there was a problem. Once we'd started having intercourse I found Ted was very sexually active. It was morning, noon and night, he couldn't get enough of it. Even when I'd made love with him that night he'd still masturbate, he seemed to need it all the time. And that began to make for difficulties: because I didn't want to have sex with him twice a day seven days a week, he saw that as a rejection of him. He never saw that all the things I was doing for him, like cooking his favourite meals, running his business for him, were my expression of love – he was convinced that my not wanting him sexually all the time was a rejection of him.

At night after we'd made love and I was ready for sleep he'd often want it again and he'd masturbate beside me in bed. Sometimes I'd be woken up at six o'clock in the morning by the bed shaking, other times I'd wake up with a crusty back where he'd masturbated and come over my back in the night. I used to feel so humiliated, I didn't like it at all. I didn't think it was right.

I discovered he was buying stacks of magazines; a friend who was broke was doing some cleaning for me and she found them. She laughed at first until she found how many they were. We threw them out but my brother Harry happened to turn up the same afternoon; he picked them up and was flicking through them when he found pages that were all stuck together where Ted had masturbated over them. That really was embarrassing, in front of my friend and my brother. He just stood there, with a funny look on his face. 'Cor,' he went, 'I grew out of that at 18!' and he threw the mag down. He was really angry, he didn't like that at all.

No, they were all adult magazines, there were no children in them – there was nothing to indicate anything more than the fact he couldn't express himself except sexually. Another thing was he used to tease the eldest girl a lot and we rowed about that. She's a very placid girl, but he kept on aggravating her and winding her up, and after half an hour she turned and slapped him round the face. He whacked her so hard on the backside she couldn't catch her breath. I went mad and I warned him never to dare to tease the children and smack them again like that. From that moment on he stopped teasing her and being mean to her in front of me. And because of that I presumed he'd stopped. But he'd begun to do it behind my back. She'd say 'I don't want to stay with Daddy, because he says horrible things.' I'd say, 'He's only playing', and I really believed it.

Things snowballed from there. I was nursing Ted's widowed mum who'd had a brain haemorrhage, and we had Susan, and on top of that the business started going down the pan; he owed £26,000, so I ended up signing my half of the house over to the bank so they wouldn't foreclose on us. At that point I took over organizing the admin. side of the business from home while he did the labour. But he was advised to declare himself bankrupt and in the end we had to sell the house anyway.

Luckily we were able to move back into my old council flat. But it was a real step down back into the past – I lost all the money I'd gained because of inflation on the house, as well as the carpets, the furnishings, everything. Ted, who in addition to all the rest was a gambler, went on losing money, and I decided the only way for us to cope was for him to agree to do things my way, and that I'd look after the money side entirely. He agreed happily, he was glad to shed the responsibility, and basically he went on doing the same work, but under a new name for the company as he'd been bankrupted.

Katie, the daughter

But, just before all that was finalized at the end of 1988, Ted was accused by our neighbour across the passageway in the flats of abusing Katie, my second child. This neighbour loved the kids and me, but she couldn't stand Ted and he claimed it was just her spite.

Now Katie, who was 3 by then, was born with a problem with her kidneys called renal reflux which she'd probably inherited from me, though they didn't call it that: it means she can't help wetting herself, but that's easy enough to cope with. Because of it she's been under a paediatrician since she was 9 months old and she's examined vaginally and anally regularly to keep a check on her.

What happened the first time was that Ted had to go to Exeter on business, and he'd taken her with him. It was 10 o'clock at night when they got back. I went to get them something to drink and Katie sat down in her wet trousers in front of the telly. Then she turned to me with her face all puckered up and said, 'Mummy, my bum's sore, it hurts.' Ted said it probably did, she'd been wet all day. So I took her into the bathroom to clean her up and as I bent over her to take off her trousers – she was wearing her pink cords and they were so wet they were really difficult to pull off – I could smell the smell of sperm. I just carried on with what I was doing, and the smell was definitely there. I undressed her, washed her, creamed her bottom, put a nappy on her, put her nightclothes on her, and took her to say 'night-night' to Daddy. Then I put her to bed, tucked her up, kissed her and walked out of the room and closed the door. I totally refused to acknowledge that I'd smelt sperm on her. I didn't want to know.

I love her, we are very close. She was often very ill as a baby because of the debilitating effect of the renal problem, and I used to look at her tiny face . . . I love her so much. But when this happened, I just didn't want to know. I put it out of my mind. In therapy I got in touch with my thoughts at the time and I was able to remember thinking – well, if he did it, I wouldn't let him do it again, and anyway, it happened to me, and I'm all right. Yes, that was a calculated decision; along with everything else I decided it was best tucked away. I didn't even talk to Ted about it.

It was really weird, I wasn't even aware why I was so worried about leaving him with the children. I wasn't aware of what was frightening me so much, I just felt uncomfortable about leaving him with the children. The Exeter trip was at the end of September, then the next weekend we went to Paris with our neighbours. The business was picking up and it was a great weekend. I'd put the whole incident of the sperm smell out of my mind. There was some horse racing (I'd arranged it as a surprise for Ted) and I gave him £100 to blow on it; he loved it, he was really happy. But in spite of all the romance of Paris we only made love once over the weekend. By coincidence he'd been using acid on his fingers in work and it was still under his nails and it had been making me feel very sore when he touched me – it was as though I had cystitis. (I didn't find out the cause of it until we split up and I'd been to see to a gynaecologist.)

A couple of days later after getting back from Paris the neighbour rang me up and very nervously asked if Ted was there and if he had a gun. Then she said that Katie had told her Ted had hurt her bottom. She'd asked how, and Katie said, 'He put a gun in my bottom and put glue all over me.' I said he had a glue gun in the car for work – and this is hard to believe, but I didn't connect the smell of sperm that night a couple of weeks ago and what Katie was saying to my neighbour. But I did ring Childline, and the lady there gave me what they now say was the wrong advice, to confront Ted with it.

So when he came in from work I confronted him. He started shouting and swearing, that the neighbour had never effing liked him, she was deliberately causing effing trouble and so on, and he wanted the doctor to examine Katie right there and then. I was petrified, because Ted never shouts, but anyway I got hold of our doctor – I was in floods of tears – and he came round straight away. He didn't examine Katie, he just shone a torch on her bottom and said 'She's got a bit of a rash, but then with her problem she's bound to have a rash.' I kept saying to the doctor, 'I don't know if Ted's done anything to her, but I can't believe he has.' I kept repeating that, and I really meant it at the time. I wasn't in touch with the smell I'd smelt only a couple of weeks before.

Because Katie was all over Ted the doctor was saying, 'She's not acting like a child who's been abused; she's not withdrawn, she's not silent.' He said, 'Your home's lovely and clean, your children are well-kept, you've always come across to me as being a very adequate parent.' And he kept quoting the Cleveland case to me, 'It's not like that here, we don't just whip your children away,' he said. He went over the way to talk to the neighbour but she couldn't convince him.

So the doctor left it where it was and there was no investigation at that time. The police were involved at one point because my neighbour came in and punched Ted in the face, and Ted said, 'You're not hitting me in my own house!' and called the police in. It came out what the argument was about, then the Child Protection people came round and investigated us all, and they spoke to the same doctor who assured them everything was fine. No, they didn't get their own forensic surgeon in.

In December when she had her three-monthly appointment with her paediatrician for the renal trouble I told the doctor Katie had been needing to pass water more urgently than before, that was all I said, and she did an in-depth examination and noted down what Katie's structure was. Then she referred me to another doctor at Guy's for the next appointment to make sure there weren't any other problems from her kidneys that she hadn't picked up, and Katie had to go to the hospital for a special renal scan. No, I hadn't said anything about the trouble with Ted.

By March I was suffering from a terrible depression, I was feeling I couldn't live with myself any more. I wasn't in touch with why, I couldn't eat anything, and I lost a stone in about four weeks. I just sat in bed and cried all the time. Ted kept saying if you don't want me any more I'll leave, and I knew I didn't want him in the house but at the same time I wanted him to take care of me like I'd taken care of him when he'd had his problems. I'd been going to night-school to study bookkeeping through all this, and when I walked out of the front door I'd creep round to the back and listen to him putting them to bed before I went off. I didn't know why I was doing it, but something made me.

The doctor gave me some anti-depressant pills and temporarily I became better. I decided to give our marriage one last go, put everything behind me and make it all work. Looking back I know I felt I could protect her and that he wouldn't do it again, anyway. For those six months I responded to every sexual need Ted had whenever he had it, and I remember thinking he won't want to abuse Katie if I respond to him. Whatever, in no matter what way, he needed it I gave it to him, and I hated every minute of it.

We went on holiday in July, Katie hadn't said a word, and when we got back we had an offer from the council for a cottage in the country. We moved, and it was marvellous, everything we wanted, a chance to begin all over again. But then in September Katie came in after Ted had taken her to the toilet and wiped her bottom, and said Daddy had put a finger up her bum. I froze on the spot. He was standing behind her, and I just looked at him and he denied it. All he said was that I'd better wipe her bottom in future because he was too rough. I left it at that, and no one said any more, but after that I stopped responding to his every whim.

Then a month later he took the children out to his Nan's, for a walk in the woods, and when Katie came back home she said in front of him he'd hurt her bum with sticks. He explained that she'd done a poo and he'd wiped her bottom with leaves. I wanted to believe him – I wasn't happy, but it wasn't enough for me to be sure. As I looked at him he just went mad. It ended with him going upstairs, and I could hear him in floods of tears up there, then he came downstairs with his suitcase and said he was leaving.

We had a long discussion, and he said why didn't I have her checked by a paediatrician, and I said, 'No, they'll find something and you'll have to leave.' Yes, I actually said that. He said they wouldn't find anything that hadn't already been done by the doctors when they were sticking tubes up her. I was shocked at that – he hadn't realized that when they examine her it was her urethra they put tubes up, not her vagina. I explained about it, and then he said there was a judge who'd told a wife it was her fault her husband abused the children because she'd kept him short of sex . . . ! He destroyed something in me by saying that. By then I'd brought sex down to two or three times a week, I just tried to keep him satisfied. But it was never enough for him, when I got out of bed at six in the morning there'd be a cold wet patch where he'd masturbated. And he was getting up at night saying the kids had been crying, but I never heard them crying.

That blew over, but from the middle of October to the end of 1989 I couldn't do anything with Katie, she was being really naughty. On the 12 November he'd been out all day with the children, and when they came in Katie was a right git. I'd been working all day on the business, and I asked Ted to put them to bed so I could get on. He took Katie up first because she was being naughty, gave her a wash, then I heard Katie cry out – it was a weird cry, not the sort of cry she'd give when she was being smacked or told off, it was almost a growl like she was angry. I couldn't concentrate with Katie crying, so I went upstairs to tell her off and she was sort of punching him and saying, 'I'm going to tell Mummy of you.'

Now over the weeks I'd been smacking Katie, I'd put her on a sweet ban, not let her play out, so many things I'd stopped her from having because she was being so naughty. So now I just got her back into bed and asked her what the matter was – why was she being so naughty? what was wrong? She looked at me with this funny look and told me to get into bed with her. I got into bed and cuddled her up close for a bit. Then she turned round facing me and said, 'When Daddy put my nappy on he put his fingers in my fanny and my bum, and he hurt me.'

I couldn't pretend it wasn't happening any more, I couldn't turn my back on what she was saying any more. I just cuddled her up, I didn't want to make a big fuss there and then, and I said, 'I won't let Daddy hurt you ever again.' As I held her she said, 'I'm not telling stories, Mummy, I'm not!' and I assured her I believed her. She was just 4 by then.

I think I was starting 'flu or something – I felt ill as though I was, anyway – and I knew if I confronted Ted right away he'd make excuses and find some way of explaining it away so I'd accept what was happening, and I wasn't willing for that to happen again. I *knew* now that abuse had taken place and that every time she'd said something he had abused her and I'd turned my back on it. I went downstairs, I didn't say anything to Ted, I put the other children to bed and finished the work I'd been doing. We went up to bed ourselves, but I couldn't sleep. I lay as far away from him as I could, looking at his face. . . . I can't remember what I thought, I know I was very detached, matter of fact – I had something I had to do and nothing was going to get in the way of it.

The next day I took the children to school and the child-minder. I phoned up Katie's paediatrician, not the local doctor this time, and I poured out everything except that business of the smell of sperm. I still wasn't in touch with that. She said she wanted to see Katie that afternoon, and that she would have to inform the Welfare, unless I wanted to do it myself. I said I did, I wanted to be the one in control now, so I rang them and talked to a social worker. I didn't like the way she was acting, she told me to get the children out of the house right away and keep them out, but I'd no intention of moving us out of our own house. Why should we be the ones who had to go?

Anyway, I collected the small ones and when I got to the hospital at 2 o'clock the social workers and the police were there. They interviewed Katie together – I thought it would be better if I didn't go in as well, she'd speak more freely without me there – and when they came out they said there was no doubt in their mind she had been abused. Then the paediatrician took us into her room with the nurse and examined Katie. Her little face when she saw the swabs. . . . She lay there and did everything she was told to do. . . . I don't know how to put it in words, her eyes – it was almost like a death in her eyes. She was looking round the room, she knew everybody there really well, she'd been going since she was 9 months; but now she didn't trust anybody and I'd never seen her like that before, all wary. She'd always been such a sparkly kid.

The paediatrician confirmed it. She said her vagina was a totally different shape now to what it was when she examined her in the December eleven months previously. She said she couldn't say whether it was the result of digital or penile penetration, and that children could be born with this shape but because she'd examined Katie previously she was certain the change had happened within the last year. There were tears in her anal passage as well, and some were old and some were new, and the new tears and the redness in her vagina meant this had happened within the last three days. Only Ted had been around Katie then, there'd been no other men with her at all during that time.

When the paediatrician said that I went numb; to survive I went numb. Then everything followed. All the people involved were very helpful, except the policeman at first. It was his first case and to begin with he was really stroppy, but after that first reaction he was very supportive. He was really shocked a bit later when he met us together as a family to see how different we were from the way Ted had put us forward; he'd been given a totally false picture of us. He's been around all the way through ever since, and he's been great. Even now he sometimes rings to ask how everything is going. Anyway, after that disclosure I went back to my mum's with the children, and that night Ted was arrested as soon as he got back home from work.

He phoned me at my mum's that same night as soon as they released him from the police station. He was in floods of tears, denying everything about Katie but apologizing for the way he'd let me down in the past, gambling and losing all our money. He said he could accept it if I decided to split up because of the bankruptcy and his gambling but not because of the other, since he hadn't done it – he wasn't going to lose me for nothing. The police had told him he couldn't go back to the house at all, but I said he could go back to pick up the van and get some money.

From that moment on he pleaded innocent all the way and would not accept guilt.

There wasn't sufficient evidence to send him to Crown Court. Nothing came back on forensic and Katie was only 4 so the CPS [Crown Prosecution Service] wouldn't let her give evidence, not even in the Magistrates Court. But he wasn't allowed to live at home any more, though I wouldn't have let him anyway, not now I was sure.

He phoned me constantly after that. I was still running the admin. side of the business from home and he was working from his sister's. He'd told all his work mates and his family that he was innocent of what he was being accused of, and everybody believed him – it was very difficult for me to carry on working for the business under those circumstances. He'd ring me and literally stay on the phone for hours, crying and protesting, and I couldn't bring myself to put the phone down. He kept saying I was paranoid because I'd been abused, and it was all in my mind. He found out from me there were a lot of people I hadn't told about him because I didn't want to spread it around everywhere, so he rang the friends I hadn't spoken to and told them personal things about me, begging them to ring me and convince me he was innocent.

It was several months later, when all this was getting on top of me and I was talking to the social worker, that I suddenly recalled the sperm I'd smelt on Katie that time. I told her about it and she seemed very dubious. I think she couldn't believe I hadn't been hiding it all along, or perhaps that it hadn't happened at all. Up to me remembering that I couldn't stop wondering if it had all been a mistake like Ted said, or whether – if only he'd finally admit he'd done it and get help – I couldn't take him back and everything would be all right again. Every time after he rang me I'd put the phone down and hit my head on the wall because I couldn't stand it any more.

At that point I knew I had to get some help, and I insisted that my doctor arrange for me to see a therapist. He did, and as a result I met Jane, who's a clinical psychologist at the hospital. Jane was, and is, marvellous. I went in there feeling responsible for everything: Katie's abuse, Ted being where he was, and terribly guilty because I'd reported it. It was as though nothing I'd found or felt could be trusted – how could I really have forgotten all the things I'd claimed to forget?

We had an assessment, and I was able to go straight on from there. I shared everything with Jane, and as time went on I arrived at my own abuse in detail. Sometimes it was awful, like when I started to keep a diary of my therapy and forced myself to write everything down that I could remember about my abuse. I found myself feeling sexually aroused as I wrote, when I hadn't felt anything like that at the time it happened. It made me feel perverse and quite ill, disgusted with myself – I was hot, sweating all over, felt sick, and when I read it back to myself I thought how could I write such a sick thing down? It was really hard to share that with Jane – I said to her, it was like I was writing a pornographic story about a small child, as if *I* was being abusive.

In June 1990 when the business was up to £900 a week turnover I passed it over to Ted, told him to take all the business debts, only £5000 by now, and that when the business was on its feet please support me. Then I went on to Income Support completely. I was still going to night-school through all this, studying bookkeeping and French now – the interest of it kept me alive – and I'd changed my phone number because I couldn't cope with him still ringing me.

In August he began therapy with a psychiatrist. He went there because he'd put himself in the Gracewell Clinic at Birmingham for a week; it should have been a month's assessment, but he came out after a week having admitted abusing Katie. He phoned Great Ormond Street, admitted it to them, then phoned me and my mum, but as soon as he realized it had to go down on paper he withdrew his confession and said he'd only admitted it so that I'd take him back.

He was suffering acute depression by this time, suicidal, and he went into hospital for therapy as an in-patient for sixteen weeks. The kids kept wanting to see him, and I needed to see him for myself because I kept picturing this ogre, this monster. But first I went to the hospital and spoke to his psychiatrist, who to my horror said she didn't believe he had abused Katie. I was very angry with her, because that wasn't what he needed to hear. I told her about the sperm smell, the paediatrician's verdict, all the things Katie'd said and the 'sticky wee' she talked about, and that I couldn't live with him again unless he admitted it and got help.

I took the children to visit him under supervision at the hospital and we all had a lovely day. It was fun again, it was as though nothing had happened. It was playing happy families, and it really cracked me up. Katie sat on his lap in the kitchen and swung her arms round him, she really missed him, and she said, 'You didn't hurt me, did you, Daddy? I was only 'tending.' Ted said straight away, 'No, I didn't hurt you.'

I was furious, he shouldn't have said that to her. She looked at me and said, 'See, Daddy can come home now.' Afterwards at home she said, 'It isn't my fault Daddy's gone away, it's Daddy's fault, he hurt me, didn't he?' I said, 'Why did you say that to Daddy, then?' 'Because I want him to come home.'

Ted went to lots of different groups protesting his innocence, including one for parents wrongly accused, then he heard about Great Ormond Street's Family Therapy groups and wanted us to go. When I went to see them for the first interview in February 1990 I hoped they'd tell me what I wanted to hear and everything would all be all right after all, but the therapist came to the same answer and I was pretty pissed off! She interviewed Ted, and told me she believed he is likely to do it again and may well have done it before. Mind you, he did come across badly. I myself have actually felt totally suffocated by him, and when he was on the other end of that phone I kept pulling at myself like this all the time, it was like he was a leech and I was sort of trying to pull him off while he was on the phone! The therapist said to me, even professional and trained as she is, she could find herself being drawn into his pleas of innocence, and the only way not to get drawn into it is to hold on to what the child is saying and other information that's come in.

No, we didn't do family therapy, now it's purely for Katie at the moment at Great Ormond Street. After she saw Ted that last time she began acting up badly again. She's a lot better now, but she does sometimes have bad dreams. What worries me is she seems to have no respect for her body. In company she'll sit and throw her legs open and fiddle with herself. It's not like a 3-year-old who's healthily curious about her body – she looks around for attention, she's almost looking for the stimulation she's not getting now. And it's not safe, it's not safe. It was her doing that that got me in touch with what I did to my step-dad. She's talked about Ted hurting her, and I wondered why she wanted the stimulation if it had all been painful, so I asked her about it. 'Sometimes Daddy did nice things to me,' she said, 'he used to blow on me, blow on my fanny.' It really hurt when she said that, because it was . . . something he used to do with me. Ted was very digital in foreplay, and other things she said he did to her he used to do to me.

It's very hard, that Katie's sexual awakening is premature and is based on the perverse actions of another person. I get in touch with that so painfully, because that was how my own awakening happened. The paediatrican says she'll always carry the vaginal scarring – when they examined her a year later it was still there, but no, it won't have any physical bearing on her later on in childbirth or in her own sexual relationships.

Finally – he can write to me but he can't phone me; I've gone ex-directory and changed the number. But he's not seeing the children any more because of what he said to Katie. He only goes to the psychiatrist at the hospital where he was an in-patient, and she believes in him completely, and tells him the reason I can't trust him is because of my own abuse. Yes, she's said that to me in person. I know it's all against the rules what she did, but that's what she believes and says. So he writes to me and I write back and tell him how the children are and what's happening to them. In a way I still need to share that growth of the children with someone.

I've put myself through ever such a lot, all my fantasies of my being wrong, and sometimes I've wondered if it was all because I was still attracted to abusing men. I made a link in therapy that Peter, the man who abused me, was very, very much in appearance and manner like Ted. That was very difficult when I discovered that. I'm afraid now for my judgement that I'll follow the pattern and chose another abusing man – I'm afraid of that more than anything. I couldn't bear for my own problems to end up harming the children again.

The future? I'm really enjoying studying now. I used to bunk off school because I never liked it, but my step-dad was into school and he made me go and I found I enjoyed it. Within a few months they put me up two classes and I started doing really well. But then I started bunking off again, I was so used to being rude and badly thought of at school I just couldn't become a goody-goody. I left school at 16 with five CSE low grades not worth the paper they were written on, but later I went to night-school to do O' levels. Now I've just finished examinations for my A' levels in psychology, literature and sociology. I think I did well, but anyway the college has already accepted me unconditionally to begin in September for three years, not quite full-time because of the children. I'll be doing the Diploma in Social Work, but later I would really like to specialize in child protection, because I know so much about it now. I hope I'll be healed enough by then.

And for the children, whether I do it on my own or with a partner, I'm just hoping to bring them up to be strong and independent. We live very poorly in comparison to the way we used to – I'm solely on Income Support of about £103 a week with three children, and it's not fair we have to live on so little now, but they understand and are really good about it. No, they don't take it out on Katie at all. My main hope is that she can come to terms with what's happened and that it doesn't continue in her future life.

I want to go on now learning things, I want to learn sign language, get a degree – there's so much. I feel pretty confident now, and I've come to the conclusion that I'm not this awful person I thought I was, and I accept that I've got flaws of imperfection and it's OK to have those flaws. Whereas at one time everything had to be spotless, the children had to be spotless, everything had to be organized, because I felt such a mess inside.

But now I accept I haven't got the money to have carpets everywhere and Laura Ashley wallpaper, I don't apologize to callers any more for the house. I don't know what life holds for me and the children, but I know where I'm going and I know what I'm doing to improve myself and to improve the lives of us as a family. And Ted's not a part of that.

A day or two after I saw Barbara I was very moved to receive the following letter from her:

. . . I have mixed feelings of the experience but meeting you and taking part in something very worthwhile was both enjoyable and satisfying. In sharing my life with you – particularly that of my own abuse – I began to get in touch with a deep inner sadness.

When I spoke of taking Peter's penis in my hand I was actually back there and could even feel the heavy weight it felt to me at 9. Soon after that experience I felt a numb, tingle sensation on my hand which I covered with the right hand. At that moment you noticed I was hurting and I knew I was but I hadn't made a link. On the train on my way home I put those two feelings together. I remembered Peter ejaculating over my hand. I felt quite distressed and touched by perversity for a while, but then became emotional and felt pity and sympathy for the 'little me'.

This was terribly important for my own healing and I'm sharing it with you in case you want it for your research but also because in talking with you I became in touch. Feeling sorry for the 'little me' has been a long slow process and you have helped me finally get there.

I would also like to say that on reflection I don't think I came across as being very supported except by Jane. I'd like to say that since November 1989 my family and friends have been wonderfully supportive and have spent many hours listening to my pain. My sister, mother and father have been particularly strong for me, and the official support of my Health Visitor rescued me from moments of despair – when I moved from her area our friendship grew. I feel this is really important because if women are to find the courage to protect their children then they need to know that they are not alone. I am touched by the support I received too from the Social Worker and the police, and the new stronger bond that developed between myself, my family and friends.

Finally I forgot to give you a poem I wrote when I was in the early throes of therapy. I feel it is an indication of just how painful my journey of self-discovery has been.

The endurance of such pain
Elicits a depth of awareness within.
The necessary strength required to survive
Depends entirely on one's own core;
But until it is explored
There is no way of knowing,
If one's core contains the courage.
To live. Or the weakness. To die.

Chapter 2

Outlines

A BRIEF HISTORY OF CHILD SEXUAL ABUSE

'Society has given men contradictory messages about their offspring. As "head" of the family, children are his property, an attitude which varies across cultural groups but one embedded in the need to prove virility, the male dominance of discipline and moral authority' (Edgar 1988a: 143). This basic concept is slowly losing its ancient power, but as long as any person anywhere is bigger and stronger than another he/she will be in a position to impose his/her needs on a smaller/weaker person unless society in the form of law or morality intervenes.

Incest itself has not always been forbidden by people of every society. It is not possible in a book of this size to attempt to disentangle the various strands of inheritance of property, convenience, magical ritual, physical and emotional desire which over the ages have led to this type of relationship. In spite of the fact that almost every society we know of has had strongly enforced taboos against incest (Henderson 1972), at certain times in a few societies intrafamilial marriages or sexual relationships have been allowed. The most famous are, of course, the brother/sister and much rarer father/daughter marriages in Egypt during the Pharaonic and Ptolemaic periods, but such marriages were also allowed in certain other ruling families, in, for example, Hawaii and among the the Incas of Peru (Meiselman 1979).

Keeping property and regal power within the closed family unit was obviously of the greatest importance in the arranging of these marriages, but in some 'primitive' tribes magical ritual also played a major part in permitting sexual relations between family members, for example in a belief that certain rituals would enhance the courage of hunters and warriors. Such ideas continue to exist – in this century there have been groups in America who still believed that, just as you can catch venereal disease from an infected partner, so you can also 'catch' purity and cure such infection by having sex with pre-pubertal daughter (Weinburg 1955).

Anthropologists such as Ford and Beach found societies where children were permitted to play sexually with each other and where parents sexually stimulated their children, masturbating them as a normal part of family contact. But such attitudes are rare. 'The taboo on nuclear family incest is more or less universal. The exceptions that are so frequently listed often serve to distract the reader from apprehending the truly remarkable degree of regularity with which nuclear family incest is prohibited' (Meiselman 1979: 3). In Western countries there have been few exceptions to the incest taboo, one being the Mormons of Utah who, until a state law banned the practice in 1892, permitted incest among their members to make certain that their children married only within their own religion.

Taboo or no, children have never been guaranteed freedom from the sexual attention of their relatives and others. One way of attempting to control the sexual abuse of children has been to regulate the age at which it was legally permissible for the young to first have intercourse. This has varied tremendously: in Britain in Elizabethan times it was 10 years of age for girls, and by 1885 the age – at that time 13 – was raised to its current level of 16, primarily to discourage the sale of children into prostitution by their parents (West 1987; Rose 1991). In Europe the age varies – a *Note on the Age of Consent* (April 1989) issued by the Spanish Embassy explains that in Spain although 'there is no specific legislation setting out the minimum age of consent . . . it would appear the operative age may be 12' for both heterosexuals and homosexuals but, in an attempt to prevent abuse, intercourse has been made illegal between the ages of 12 and 18 if deception is used or a position of authority is taken advantage of. However, this may be so difficult to prove or disprove, the *Note* suggests, that 'the operative age cannot safely be given as under 18'. In Italy sexual relations are permitted between children over 16 and under 18, but an adult over 18 may not have intercourse with another young person still under 18. In the different states of America the permitted age ranges from 12 to 18.

Until 1908 incest in England came under the jurisdiction of the by then almost defunct Ecclesiastical Courts, who were mainly concerned with the sinfulness of the blood-link rather than with the criminality of the sexual abuse of a minor. A contemporary study suggested that to make incest a secular criminal offence would mean acknowledging 'publicly the existence of such "unnatural vice" ' which would 'tarnish the reputation of the Victorian family as a repository of the highest Christian virtues' (quoted in Scott 1989). Legislation would also mean state interference in the family, until then a unit sacrosanct in the eyes of the Victorians.

But towards the end of the nineteenth century the newly formed National Society for the Prevention of Cruelty to Children together with the National Vigilance Association (an interdenominational Christian movement) attempted to change the situation and to prosecute incestuous fathers, arguing for the criminalization of incest. Dorothy Scott (1989), to whose paper I owe much of this last information, points out that they did not expect this to deter abusers, and it was accepted that there was a public reluctance to report cases, but they wanted the change because of its symbolic value 'in expressing the moral values of the society'. England's colonies, with similar Victorian ideas about the family, were also beginning to face the problem of incest. During a debate on the introduction of legislation in the State of Victoria, Australia, one argument against it was that it would be better 'that a few persons should escape than that such a monstrous clause as this should be placed upon the statute book of this colony'. In spite of further opposition on the grounds that 'the contempt of the community . . . would come home to [the abusers] more than the punishment provided in this clause', a bill making incest a criminal offence was passed in Victoria in 1891. In England it was not until 1908, after the passing of the Punishment of Incest Act, that incest was finally taken out of the hands of the Ecclesiastical Courts.

The subject itself, however, remained virtually taboo in spite of Freud's, and later Kinsey's, work. Because of Freud's later opinions (originally he had specifically identified child sexual abuse as the cause of the clinical hysteria he diagnosed among so many of his patients) those who followed him came to believe that most victims were either fantasizing their abuse out of an Oedipal desire for sexual relations with the father or they themselves had seduced their fathers into abusing them. Either way it was the victims, not their fathers, who were at fault (Renvoize 1982).

After Kinsey's 1948 and 1953 studies into human sexual behaviour it became easier to discuss sex in all its forms publicly, but the fear of holding up much-needed reform in attitudes to sexual matters in general led concerned professionals to back-pedal on the subject of child molestation, saying it was infrequent and exaggerated by the media, thus leaving themselves free to concentrate their reforming efforts on what they saw as more pressing issues (Finkelhor 1979a). Now, however, a combination of factors has at last led to the opening up of the subject, to the extent where, as one cynical editor put it, child sexual abuse has become 'the flavour of the month'; but, as the scandals of Cleveland and other recent revelations have shown, most people – professional and lay – continue to find themselves unable to accept the appalling reality of its prevalence.

DEFINITIONS OF INCEST/CHILD SEXUAL ABUSE

This book is concerned with the most common form of child sexual abuse (c.s.a. in abbreviation); that is, abuse committed by someone known to the victim. Stranger abuse is much rarer, and, although certain aspects of treatment of both have much in common, on the whole a very different approach is required, not least where the rest of the family is concerned.

In previous years, sexual relations with a very close family member were mostly referred to as incestuous, but the legal definition has always been so narrow that many cases, which would have had the same emotional effect on the victim as legally defined incest, could not properly speaking be called that. So for practical purposes the definition of incest gradually became broader, until now the word 'incest' is not often employed, the phrase 'child sexual abuse' being used where appropriate instead, although very often the abuser in any particular case will in fact be the biological father or a stepfather. I suspect also that, in addition to the legal problems involved in labelling, the intense moral disapproval mentioned earlier lingers on and that many people, professionals included, find it easier to cope with the thought of what is implied when the act is sanitized by calling it something less direct than incest.

Let us look, then, at a variety of definitions of what is meant by incest and child sexual abuse, and arrive at our own version of the latter which will include the former. To start with, in English law incest is sexual intercourse between a male aged 14 or over and a female whom the man knows to be his daughter, sister, half-sister, granddaughter or mother. If the female is under 13, the crime carries a possible sentence of life, the same as for rape; if she is over 13, seven years is the maximum sentence. In fact the courts rarely give a sentence greater than two to five years. Even if both participants are adult and fully consenting incest is still a crime. If a woman over 16 has intercourse with her father, brother or half-brother, son or grandfather this is also legally defined as incest. Step-parents, adopting parents and non-blood-related guardians will not be charged with incest but with indecent assault when the child is under age or with rape if she/he did not consent.

Scottish and Northern Irish law differs from English law in certain ways; for example, in Scotland sexual intercourse between uncle/niece or aunt/ nephew counts as incest. In America and Australia the definition varies among states, as does the punishment. But in many countries the law is under scrutiny and is subject to change: to give a single instance, in 1981 the Government of the State of Victoria changed their law to make males and females suffer the same penalties, and included mothers as possible offenders in relation to sons.

One major problem with the current British legal definition of incest is that intercourse is the sole act referred to, intercourse meaning the penetration of the vagina by a penis. But intercourse is by no means the most common abuse; buggery is often preferred regardless of the age or sex of the child, and as this cannot be counted legally as intercourse such abuse has to be prosecuted as sexual assault. The Indecency with Children Act passed in 1960 means that acts not involving touching a child, such as masturbating in front of her/him or inducing the child to masturbate the abuser, can be charged as 'indecency "with or towards" a child of either sex who is under the age of 14'. It is irrelevant whether the victim is male or female: the penalty of a maximum of two years' imprisonment was increased to seven years by the Sexual Offences Act 1985 (West 1987). Offenders who keep up with the law know perfectly well how difficult it is to bring successful prosecutions under any definition. Many have already learned that DNA testing is being used in investigations, and so oral sex, which is undetectable unless the testing is carried out immediately, is increasingly becoming the favoured method.

Since for all these reasons the law on incest is becoming less relevant even where close family members are concerned, let us consider the various criteria which constitute the broader term 'child sexual abuse'. It will be helpful to forget the law at this point, and to take a child-orientated point of view. It is the child's perception of what is happening to her/him that should be our major concern, bearing in mind, though, that when violence is not used small children often do not realize they are being abused until they are older. This does not necessarily make the after-effects of the abuse any less gross. Anna Freud emphasized this when she wrote that the victim 'cannot avoid being physically aroused and this experience disastrously disrupts the normal sequence in his sex organisation. He is forced into premature phallic or genital development while legitimate developmental needs and accompanying mental expressions are by-passed and short-circuited' (Freud 1981: 33–4).

After the public inquiry carried out by Lord Justice Butler-Sloss into the Cleveland affair, in September 1988 the British Law Society Local

Government Group and the National Children's Bureau held a widely based conference whose opening speaker was the Lord Justice herself. To begin with, the conference attempted to produce a definition of c.s.a. from which they could work. After much discussion they concluded, 'The consensus view was that although certain acts quite obviously constituted child sexual abuse – and this was not confined to physical contact, far less penetration – the parameters of the problem were not yet definitively drawn. Some doubted whether it would ever be possible to have an unequivocal definition. At local and operational level, however, it would be essential to have some measure of agreement both within and between services as to the boundaries of concern or referral.' And later, 'What is very clear is that child sexual abuse within the family cannot simply be equated with incest. . . . [Its] essence . . . is that it involves the sexual exploitation of a child by an adult; or, as the Cleveland Inquiry Report itself expresses this, "the use of children by adults for sexual gratification" ' (Davie and Smith 1988: 10, 80–1).

Even simpler is Fraser's useful definition: 'the exploitation of a child for the sexual gratification of an adult' (Fraser 1981). The Queensland Centre for Prevention of Child Abuse (Australia) in their *Fact Sheet 4* write, 'Sexual abuse is the exploitation of a child by an older person or an adult for the sexual stimulation and/or gratification of that person.' They continue, 'Sexual abuse of children can take many forms from exposure, fondling, voyeurism and exhibitionism, to sexual intercourse, incest, involvement with pornography and child prostitution. It is rarely a one-off event. Inappropriate sexual behaviour should not be confused with affection or playful physical contacts between an adult and child which are essential to a child's healthy growth and development.' In 1984 a South Australian Government Task Force defined c.s.a. as 'the imposition of explicit sexual activity on a child who lacks the power and authority to prevent being coerced into compliance' (Winefield and Castell-McGregor 1986: 27). More elaborately, in their book *Child Abuse* the Kempes suggest 'the involvement of dependent, developmentally immature children and adolescents in sexual activities they do not truly comprehend, to which they are unable to give informed consent, or that violate the social taboos of family roles' (Kempe and Kempe 1978).

David Finkelhor regards age discrepancies between victim and abuser as being of major importance: he considers c.s.a. has occurred where there has been an encounter between a child of 12 or under with a person of 19 or over; between a similarly aged child with a person under 19 but at least five years older; or between a child/adolescent of 13 to 16 years and a partner at least ten years older (Finkelhor 1986a). But although this definition is useful, as we will see later in Chapter 6 when we look at adolescent abusers, it can sometimes be very difficult to decide whether an incident has been actual sexual abuse or simply youthful curiosity. In an interview, Detective Inspector Bob Taylor of Albany Street Police Station, London, commented:

> We've had quite a few cases recently with teenage boys – and younger – abusing children younger than themselves. Sometimes you think to yourself, is this sex abuse or is it the things children used to do when you were young? . . . One case we had concerned the two sons, about 12 or 13 years old, of a child-minder. They were helping the little girl the mother was looking after to go to the toilet – the child was quite young, 4 or 5, and one of them interfered with her. The girl mentioned it to her mother, who told a friend who was a nurse, who reported it. It turned out he'd touched her a bit in the course of helping her go to the toilet. Now was that actual sex abuse or was it just curiosity? Sometimes you get a boy of say 14 who had full intercourse or buggery with a girl of 7 or 8, and that's another matter altogether, of course.

Juliette Goldman in a new book gives a shortlist of various professionals' definitions of c.s.a., most of which consider age discrepancy to be a 'defining characteristic' (her own preferred definition). Two – Finkelhor and Lewis – also include as a characteristic that the 'respondent considered the experience to have been sexual abuse' (Goldman in press).

Tilman Furniss points out that the difference in social attitudes towards child physical abuse and child sexual abuse is an important cause of the problems of definition of the latter. With the former it is mainly a question of how much physical violence is permitted; with the second virtually no sexual violation is permissible. 'Whereas a "bit of violence" is acceptable, "a bit of sex" is not.' In sexual abuse, regardless of any psychological damage to the child, legal and protective interventions take place which in themselves may in fact inflict secondary psychological damage (Furniss 1991).

Particularly because of this last aspect it becomes obvious that workers in this field have an urgent need for a definition in which c.s.a. is outlined as clearly as possible without it becoming too cumbersome for general use. In my 1982 book on incest, my own very broadly based and rather cumbersome definition of incest was as follows:

> a sexual relationship that may continue for years or be expressed overtly by nothing more than a single act, that takes place between a young person under the age of consent and an older person who has a

close family tie, which is either a blood tie as with father/daughter/son, mother/daughter/son, brother/sister, or is a substitute for such relationships, as with step-parent or parent's lover where the substitute has effectively taken over the role of the missing parent. The sexual act/acts can vary from exhibitionism to full intercourse: the only essential is that they shall be perceived either contemporaneously or later by the younger person to be of a sexual nature and of sufficient intensity to cause disturbance in that younger person.

(Renvoize 1982)

After picking out key words and ideas from the various definitions above, I shamelessly present my own offering for a definition of c.s.a., a borrowed amalgam of phrases and wisdom from three continents, which, though quite a mouthful, contains I hope most of the essentials:

Child sexual abuse is any type of sexual exploitation of a child or adolescent by any older person or adult for the stimulation and/or gratification of that person, which is not necessarily confined to physical contact and which may range from exhibitionism or involvement with pornography to full intercourse or child prostitution; where the developmentally immature victim lacks the authority or power to prevent her/himself being coerced into activities to which she/he is unable to give informed consent, which she/he does not properly comprehend but which – either at the time or later – the victim considers sexually abusive.

EMOTIONAL, PHYSICAL AND SEXUAL CHILD ABUSE

While I find it impossible to imagine a child being *sexually* abused without it also being *emotionally* damaged at the same time, until recently the various types of abuse have generally been considered separately. Current clinical thinking, however, is beginning to accept there are more connections between what is normally recognized as child physical abuse (c.p.a.) and child sexual abuse (c.s.a.) than used to be thought.

There have always been some professionals who feel that by the very nature of sexual abuse with its accompanying age discrepancy a kind of violence has to be taking place. Dr Jane Wynne, Consultant Community Paediatrician, Leeds, discussing this subject with me, commented, 'My view is that if a six-foot man lies on top of a 3-year-old, that's violence. Just as if a 17-year-old adolescent at school buggers a 13-year-old boy who can't do anything about it, that's violence too.'

The few statistics available at present suggest the connection is less uncommon than was previously assumed, lying somewhere between 5 per cent and 31 per cent. In a study of the clinical experiences of a random sample of registered South Australian psychologists, 149 who completed questionnaires reported that they had found associated physical abuse in 30.9 per cent of cases of c.s.a. (Winefield 1988: 16). Earlier, Helen Winefield together with Sally Castell-McGregor had carried out a study of the experiences of c.s.a. cases of a representative selection of South Australian non-specialist general practitioners (the final sample numbered 193) and found that 'associated physical abuse was evident in 10.7 per cent of cases' (Winefield and Castell-McGregor 1986: 312).

The American National Reporting Study of Child Abuse and Neglect, 1978, showed that of the sexually abused children reviewed 20 per cent of the boys and 5 per cent of the girls had also been physically abused. In light of these figures Finkelhor suggests that, unlike girls, many sexually abused boys may come to official attention through their physical abuse rather than their sexual abuse. Using the same source he finds that mothers who sexually abuse are more likely than similarly abusing fathers to combine physical with sexual abuse – over half of them did so (but in this purely American study a large number of the mothers who sexually abused their children were from poor black families, a fact which limits the international value of this particular finding) (Finkelhor 1981a).

In a study of 206 abuse cases at the Child Protection Unit at the Royal Children's Hospital, Melbourne, 102 of the young victims had been physically abused and 104 sexually abused. Fourteen of these 104 victims of c.s.a. had also been physically abused and ten of the fourteen had suffered 'direct physical aggression resulting in bruising, lacerations or burns' (Hiller and Goddard 1990). Chris Goddard, Monash University, Melbourne, told me, 'Too often sexual abuse is seen as an isolated act, and very often we should be looking at it within the context of other things that are going on in that family. Often it's situational violence – physical violence used against the child's mother, for instance, and physical and sexual abuse used against siblings.'

In the Greater Manchester area of the UK the regional profile of child sexual abuse registrations 1988/89 showed that in the majority of cases abusers used more than one coercive technique, child/adolescent abusers using threats and physical force more frequently than any other method, with 70 per cent of their victims having suffered this. In all, of the registrations of c.s.a. in general, 18 per cent of the victims had been physically forced and 18 per cent physically threatened (NSPCC 1989).

Finkelhor was concerned, in 1985, that professionals already working in the field of child abuse should ask themselves just how sexual abuse differed from physical abuse, in order to avoid mistakes caused by using the framework of c.p.a. in thinking about the identification, treatment and prevention of c.s.a. In his paper he gives six ways in which they differ, the first being that, while c.p.a. is committed more or less equally by both men and women, the great majority of sexual abusers are male. Secondly, he claims, 'overwhelmingly' it is parents who abuse children physically, while much sexual abuse is also perpetrated outside the immediate family by extended family members, neighbours or 'caretakers' such as teachers. Thirdly, in most cases of c.s.a. there is little physical trauma, 'actual full-fledged' physical abuse occurring in only around 5 per cent (sic) of recorded cases of c.s.a. Fourthly, he points out that offenders get actual enjoyment out of the act of sexually abusing children and, fifthly, that the criminal justice system involves itself in cases of c.s.a. far more directly than it does with c.p.a. and has done so for some time. Finally, unlike c.p.a., he believes, c.s.a. is more likely to occur in the 'middle' classes than in the lower socio-economic classes, and the median income in reported cases (1985 figures) was $2000 or $3000 higher than in families where physical abuse had taken place. In addition, he also points out the greater difficulty of identifying c.s.a.; the problems of motivating a desire to change in offenders who are getting sexual pleasure out of c.s.a., as against the more easily treated aggressive behaviour of physical offenders; that for various reasons doctors and psychiatrists are more uncomfortable dealing with c.s.a. than with c.p.a.; and that – arising from the contradictions in our culture concerning sexuality – c.s.a. prevention is even more difficult than c.p.a. prevention (Finkelhor 1985).

Another important difference between the two types of abuse that must not be overlooked is the effect on the victim and on the family of the extreme secrecy invariably insisted on by the abuser. This secrecy is of a completely different nature to the silence that might be imposed on physical abuse victims, the obviousness of such abuse in any case being much more likely to be spotted by outsiders. The damage sexual abuse inflicts on children, with the learning of sexual responses at inappropriate ages together with the dangerous expectation of reward, is intensified by the isolation from peers and others as a result of the enforced secrecy.

But while there are unquestionably large areas of c.s.a. and c.p.a. which will always have to be treated differently and with specialized expertise, it will be helpful for newcomers to the field to remember to keep the connections in mind. Adrian Ford, Director of the Scarba Family Centre near Sydney, told me that he finds

an enormous overlap of all four forms of child abuse – emotional, physical, neglect and sexual. So I'm intrigued that, in spite of this, sexual abuse – probably because of its horror – has been separated out from the rest of the child abuse spectrum while all the others are accepted as normal. You know, 'well, this or that happens in every family, but sexual abuse doesn't'. I think it's almost a way of trying to deny that c.s.a. itself is comparatively normal – that in fact it happens again and again – because everyone can rationalize away the other forms of abuse, to some degree or other they've happened to all of us – but people get stuck on sexual abuse. . . . If I'm presented with a child who's been sexually abused, I know more often than not I will find something of at least one of the other four types of abuse in both the parents, and that that threat's been there from generation to generation. . . . My feeling is that it's much less likely that a person who hasn't been at all neglected or abused will link up with someone who has. We do have this uncanny ability to link up with partners who fundamentally have had extremely similar experiences but which superficially appear incredibly diverse.

(personal communication)

This multi-generational/multi-abuse aspect was confirmed in Williams and Finkelhor's review of thirty recent studies of incestuous fathers. They report that the 'rates of physical abuse in the backgrounds of incestuous fathers ran consistently higher than rates of sexual abuse'. Their final conclusion was that on current evidence physical and other forms of maltreatment were more prevalent – by a factor of at least two – than sexual abuse in these fathers' backgrounds (Williams and Finkelhor 1988).

After seeing Adrian Ford I discussed what he had been saying about the question of separating out the different types of abuse with Cath Laws of the New South Wales Department of School Education. While Laws thought that the dynamics animating the two types of abusers were very different ('I mean, how does the physical abuser make sense of what he's doing, as opposed to the dynamics of secret sexual incest?'), she agreed that from 'a child's perspective it's probably very similar, except that the secrecy about it is probably very different. And again, I think the children make sense of getting a whack across the face quite differently from being sexually abused. They don't see their parents as betraying them so much, because everybody gets a whack across the face, you see it on TV. I think too the betrayal of trust in sexual abuse can have a bigger impact than physical abuse, but it's still devastating for all kids.' She also pointed out a major difference in the teaching materials produced for the prevention of abuse: 'In sexual assault you want kids to be assertive and to say, "No", and to "go and tell". In physical assault you almost want kids to know when to shut up until Dad or Mum have had time to calm down, so there's a different dynamic in terms of keeping safe.'

It is crucial too to consider this difference when deciding what action should be taken when abuse is discovered. Child sexual abuse rarely threatens life, while physical abuse, especially to an extremely young child, can. The preferable option with regard to the latter may well be an immediate – even if temporary – removal of the child but, as we will see later in the section on treatment in Chapter 9, precipitate action involving removal of a c.s.a. victim without proper consideration and preparation among a number of concerned helpers may intensify the psychological damage already done to her/him.

Finally, it has become obvious that much more research needs to be conducted into these connections and differences, not least in order to aid those who work with child victims of multiple abuse, where 'the task of treatment is to identify, neutralize, and unlink traumatic memory and cue traces, and to correct the cognitive distortions and meanings set during the abusive experience' (Burgess *et al.* 1990).

ATTITUDES TOWARDS CHILD SEXUAL ABUSE

Anne Bannister, team leader of the joint NSPCC and Greater Manchester Authorities C.S.A. Unit, writes in her paper on the Cleveland Report 'Conclusions from Cleveland', 'One problem which has not been fully addressed by the report is the effect of differing philosophies as to the causes and management of child sexual abuse. Practitioners using a feminist perspective are unlikely to reach easy agreement with those working from a dysfunctional family viewpoint. Those who use a "sickness" model will be unhappy with a wider social and political viewpoint' (Bannister 1988a). So let us look at some of these differing viewpoints more closely.

In their book *The Protection of Children, State Intervention and Family Life*, Dingwall *et al.* reject 'fashionable radical allegations of over-zealous intervention by health and social services' and feel that 'if anything, justice for children may require more state action rather than less'. In discussing 'the Dilemma of Liberalism' they write:

[A]gencies will always fail to recognize more than a selected proportion of child mistreatment. They cannot be given the legal power to underwrite an investigative form of surveillance without destroying the liberal family.... [But] liberal theorists ... have repeatedly insisted that parents cannot have unrestricted liberty in child-rearing. The parent/child relationship is an unequal contract, which children do not enter freely. At the same time, both children and society ... have a vital interest in the success of that relationship, in cultivating the capacity for responsible moral action. The only body with the legitimacy to survey the whole population is that which, in liberal principle, is accountable to the whole population – the state. Whatever machinery is devised, however, it will always remain vulnerable to criticism from Utopian libertarians whose ideals break on the brute physical reality of children's dependence on adults.

(Dingwall *et al*. 1983: 220)

Don Edgar, Director of the Australian Institute of Family Studies, has no doubt where the main blame lies:

Child abuse is not a matter of personal aberration or 'sickness'. It is socially produced and maintained. The two major conditions which predispose families to violence, including child abuse, are inequality of resources for power based on age and gender, and the privacy of family life which reduces accessibility to outside agencies of social control. Added to this is the pervasive normative acceptance of (male) violence as a means of resolving stressful situations.

(Edgar 1988b)

He therefore calls for the removal of inequalities in society, for surrounding the families with community networks of support, and for public education in parenting and 'respect for one another's dignity'. The training and experience of professionals such as doctors and social workers works against their accepting the full impact of social forces, and they mostly see the problems in individual, psychological terms. Counselling, Valium, etc., can only be temporary measures – without changing underlying social structures there will never be sufficient workers, time or money to cope. The move towards self-help through social support networks is growing in response to the need, but community networks cannot provide the answer alone. Arguing the need for a new social approach to prevention, Edgar writes:

Public attitudes towards child-rearing and individual rights within each family must change so that violence and abuse are seen as both illegitimate and ineffective ... above all, families need to be brought out of their isolation, to be 'resurrounded' not by prying bureaucrats or social work busybodies, but by activating social support networks within neighbourhoods. Child abuse is not a matter only for protection agencies and formal intervention. It is a disgrace requiring total community action and reorganization.

(Edgar 1988b)

Discussing the subject with me he also referred to the problems of dealing with lawyers who still have difficulty in accepting the fact of child sexual abuse.

Counsellors, who are compulsorily involved in any dispute over custody or access in the Family Courts, have been psychologically trained, but the judges, the registrars, the lawyers, have not, and they find great difficulty in accepting the counsellors' reports as being reliable. They're a bit like Freudian Vienna – middle-class men don't do that sort of thing. It's not just in the area of c.s.a. – it's the whole attitude of many male lawyers and judges to the revision of laws on property, rape in marriage, whatever. Most of the opposition to mandatory reporting and much of the difficulty in the Family Courts' handling of c.s.a. has been produced by lawyers who are defending male clients. They don't want to believe it happens, and they have the attitude that, if it does, it was probably provoked and therefore excusable. Of course there are some terrific people who think family law and children are the most important things to work on, but the attitude I've been talking about is still far too common.

But it is not only lawyers who have this mental block. Consistently over the years I have found people of every kind in every country I have visited, including my own, claiming that, although child abuse obviously exists elsewhere, 'it does not happen *here*'. Intending to visit India on my way back from Australia I wrote in advance to the heads of the sociology departments of Bombay and of Goa, having heard reports of child prostitution and other abuse. They responded very courteously, one writing, 'Fortunately in India child sexual abuse has not yet become a serious problem. Only occasionally we come across some cases of rape involving girls', and neither professor knew of any Indian studies on the subject nor of anyone they could suggest I might meet. My attempts to meet with police never came to fruition, and I eventually realized that a fortnight was too short a time even to begin to approach such a complicated subject in a country like India. Just before leaving Australia, however, I had been told by a colleague there who has adopted an Indian child that she had been sent several Indian middle-class women's magazines and that two of them had serious articles on c.s.a. in India.

But this official denial may soon change: the following year, 1991, an Indian Airlines stewardess stopped a 65-year-old Saudi man from taking his weeping 10-year-old bride out of the country. Little Ameena had been sold to him by her impoverished father, a rickshaw driver, a practice that it now appears is not uncommon. As a result of the air crew's intervention the child was taken off the plane but to their distress she was locked up in a home for delinquents along 'with thieves, prostitutes and the insane'. Her story was soon raised in parliament in India where women MPs demanded 'an inquiry into the traffic of Indian children for sex', the suggestion being that the Saudi had bought her to sell to clients. 'But while the political issue rages, Ameena is languishing in the detention centre' in danger of further abuse (*Independent* 12 August and *Independent on Sunday* 18 August 1991).

Dr David Wells, Forensic Physician (he rejects the old title 'Police Surgeon' as an anachronism) for Melbourne, told me: 'Quite consistently, if I talk in a country area or a country town, you can almost predict you'll get a number of individuals who'll say, "Well look, isn't it horrible what happens in the big cities, but thank God we live in this country town; we've no cases here, and we've never had one" – and yet we're talking about a town of 10,000 people!'

Talking with British Consultant Paediatrician Jane Wynne and her colleagues Helge Hanks and Chris Hobbs, they discussed how there were still some psychiatrists who could not accept how many patients had been sexually abused. Wynne: 'We have some good ones here who know the majority of the children referred to them have been abused, but others will not accept it. Goodness knows why they think the children are disturbed, because there's very little major psychiatric illness in childhood.' Hobbs: 'There's a child here who's being abused, nobody's disputing that he's psychotic and also a slow learner, but they say, "this child's having problems: one is he's being abused and one is he's a slow learner" – there's no way they will see these problems are related!' Wynne: 'I was very recently told by a consultant psychiatrist that he'd seen thirty of his patients during the last four weeks who'd told him they'd been sexually abused, but he insisted that was only secondary, their real problem was they were mentally ill. He would not make the connection – but thirty in a month!'

The people most frequently accused of obstructive attitudes in the past were the police, but there has been a fundamental change in police attitudes towards c.s.a., with excellent results in many places. But any force is as good as its workers on the ground, and occasionally policemen who have not been specifically trained to deal with c.s.a. come into contact with victims, with unfortunate results. In the above discussion Jane Wynne reported that the previous week she had dealt with a young girl who had been seriously abused over many years, and was now behaving in a very promiscuous way. 'The policeman, who obviously considered she deserved all she got, said to her, "You're nothing better than a whore, are you!" It's still a common attitude, along with if a women doesn't have bruises she must have enjoyed being raped.'

But Detective Inspector Dave Compton of the Southgate Protection Team near London is very pleased with the general changes in police cooperation, and spoke of the numbers of abusers his team has chosen not to prosecute (in the last two years about half as many as those they did prosecute), though they had enough evidence to do so.

> The police have moved forward a lot in their attitude towards victims. This is the first time I've known in twenty years of police work where the Metropolitan police policy document's first line quotes that the welfare of the child is of paramount importance. So where in the past we've always gone out to get the bad guys and prosecute them, now, we look at the needs of victims first. I think that attitude has spread throughout the country to the police in general, looking at it from the point of view that the victim is the most important aspect of the inquiry. ... We're realizing it's an area that has been totally nelected. In the past we would never have spent the time we do now with children.
>
> (personal communication)

Chris Goddard, Senior Lecturer in Social Work, found much difficulty in attempting to track a number of c.s.a. cases through the criminal justice system in Victoria for a research project under the auspices of the Law Reform Commission of Victoria. Each case followed up had been known to the police and was now being investigated through police records as to its outcome. One of the eventual findings of the study was that many cases had been 'lost', and 'that cases do not appear to be entering the protective service system in large numbers from the police'. A subsequent conclusion reports 'it is clear that a number of informal (and probably organizational) "screening processes" operate to "filter out" very substantial proportions of cases ... it seems more than likely that the processes of denial of the very existence of child sexual abuse that are found among the wider public operate also behind the scales of justice' (Goddard and Hiller 1989).

The feminist viewpoint, that c.s.a. is a women's issue about abuse of power and acts of male oppression, is less often stressed nowadays since it has been accepted that a high proportion of victims are boys, though it remains true that in most cases the abuser is male. Adrian Ford, whose comments we have just seen, thinks that because c.s.a. is

> an experience everyone has some sense about deeply inside themselves – it's normal rather than abnormal – people need a scapegoat. They need to say there's these bloody awful men who've done all these terrible things, or they say there's these provocative kids who do all these things, or there are these dreadfully poor families who live in all the grotty areas of the world. . . . The only way people can cope with the grossness of it when it gets to the most horrendous levels is to say there is this terrible individual or this terrible family or terrible suburb or terrible child. So you deal with it by blaming it on to someone, or you get into the helping system and say it's all the police, or all those bloody social workers, or all those bloody doctors, and you just deal with it by pushing it away.
>
> That's why for me it's much better to just sympathetically try to explore what it's like for the person in front of me, be it either the father, the mother or the child, and to understand what is their particular experience. Otherwise when one is confronted with these horrendous incidents, if we make judgements, or say this is the way the world works – that puts it away from me. Getting to the wonderful Californian thing where I'm OK, you're OK, is a long way to go for most of us, and it's great when we can, but it's more common, I think, to go out of that state, and put it away, say I'm OK, you're not OK – then you become safe.
>
> (personal communication)

Lastly, we need to look at the fact that the change in attitudes towards sexuality over the past two decades has spread to the school playground. This has been more noticeable in the last few years, partly no doubt as a result of the influence of home videos and of soft porn magazines. This means that many children have a more intimate knowledge, albeit superficial, of sexual matters, which adds to the difficulty of those investigating the possibility of sexual abuse. Jane Wynne again: 'I was very surprised, I heard kids in the playground singing this very lewd song about "if you go down to the woods today . . ." and then there's a bit about "licking his knob" or something. Five years ago the fact that kids had that knowledge would have worried me: if they went from talking about it to *doing* it I would still be worried. . . . I suspect that a high percentage of those that move from talking about it to doing it have been abused. But all the same, yes, attitudes are changing, and I think perhaps parents are not watchful enough.'

Chapter 3

Myths

There are various myths about children and child sexual abuse, one or two with a basis of truth, others totally false. There is the one that young pubertal girls are the main target of sex abusers: we will see in Chapter 5 that sexual abuse may in fact begin within a few days of the birth of children of either sex, and that, although research statistics are far from clear as yet, it does seem that the majority of victims are pre-pubertal. Another myth is that sibling incest is OK, and another that most mothers of sexually abused children collude. Yet another myth is that 'nice' middle-class families 'don't do such things'. And who would ever suspect that a dear old grandfather could possibly think of doing anything 'nasty' to his sweet little granddaughter, or, even more unthinkable, to his little grandson?

In this chapter I will be looking at some of the above mainly from the point of view of the reality behind the myths, in two cases using long case histories which illustrate many other aspects of c.s.a. as well as the most obvious one. Sibling and grandfather sexual abuse will also be examined in Chapter 7, which deals with families; we must always remember, however, that while grandfathers do commit a significant amount of child sexual abuse it is a myth that dangerous numbers of 'dirty old men' lurk out there searching for vulnerable children to abuse.

As we will see in Chapter 6, while c.s.a. is committed by abusers of all ages the well-researched NSPCC regional profile for Greater Manchester found the mean age of the abusers on their registers was 34.6. The Goldmans believe that most abusers are even younger, tending to be in their twenties to early thirties (Goldman and Goldman 1988a). Stranger abuse is *not* the main fear: it is among family members and acquaintances that the worst danger lies.

MAINLY GRANDFATHER ABUSE: PETER'S STORY

Let us start with a combination of class, grandfathers and collusion. Peter, 46, bright son of English upper-middle-class parents, has not yet quite succeeded in overcoming the trauma inflicted on him by his grandfather, a Russian prince. By the time he reached adulthood two or three other early assaults would probably have been put aside as unfortunate – but alas not uncommon – experiences; but his grandfather's more serious abuse together with his father's unloving behaviour resulted in his having to undergo a series of therapies, the last beginning a few years ago when old memories resurfaced. Peter, now living in America, contacted me to tell me his story, and the following is a compilation of letters, group therapy print-outs and a personal audio-tape.

I thought the issue of grandfather/grandson molest was very common because of my own experiences, but since very little is written about it I would be very glad to share my history with you if it will help other grandchildren.

It might sound odd, but in spite of everything that happened I was proud of my family. On the one hand, there was my father, a geneticist responsible for developing a new breed of cows, and, on the other, my mother's father, an inventor and early aviator, descended from an old Russian family of the highest standing. He had come to Britain as a military attaché during the first war and subsequently married into a well-known British family. Socially, my grandfather was a very charming man, but the relationship between my mother and him was not good, in fact she strongly disliked him. Also her father hated his own father vitriolically – I don't know what happened between them.

I was born in the West Country at the end of the war in 1945. Part of our home had once been a bishop's palace but most of it had been torn down during the dissolution of the monasteries. There was a rose garden and a dovecote, walks with our governess by old mill ponds picking blackberries – a truly idyllic environment.

But not everything there was rosy. When I was 4 years old I found Toto, our dog, dead in the cowshed, blood coming out of her mouth. I ran off in tears. Afterwards I often went by there, hoping to find Toto wagging her tail. One day our cook's son, who was what was then called a 'half-wit', asked me to suck his penis. I said no and when he asked why not I said because water came out of it, and he said his hadn't done that for a hundred years; it was dried up now and tasted like a stick of Brighton rock. At 4 that made sense. I had been told about private parts but no one had told me what 'private' meant, and a mouth wasn't private, was it? Afterwards I ran in crying to my governess.

In 1951 we moved to a larger but very run-down farm in the same county. Our family was very isolated, and having a series of governesses added to the isolation. My sister and I went to a local school, eventually as monthly boarders, where I was beaten, naked, about twice a week. Then I was sent to a term boarding school.

It was around 1953 when my next abuser, my grandfather, moved in on me. It was Easter Day when he came into my room at the farm and asked me if I would like him to make me happy. Naturally I said yes, and he put his hands in my trousers and fondled me. For the rest of his stay he was always after me, giving me 'hand-jobs'. About that time I stopped sleeping in my own room and slept on the floor in my sister's room in a sleeping bag.

Later, my sister and I went to London to stay with my grandparents. In the morning we used to go into their room for 'coffee'. I would sit on my grandfather's bed, she on the other side on my grandmother's. He used to pull a blanket over the two of us, and masturbate me and make me do it to him. My grandmother always used to take my sister out all day, and I was left alone with him. One day after lunch I walked past the bathroom. He was there, fully dressed but with his flies undone and his shirt sticking out. He told me to come in and asked me to suck his penis – it was not properly erect because I remember the foreskin was not pulled back very far. From then on that was his most common request. I used to beg him 'no', but he said since he had 'made me happy' I had to make him happy too. I had always been taught to obey my elders and betters so I did what I was told.

I remember the start of every time: it smelt terrible, it became erect ... sometimes he would ejaculate into the sink or a handkerchief. My mind would freeze, it seemed as though there was silence everywhere, that time had stopped – I'd forget I was there, I would come to later. I longed for help, but there wasn't anyone there who could help me. And if I told, who would believe me?

The most amazing thing was what happened at night. Every night when we'd all gone to bed and all the lights were out I'd hear this shuffling noise as this man would come into my bedroom to 'reward' me. He would make me stand up and then he would take my penis and put it into his mouth and make me urinate into it. His signal when he was too full was he would clench my buttock and I'd have to stop; when he swallowed he'd release it and I was to continue.

Every day it would all happen – wherever I went he was there. I'd get into bed with my grandfather and my grandmother would go out and make coffee and it was hand-jobs. . . . Then we'd have tea, and dinner, then we'd go to bed. After about twenty minutes or half an hour I'd hear him coming. The wait was horrible. I was in a state of absolute terror. I was totally helpless, completely at sea. No one to turn to. I tried to get some reassurance I was all right, but how? My head felt frozen up. I felt like I was nailed to a wall.

My sister escaped everything except this fetish he had with urine. She used to get sore from his moustache. He only did that part of it in London; in the country he never did anything but hand-jobs.

When I was 9 the local garage man started in on me also. I had a bicycle that was forever breaking down – I was always given second-hand things, they were always breaking. Raymond would fix it on condition that I masturbate him. That went on for several years and ended in a futile attempt at anal sex, when he came with his penis between my legs. How the hell do you think I felt? Another man ejaculating over your testicles!

My grandfather died in 1955 of an ulcer. I asked my parents what an ulcer was and they said, 'It is like the boil you have on your tummy', and indeed I did have a large boil. Imagine how I felt, had I caught the boil from him? Was I going to die too? . . . I've sometimes wondered if the ulcer that killed him was caused by the enormous quantities of urine he must have swallowed from the two of us.

In 1957 my young brother aged 4 – a very lively character, though I don't think my parents liked him, he was a 'mistake' – was killed when he was hit by a train. My father had been working in a field nearby and didn't see him on the line. Yes, I do think his negligence was directly part of my brother's being killed. It showed up what a neglectful family it was. They didn't give him a gravestone and they never talked about him again.

In 1959 I was sent to a well-known public school in Dorset. It was a rigorous extrovert sort of place, given to cold baths every morning and runs before breakfast. What had happened to me over the years had made me very destructive and distrustful, and when my brother died the terrible nightmares I'd had for a long time became nightly. My grades started to decline and finally the school sent me to a child psychologist for a year. But the therapy he gave me was zero, he only ever asked me one question on sex. That was therapy attempt No. 1.

In 1961 my parents moved to my grandmother's ranch in Texas. Leaving school I followed them in 1962 and went to college, but it was a disaster since the syllabuses had nothing in common. Things took a turn for the worse. My father was verbally and mentally very abusive – recently my sister told me she also remembers him beating me to the point she was afraid he would kill me, but I don't hold that as a memory, only as a vague impression and a few nightmares. One evening my father and I were having a row, I was pointing out to him what a lousy job he had done, and later when he walked past my room I grabbed a scalpel and stabbed him in his left shoulder. A day or two later things were getting worse and that was when I tried to blow my brains out but failed.

The school disaster was resolved by my going back to my old school in England, where things went from bad to worse. The best description I can give you is the last year there I felt I was drowning. The year before I'd been tops in physics, tops in maths, but after that there was a very rapid deterioration. I'd been to the masters to discuss the nightmares I had been having four or five times a night, three or four times a week. Then, two weeks after my parents divorced, a master confiscated a TV I'd hidden, it was absolutely against school rules. I retrieved it and he found out. He threatened to put me on the maximum school punishment and I said if he did that I'd kill myself. Next thing I knew I was confronted by a psychiatrist who asked me about my nightmares, and I was carted off to a real live loonybin not far from my school, full of genuine nuts all much older than me. A wonderful place for someone trying to avoid older men!

I was questioned among other things about the dream diaries I had been asked to keep by the first therapist. What worried them, I discovered much later, was 'the psychotic content of the morbid dreams', and I was diagnosed as being schizophrenic. Did they seriously expect a 17-year-old boy in deep trouble to tell them what had happened to him?

I managed to escape electric shock therapy, but they filled me with drugs. I learned later the doctor who was in charge was an expert in the use of chlorpromazine in the treatment of chronic psychotics, so everyone there was psychotic and schizophrenic. My lungs hurt, people were dying, it was like a horror movie.

Six weeks later my father arrived but I had to stay in the hospital for another two or three weeks. And that was the end of therapy No. 2. The secret of my abuse had held, no one had asked or found out about my past.

Quite recently in my current therapy I managed to get hold of a number of letters written about me that had passed between the various doctors involved with me in my early years. Something I'm very proud of is how I have disproved their diagnosis and prognosis. One of those doctors had written, 'Nevertheless, despite undoubted improvement he is clearly suffering from this severe psychotic illness and the prognosis must inevitably be a very guarded if not poor one from every point of view. It is essential that he remains on these drugs indefinitely.' Elsewhere they had described the prognosis as 'doubtful in all aspects'.

I then went to a 'crammers' in London which helped me scrape through my exams. That winter, when I was 18, two people tried to assault me. One, an American, was giving me a ride home in his car when he reached down to molest me. I managed to jump out and run away. Then another man, my final molester, tried the same thing in a cinema. I'd finally had it up to here. I dragged him out and held him against a lamp post and proceeded to kill him. The police arrived, he was still alive. I told them what he had tried, he was arrested and placed on trial. The school wanted me to drop the case, but I wouldn't. After two sessions the witness dropped out and the man was acquitted. But I had been validated, by the police of all people! That was an important turning point – at least somebody believed me.

After two terms at college studying for a physics degree I quit. I had the luck to be able to stay with the doctor father of a friend of mine. I was able to talk to him, though not about the molests, and he got another doctor to review my case – he decided I definitely had not been schizophrenic. Unfortunately money ran out before anyone had figured out more about me, but I scrapped all the drugs I had been put on to and felt much better for it. That was therapy attempt No. 3.

[Peter found difficulty in getting a job because of his hospital experience but, a self-confessed over-achiever and workaholic, once he had started work he prospered, creating several well-received computer program designs. Later, having married and moved with his wife to Colorado, America, he designed various highly successful programs in computer data-processing, and achieved his ambition of qualifying as a pilot.] In effect during that period I ran two parallel careers with my computing and flying. For quite a while I worked during the day in data-processing and at night I would fly freight. Then in 1987 I joined one of our major airlines as a pilot. That was when my fourth therapy started after two triggers brought those memories back into focus. I had never forgotten them, merely repressed them. I'm glad I had because it gave me time to get a therapist who knew what she was doing. In 1960, 1963 if I'd told what had happened I think they would only have loused things up and I'd probably still be there.

This new therapy hasn't done as much as I would have liked, but it has certainly helped. The best thing it has done is I can talk about all this stuff, answer questions like – did I like this happening to me? Physically, obviously, some of the things, yes. Mentally, no. I'm no longer ashamed by what happened, no longer ashamed of the stay in hospital as I now know why it happened. And I've been able to talk to my sister. It turned out she had undergone similar experiences to myself, but when the cook's son had tried to abuse her she ran away. Raymond also tried but she simply raised her knee at the appropriate time and that was the last time he ever tried anything. The third person, my grandfather – he constantly exposed himself to her, and of course there was the urine fetish. It beats me how anyone can do that to 5, 6, 7, 8-year-old kids, it absolutely amazes me. As far as my father goes, I still don't talk to him, but I don't hate him as much as I used to.

Did my grandmother know her husband was doing this? In retrospect my sister and I – and now my mother also – believe she knew. That was why she always took my sister out shopping every day, that was why my mother always had a companion when she was growing up. Hearsay from relatives implies he put 'the moves' on my great aunts also, but I cannot verify that.

So, the gist of it is I'm still a bit of a workaholic, still somewhat insecure professionally in spite of my success, and I am still very self-critical but less than I was. For hobbies I make stained glass, garden an acre of land, grow oranges, peaches, figs, and fly or compute for fun when I'm not doing the one or the other for work. So for someone with a prognosis of poor and doubtful, I think that proves they were wrong, don't you? Yes, I'm proud of that, very proud, and not ashamed to say so, under the circumstances.

My intent in all this is to point out that 'nice, very respectable families' are just as bad as the slime at the bottom of the barrel. These people were looked up to, socially, financially: it wasn't just my grandfather's Russian background – my sister through marriage is a viscountess, my grandmother's family a household name. And yet, look what's happened to us!

All the same, when in groups I'm sometimes asked whether, if I could go back and stop all this from happening, would I?, I've shocked people by answering that I'm not sure – it is because of all those things that happened to me that I've wound up very successful in my careers. If none of those things had happened what would I be now? An accountant, an articled clerk somewhere? Whereas now I'm pretty much of a free spirit, and my wife is supportive of that.

[Peter's description of his relationship with his wife, his parents' – particularly his father's – reaction when he and his sister confronted them with the truth about what had happened to them in their childhood, and also of his own experience of what he calls 'psychological splits – dissociation', appear in Chapter 8.]

We will look more closely in a few pages at the question of mothers and collusion which is touched on in Peter's story (the grandmother in this case), but first a few comments on class.

CLASS

It is fairly widely understood that every type of child abuse occurs in every class, but it will be interesting to note the remarks of a few professionals on this subject. When I asked Juliet Harper, Senior Lecturer in Psychology, Sydney, about her opinions on the differences between classes, she made an important point:

> The children referred to me have all been of low socio-economic status from fairly dysfunctional families, so some of the disturbances I have been talking about may not apply in your better-class homes where there's enough financial coverage to make sure they're not deprived of resources in addition to other problems. It is difficult to explore differences between the classes because they don't get referred to me, I don't see many privileged cases. With the well-off ones you can't really get a sample, they go to a private psychiatrist and the files aren't available – now, it's true they're supposed to notify, but of course they don't. And if you did get a sample it would be a very skewed sample of the middle or upper-middle class, it would be the ones who have been found out or where the mother was very hostile to the husband, rather than cases where the mother didn't believe it had happened.

In Peter's case all of his therapy has been entirely private and it is very unlikely that any details of his case have ever been entered into any statistics. D.J. West, however, in his book *Sexual Victimization* describes his meticulously selected retrospective study of 452 women from two health centres in which he claims the whole range of social classes was represented, although again presumably private patients rarely go to health centres. West found that, judging by the 'reported occupation of their fathers during their childhood, and the present occupation of the main wage earner in the home, there was no significant difference between the women who admitted having suffered childhood sexual abuse and those who denied they had ever experienced it, in either socio-economic class of origin or present socio-economic class.' But he did find that the women in the sample who had been abused were less likely to have been educated beyond 'standard schooling'. 'If further education reflects higher intelligence or social sophistication, then these qualities among the "non-abused" women might possibly have rendered them less vulnerable to molestation or better equipped to avoid it' (West 1985: 72).

As we saw earlier, Finkelhor finds that in America c.s.a. is more a middle-class phenomenon, but is not as closely tied to any particular class as is physical abuse, where the median income is $2000 or $3000 lower than in families where c.s.a. has taken place (Finkelhor 1985). In another paper he suggests that some reported figures showing an opposite result are likely to be a misleading 'artifact of reporting' and claims that epidemiological studies of c.s.a. have repeatedly failed to find higher rates of c.s.a. in poorer families (Williams and Finkelhor 1988). But in an even earlier study he had found the situation different when it came to boy victims of sexual abuse, where the social background was much more likely to be similar to that for other types of child abuse, with the families being poorer (62 per cent of the boys' families receiving public assistance as against 40 per cent of the girls'), more likely to be broken, and the boys likely to suffer physical as well as sexual abuse (Finkelhor 1981a).

Ray Wyre, whose Gracewell Clinic in Birmingham, UK, is proving how effective the treatment of offenders can be, remarked à propros class, 'Offenders come from all walks of life, so we create the ethos where they help each other. We've got teachers here at the moment, so we can use that mix to help and support each other.'

On the other hand, Tony Vinson, Professor of Social Work at the University of New South Wales, comparing the 'grounds for registration of children within high and low status groups', found a 'gross over-representation of residents of low status areas' in all types of abuse. This was equally true for sexual abuse. As many as 85.6 per cent of the lll reported c.s.a. cases were placed in the low status group, this actually being the lowest percentage of those so placed apart from that for drug abuse, where 'only' 77 per cent of fifty-three cases of such abuse came from low status groups. The highest percentage recorded – 93.9 per cent of 296 cases of neglect came from poor families – is not surprising, but that so high a figure, 85.6 per cent, of sexually abused children should be from low status groups certainly gives a very different picture from the other reports we have been looking at. Vinson commented that while 'the nature of the relationship between officially recorded abuse and socioeconomic status is not clear [it] is possible that even the massive concentration of notifications in low status areas of New South Wales may largely be attributable to the greater social surveillance of such areas' (Vinson 1988).

Don Edgar – whose thoughts on the necessity for removing inequalities between families, if child abuse is to be dealt with in any systematic way, were quoted at the end of Chapter 2 in the section on attitudes – would not be surprised at the above figures. As he says, 'It should be obvious that child abuse is socially produced, just as are child care and other styles of parenting.' But the second part of a later remark of his reminds us of Peter's comments on his own upper-class background, 'Lack of income and other basic resources, together with isolation in the family home and the so-called "neighbourhood" is a deadly combination.' And we are reminded again of Peter further on in the same paper, 'It is ironic, indeed, that the very privacy of family life which we hold so dear is a major cause of family violence, child neglect and abuse. In our scramble to assert the family's right to privacy we lay open the channels for abuse of the rights of particular individuals within those families' (Edgar 1988b).

Perhaps this privacy of the family is a far more important factor in c.s.a. than is class itself. Abusing families notoriously 'keep themselves to themselves', none more so than the families where child sexual abuse takes place. I feel that Vinson's figures showing such a predominance of c.s.a. among the socially underprivileged as against the better-off may be, as he himself seems to suggest, 'an artifact of reporting', to use Finkelhor's phrase, and that when thinking about the relationship of class to c.s.a. we must always bear in mind Juliet Harper's comment with which I began, that the better-off are adept at keeping their problems to themselves, out of the way of any statistics makers.

MOTHERS AND COLLUSION

Referring to non-intervening mothers in sexually abusing families, I wrote in 1982 in my book on incest, 'How far these mothers are consciously aware of the sexual activity is a subject for disagreement.' Not much has changed in the last decade. It is still quite impossible to give statistics, and probably this will always be so. But now that c.s.a. is talked about more openly in public so that children – through schools and the media – are becoming aware of their right to an abuse-free childhood, one can only hope that eventually most mothers will be able to 'hear' what their children are telling them and be able to bring themselves to take action.

There will always be some mothers, though, who themselves have been so damaged in their own childhood that they cannot face the distress of their children. Anne Bannister points out in her NSPCC training booklet that an abused girl who has been victimized 'may accept the victim role as her role in life' (Bannister 1988b). As an adult (though Giarretto at a conference remarked, 'If the mother knows what's going on and doesn't stop it she's not acting as an adult – that doesn't mean she always knows, she sometimes doesn't'), she may ignore the abuse or in some way 'disappear', by literally removing herself to a sick bed or by absorbing herself in work or by so isolating herself emotionally from the family, particularly from the victim, that she might as well not be there. To recognize what is happening means mothers would have to relive their own old traumas, along with the ancient guilt and the new guilt that they have not been able to protect their own children. Just as they feared when they were young that they must be dirty and deserving of what was happening to them (many victims are told exactly that by their abusers), now this is doubly proved to be so by the fact that they have chosen another abuser for their partner, thus putting their children at risk (remember Barbara's fears of continuing the abusive pattern in such a way). It takes strength to face up to so much pain, and such mothers usually have more than enough to cope with in just surviving.

Of course not every mother of an abused child has been abused herself, but very many have been, and while we will look more closely at mothers as a whole in a later chapter, my aim here is to consider solely this one aspect of collusion. Mothers who not only knowingly collude but who also actively join in the abuse are rare, and will also be considered later. Far more frequent is the case where the child tells the mother what is happening and the mother refuses to listen, sometimes accusing the victim of lying, sometimes punishing her/him for being disruptive. Few children risk telling a second time.

It is very difficult for people to accept that such mothers often do not remember their own abuse with any clarity, and may indeed have totally blocked it out. 'You'd think they'd do anything to avoid their own children having to go through the same suffering they went through,' people say. But this is to not understand the extraordinary power of the mind to find ways of keeping the body functioning more or less adequately, at whatever eventual cost. Anything rather than remember, anything rather than recall the pain and live through it again. It's a bit like driving down a fast road at night with blinkers on in order to avoid being dazzled by oncoming cars – you might avoid a collision, a breakdown, if you are very lucky, but crashes are likely to be happening around you. In Barbara's story in Chapter 1 we saw quite clearly the difficulties an abused mother faces when her own dearly loved daughter is abused. The sperm that Barbara smelled on 4-year-old Katie's trousers so shocked her she was able to block it out of her mind until much later, after her husband had been removed from home.

There is heavy pressure on any mother of any abused child to keep quiet: for a start, disclosure to the authorities will mean the probable loss, perhaps for some years, perhaps for ever, of the breadwinner, with consequent loss of income. In cases of sexual abuse the break-up of the family may bring some relief at first, but the mother will probably also

was conscripted, and went into the Korean war. He got
had terrible nightmares when he came home. My next
have tried it on, but I was old enough to say don't be silly.
he was older, a sort of father figure. Looking back, I was
le messages all the time at home. My mother must have
was going on, this was our *home*, she *must* have known. But
so private. I never undressed in front of my sister, I never
nybody, not even my sister, we didn't discuss anything, not
ing. My mother never told me the facts of life – I'd started
ing. My mother never told me the facts of life – I just think we
out a couple of years before she had any idea. I just think we
private, it's peculiar. [The girls were unusually isolated
both went to private school, with ballet, dancing, and other
as a very inferior school, but we were dressed up as dolls,
ing was immaculate, we never mixed with the children in

I talked to my sister about what Donald had done she told
my mother said was, 'If that's what happened, then you
My mother was one of these women that says boys will
so it's up to girls to say 'no'. That's what was always
ll through our life. I think my sexual hang-ups were a lot
happened to me with Donald, but also what was being
all the time. There was something about the family. . . .
other had committed suicide when he was a young man,
ran away from home at 15 after her mother died and got
. She must have wondered at the pattern when both my
breakdowns when we had babies.

oo in our house, really, my father was very narrow-
dn't tell jokes. I mean we were a happy family, but,
ne was listening. My parents quarrelled over mum's
th money and dad worked all hours, they even had
nd I'd sit under the table or out on the porch crying, and
d be laughing. It was a way of life. No, my father didn't
ny mum used to hit him more than anything! Once when
y dad came in one night very drunk, and after she told
o me and my husband and told us what he'd had to put
'Your Mum's not like a woman, she won't, you know
not that way.' So it all came out. We said to her, 'Oh,
t get six children by not sleeping in bed with a man',
and says, 'I was a victim. You don't have to be sexy
. I was a victim.' So that was around all the time I was

realize she will deeply miss the presence of the abuser. He is likely to be
the only adult in the family apart from herself (though in many cases the
man will have made emotional and physical demands on her like the child
he still is in many ways, and although she might deny it she would miss
this aspect of him as much as she will miss his male company – after all,
she chose him as her partner). She dreads having to cope with the reaction
of neighbours and relatives and, if she works, with that of her co-workers
and employers. In addition, she may have disturbing feelings of jealousy,
together with doubts about her own attractiveness. She may feel anger,
bitterness towards the child who has stolen her lover and, above all, guilt,
guilt that she is so worthless as to put her own feelings before the needs
of her child. This process may not be conscious. To voice her suspicions,
even to herself, is immensely difficult. To go even further and to break
the secret by dragging it out into the public arena is something which – as
an abused child she would have been taught must never, ever happen –
requires almost unthinkable bravery.

In an interview Adrian Ford, Director of Scarba Family Centre,
Sydney, told me:

> If the mothers have been abused they have to avert their gaze because
> they fear they're being abused again and they're powerless to stop it
> just as the child is. You have to understand the mother's powerlessness
> and her collusion because of her powerlessness. They don't always
> know themselves they are colluding because there are conscious and
> unconscious processes at work and the experiences they've grown up
> with is something they're still having to come to terms with. It is in-
> credibly painful for them to face the fact that it's happening again, and
> I think one way of coping is to not really see, it's a hoping it might go
> away, just like the sexually abused child herself who hides under the
> sheets is hoping it's going to go away. . . . Do they acknowledge it to
> themselves? I don't know. It's very difficult, rarely do you get people
> who say I know it happened. Much more it's almost a preconscious
> stage, you get a sense they know the child's been in the room, though
> they had arranged for the father to look after the girls while they went
> out – there's also a sense they don't want to know, understandably be-
> cause it's too horrendous. I think it is too strong to say mothers know,
> I think people can only know after a great deal of pain themselves and
> a great deal of very specialized help to be able to get to know.

'Collusion' is not easy to recognize. Mothers in sexually abusing
families are often compulsive caretakers. In a practical sense they look
after their children competently, frequently appearing caring and close.

But if the victim tells this type of mother that she/he is being abused the mother will probably not accept the accusation but may well 'take token steps to disprove the allegations' (Furniss 1991: 48). We might remember that, after Barbara had assured her local GP she couldn't believe Ted had touched Katie, the doctor told her 'Your home's lovely and clean, your children are well-kept, you've always come across to me as being a very adequate parent.' It must have been obvious she dearly loved her daughter; it is difficult to blame the doctor for not looking closer.

SIBLING INCEST

Sibling incest may easily be taken too lightly. Children exploring together, what can be the harm in that? In fact, over the years I have spoken to a surprising number of women whose lives have been made miserable by incestuous assaults on them by their brothers, mostly much older but not necessarily so. That I have not personally heard from similarly affected men is probably purely due to the continuing reluctance of males to admit they once had to play the 'feminine' part in sex.

Small children sharing a bath in a loving family without secrets are as much a delight to watch as a bundle of kittens romping together. Of course they will be interested in each other's differences although this soon passes with custom, and there is nothing to be worried about in mild sessions of 'playing doctors'. But sensible parents will be alert to any sign of tension among the players, any unexplained change of attitude; the fact is that actual sexual *abuse* by siblings can do as much damage as any other kind.

When sexual exploring, such as looking, exposing, touching, is mutual and appropriate to age, and is a comfortable albeit exciting experience, in 'normal' families this most likely will be a formative, positive experience. But where any force is used, and where difference in age means the older child wants something more advanced and beyond the age-appropriate requirement of the younger, emotional and/or physical pain maybe inflicted – even, in severe cases, life-long trauma.

Diana Russell writes, 'One of the consequences of the myth of mutuality may be that when brother/sister incestuous abuse is discovered or reported, there may be even less support of the victim than in other cases of abuse.' In her retrospective study 78 per cent of women who had sexual experiences as children found their experiences with brothers to be abusive, as did 50 per cent of those whose were with sisters. Eighty-five per cent reported the experience was totally unwanted and only 2 per cent had more or less desired it. Forty-eight per cent had been extremely upset

after their brothers' abuse, and 2 reports that 'incestuous brothers relationships with their sisters or, most other incest perpetrators' (R Harvey for this information fr Welfare, Adelaide.

Brenda, who is now 47, first wrd abuse as a child at the hands suffered a breakdown after hav worked with a counsellor she problems being her sexual rela had one sister and four brothe occasions if Donald had abuse with this for so long it just pu fighting. I realize many othe anyone could do to anoth maladjusted children and I disturbances and reasoning v going on the exterior, but th

She kindly agreed to me having meanwhile undergo is clearer now as to what h When she talks she flits while admitting being terri bear to let her mind settle in her mind, possibly cul especially noted in this single occurrence just ha

(For the sake of clarit edited more heavily than

Yes, my sister was assa last born. The age gap years, but the gap with and she's four or five anyway she was old e her, I never asked her band. I've no idea ho me he did interfere w far. But something m

Donald malaria, an brother mig But Donald getting doub known what we were all bathed with a sex, not anyt my period ab were all very because they subjects.] It w I mean everyt the road.

Later after mother and all asked for it.' always take it instilled in us to do with wha said around us Well, mum's br and she herself married early. sister and me ha

Sex was tab minded. You d underneath, no extravagance wi physical fights, a my brothers wou abuse *her*, it was I was grown-up him off he turned up with all his life . . . sexually she' come on, you don but she turns roun to have six childre growing up.

My father was very nice, but . . . I didn't know then, but now I'm sure he knew about Donald. I think he knew about my sister at least. There was a lot of hostility between my dad and Donald. But we were all really spoiled, we all had the best of everything.

I didn't remember properly what happened until I went for therapy, after I wrote to you. I went there with my husband once a month for two years and it had got to the point where I thought it hadn't happened – in spite of all that talking I didn't believe that someone could have done that to me. So they suggested I write to my brother and tell him I needed the answer to some questions. I had to be ever so careful what I wrote because of his wife, so I asked him to ring me. My parents had just died and with all this happening he got an ulcer, and from me contacting him his ulcer flared up and he went into hospital. There it was, all put back on me. I thought, *I've* made him ill, I've done this, I've done that. But in the end he came and talked.

There was a lot I didn't know, like I didn't know he'd started on me as early as 2. That was the worst thing. He was babysitting and it started off as a game, and he said it just got out of control. He said, I'm sorry, it was my fault, and he cried. He made me feel terrible.

What had he done to me? It's still difficult to talk about it. . . . He penetrated me. He had intercourse with me. No! Not at two, I wouldn't think. God!! He wouldn't say exactly what he did, so I don't know. All I can remember is the army bit, being in his bedroom when he was either on leave or home. I can see his kitbag, I can see his uniform, so whether he was in the army then and on leave, or demobbed, I don't know – that's the only time I can actually see him doing it. I was in the Juniors, 7, 8, but it might have been going on longer, that's the only time I can be sure. He wouldn't say anything about what happened when it started, he confirmed it about the army. At therapy they tried to get me to write a diary to help me find out when it happened, but I just couldn't do it. I don't know how old I was when he first penetrated me.

There were six of us altogether, and we used to have a key on a cord behind the door – you'd put your finger through and flip the key through, and I can remember the two of us being in the house on our own, and him winding that key round the door knob so that people couldn't pull it through, and I can see him locking the back door. You know, I have pictures of things. . . . He was always bigger than me, so I can't see him as any special age. He did body-building, weight-training, so even if he was 16 he would still have been much bigger than me. Was he gentle with me? All I can say is he took what he wanted. It didn't matter about *me*. They asked me at the clinic if I'd enjoyed it at all, or the attention, and I said I don't remember, but I hope I bloody well did, 'cos I paid for it! But I didn't need that kind of attention, I got a mum and dad that loved me, I didn't need it. Yes, he hurt me. He frightened me, he hurt me.

Maybe I didn't want to grow up, but I was a very young little girl at 14, I wasn't promiscuous or anything, I was still wearing my ankle socks at 14. I never wore a tight skirt, and I mean, even now, I think lots of things are common, and it's all mixed up with how you see somebody that's slept around or whatever – I can't define it. My husband said sometimes, you're frigid, there's something wrong with you, and there was, wasn't there!'

I met my husband at 17. I'd had one boyfriend before but when he came on a bit I got very frightened and pushed him away. But my husband was very gentle with me, and that's why I chose him. I'd known him about a year when we first made love. No, I was as curious as he was. At first it was all new: we never did it in luxury like, it wasn't regular, just a quick fumble. He didn't know anything, and I never knew anything, and the first time he done it he just penetrated me. But even then I would bleed.

Then when I was 18 I had appendicitis, and the way the doctor examined me, it started off memories. I didn't want to sleep with my fiancé any more, I didn't want to stay engaged. I think that's what started it off, going to hospital. The doctor put his index finger up my back passage, I wasn't expecting it. Had my brother done that? I've no idea, but I don't think he'd have been so sordid.

When we got married the first year was difficult, because I kept bleeding, and I had mastitis. My GP sent me to see a gynaecologist who examined me, and he said, you poor lassie, and he said it would be best to have a baby and breast-feed him.

I had a hysterectomy a year ago and was in hospital for six weeks. I had tubes in me when I came out, and it's taken me a long time to get over it. I mean, even now, we haven't got a sexual relationship as such at the moment, partly because of the operation, and partly because of all this. It's like whenever I'm with my husband, whatever it is triggers off something, you know, like the breathing in my face. I mean, there is a problem, and I can't get rid of it. I get them both confused, what's actually going on.

The treatment's not solved it as yet. I suppose I'm not one of their success stories. They've helped me. But I still can't talk to my husband. He thinks it'll all go away, he says just relax and forget about it. At times, after we've had intercourse or something, I'll come down and I'll cry. I've never ever climaxed. I can't let go. I can't let go in anything. Yes, my husband knows what to do, but when I get there I can't let go. When I had counselling by the Marriage Guidance people I began to get feelings, but when that happens I have to push him away, and I cry, I sob. This is where I am now. That crying comes from the bottom of my boots, it is totally out of control. Instead of getting a climax I shut it off and cry. It devastates me, it makes me feel suicidal. I can't function as a woman.

It all got to a head, my health, everything. I got to the point where I didn't want my life to go on, I was just being tormented. I wish to God I hadn't told my husband about my brother, because it's made it worse – things didn't get better, all I was doing was putting him through pain. He'd already been through it, he'd come from a very disturbed background; his father was a batterer and his three sisters were taken into care because of the home life, so what hurts me is that he needs what I can't give him.

Sometimes I feel like being really violent towards him, I really want to hurt him. But no, I can't tell him that, bless him. I tried, at the clinic, I said I just want to die, and he turned round and said if you feel like that, then I can't help you. That's the problem, it's why I can't let go, because I know that if I fall he's not going to be able to catch me. It's . . . if I let go, what am I letting go to? Where will I end up? He won't be able to help. Like when there was money difficulty, he just turned to me and said, look what you've done to me – that's what he says, he can't help himself. If there's a crisis in the family, he can unload to me, but I can't to him. Although he's good and he's kind, it's *my* problem. And what am I doing to him? In a way, although we're very close, it's a very destructive relationship.

I can't do with any more let-downs in my life. There's been a lot of incompetence in people dealing with me, in hospital and all that, but that's the story of my life. I think, did I create these problems, what is it about me that makes everything go wrong? I can't see myself moving on. I feel like my life's over.

It's very difficult telling people that, because they feel they've got to give me a label, give me drugs, give me this, give me that. Though this new man I'm seeing, he's an obstetrician and a top man in the field of hormones. He's very nice, and when in the end I told him about Donald he confirmed I wasn't going mad, it was the hormone deficiency, and he said no wonder you've had trouble with your waterworks. One of my only memories with Donald is sitting in the toilet crying because it burned . . . whether all the illness I've had is tied up . . . I'm going back to see him and I'll ask him what he meant, and maybe in a year or so I'll get it all sorted out. Right now, like when I'm talking to you, everything's muddled in my head, it's like a piece of string, and until it's all unravelled. . . .

One last thing that's worried me is that at the clinic when my brother came he kept calling me Sally, that's the name of his own daughter. They noticed it too. He's had terrible troubles with her. I only get it through the grapevine, she's grown-up now, but she was seeing child guidance, she didn't want to be a woman, she wanted to be a little girl, and immediately I thought, ooh! That, I'd never forgive. He's ashamed of what he did to me, he says, but he hasn't learned. Admitting doesn't make them better people.

At least my own two boys are fine. They went once with us to the therapy clinic for a family session, and I was glad they could see my children don't have any hang-ups. One's got his degree now and, anyone can see, there's nothing unhealthy about either of them whatsoever.

Incidence of child sexual abuse and how to discover it

HOW WIDESPREAD IS CHILD SEXUAL ABUSE?

'We wholly accept that the true extent of child abuse is, and will necessarily remain, unknown. However, increases ... in the number of cases reported may well reflect a considerable increase in the actual incidence of offences committed', and 'In recent years substantial and apparently unremitting rises in the number of sexual crimes committed against women and children have been recorded' (Pigot Report 1989). 'Given the nature of sexual abuse, its secrecy and sensitivity, it is unlikely that an accurate assessment of its incidence will ever be established' (Steven *et al.* 1988).

One of the first questions I am often asked is, how common is child sexual abuse? When, in 1982, in my first book on incest I gave the figure of one in ten females having been abused (mainly based on Finkelhor's excellent studies) the shock/horror was almost universal, up-to-date workers in the field excepted. Even at the time of Cleveland (1987) MPs, doctors, moralists, were still able to express in the media their appalled horror at the behaviour of the beleaguered Cleveland doctors, virtually presenting them as perverted freaks. In fact, contrary to media myth, of the 121 cases of suspected c.s.a., only twenty-six were eventually judged by the courts to have been wrongly diagnosed (Campbell 1988).

It *is* difficult to accept the huge numbers involved – it seems probable that nearly one in three women have experienced some kind of sexual misuse/abuse in their childhood, as have, Furniss suggests, between 20 and 40 per cent of boys (Furniss 1991) – and we have to move from that understanding to considering how to cope with such a fact.

Reporting of c.s.a. is so sketchy and incomplete that few researchers are prepared to stick their necks out and hazard more than a guess at the actual figures involved. It is helpful to remember that we should not assume all sexually abused children are necessarily psychiatrically disturbed. Quoting a properly structured random study in San Francisco (Russell 1983) which showed that 38 per cent of women had been sexually abused at least once by the time they were 18, Tilman Furniss points out that these numbers were based on 'a normative and not a mental health definition', and that the conclusion cannot be drawn that 38 per cent of San Franciscan women are psychiatrically disturbed by their abusive experience. But, he says rightly, however disturbed or not such women may be, the sexual abuse 'in normative terms [is] still abuse and should not happen', and the abuse must be judged in those terms. Equally it must not be argued that because it is so common – indeed, almost 'normal' – we should cease worrying about it (Furniss 1991).

In 1985 Finkelhor reported that studies done on non-clinical groups suggested that between one-fifth and one-third of all women had been sexually abused as children (Finkelhor 1985). This is a higher rate than that arrived at in his earlier well-known study of 795 New England undergraduates (1978), which showed that 19 per cent of the women and 9 per cent of the men had been sexually victimized, but since these students were psychiatrically fit enough to study it may be assumed the most severely damaged victims of c.s.a. were not among them. This study has been replicated in other parts of the USA and in Canada, Britain and Australia. The Australian study (Goldman and Goldman 1988b) of 991 students showed that around 28 per cent of Australian girls had reported some kind of sexual abuse during childhood and adolescence, the vast majority of abuse happening before the age of 12 years, i.e. pre-pubertal. Again, about 9 per cent of boys were sexually molested, the majority also before the age of 12 years (Goldman in press).

Statistics issued by the New South Wales Department of Education in their *Child Protection, 7–12* (NSW Department of Education 1989a: 113) show that 30 per cent of girls and 10 per cent of boys have been sexually assaulted by the age of 18. Libby DeLacey, head of the Division of Education, Griffith University, Queensland, told me, 'I did a retrospective study over four semesters of what my students judged to be abuse, and 32 per cent of them recorded experiences of abuse, most of these female students, and the bulk of the abuse was sexual abuse. To make sure experiences of the kind one giggled about weren't counted we asked for severity to be marked according to importance. Now, this is the elite in our community, the best protected, the best informed, so one wonders what the results would be if we did a grander scale project.'

The earlier-mentioned study carried out by Professor Donald West (Director of the Institute of Criminology at Cambridge) found that 42 per cent of a mixed social group of women from two health centres and 54 per cent of a group of female students reported at least one sexual experience in childhood, ranging from an obscene phone call to intercourse. Half the total number of women had been under 12 at the time, and fifteen were under 9 (*The Guardian* September 1984). A survey sponsored by the Economic and Social Research Council and carried out by the North London Polytechnic's Child Abuse Study Unit found even higher figures and concluded that 'most women and more than one in four men were sexually abused in some form during childhood', nearly one in three of these being assaulted before the age of 12. Almost none of the incidents were reported. Twenty-seven per cent of the assaults were flashing and 23 per cent touching. One in twenty of the women and one in fifty men had been raped, pressurized into sex or forced to take part in masturbation (*Independent* June 1991).

In May 1986 the women's magazine *Woman's Own* (UK) published a well-planned questionnaire about rape to which 25,000 of their readers responded, this being the largest number of replies on a single subject they had ever received. Of the respondents 12 per cent said they had been raped, 14 per cent of whom had been under 10 at the time, while a further 29 per cent (of the 12 per cent) were aged between 10 and 16 and 41 per cent between 16 and 24. The majority of those aged under 16 were raped by a relative; 39 per cent of these were under 10 years old and 20 per cent were between 10 and 16. Seventy-six per cent of the rape victims had not reported the attacks to the police (*Woman's Own* 1986).

Official figures are much lower. The UK Department of Health's figures from the Child Protection Register for the whole of England up to 31 March 1990 show, out of a total of 22,500 girls *on the register*, 20 per cent were there for sexual abuse; of 21,100 registered boys, 7 per cent were there for the same reason (Department of Health 1991: 13).

The difficulty of finding out the truth about the numbers of sexually abused children is well illustrated by the following extracts from an interview I had with Lewis Anderson, Intermediate Treatment Officer, North London. He has been working for some years with young boys who were skirting perilously close to trouble, and there had been some suggestion that a ring involving adults might be operating in his area. Anderson's comments on how he dicovered a large number of local boys involved show how acute observers need to be:

> For our summer scheme we had sixty or seventy local kids coming in, most of them knew each other from school or the estates, or from hang-ing around the snooker halls, amusement arcades. The summer

holidays were coming on and every kid in the area was encouraged to come on one of the weekly coach trips we organized down to places like Margate and Great Yarmouth, forty or so at a time. It had become obvious that the ones not involved in the so-called rent boys scene were getting quite hostile to the four who were clearly identified as having been so. Those boys were getting their backs to the wall, really. The only ones they felt comfortable with were each other; although they knew most of the other kids they were fairly ostracized. They got a lot of common abuse, verbal stuff. The kids that knew nothing about it caught on within a few days and in turn would start dishing out this verbal abuse.

The lads I was working with over this, when they were messing around getting into the canoes and so on they were just like normal kids, and it was one of the few times they could relax, particularly when it was only their group and they weren't getting abuse from other kids. But on the long trips the whole thing was getting out of hand. I tried to shelter them as much as possible but it put me in a very difficult situation, it wasn't the sort of thing I could confront the others with without making a whole issue of it and putting the ones who were verbally abusing in a very difficult situation.

Then one of the youngest kids, he was about 13 at that time – up to then he'd shrug his shoulders and say it didn't matter to him – and we'd been coming back from a long trip to the seaside and this whole thing had been building up on the coach. There were a number of other kids leaning over the seat addressing this boy, giving him a lot of verbal, telling him he was a rent boy, he was gay and he had AIDS and all this stuff. I think he was at the point where he'd just had enough basically, and he jumped up and went round the coach saying, 'I don't know what you're talking about, I've seen *you* and *you* up at so-and-so's place!' and the kids he'd spoken to go a bright red, sit down really quick and drop out of this conversation. He went round the coach and he slowly identified around in the region of fifteen or twenty kids in the coach. It was enough for them, they sat down and stayed out of it. The ones he didn't identify continued their verbal. No, he wasn't boasting or anything, just saying it quite calmly, matter of fact. 'I've seen you up at Harry's, I've seen you up at Stan's, you hang around with so and so' and it shut these kids right up.

It absolutely horrified me, because if those four kids hadn't been on the scheme it would have been a normal scheme for us, the normal kids we deal with day in day out, general run of the mill young offenders. I hadn't realized until then that so many of them could be involved in this sort of abuse in some way – it was obviously on a much bigger scale than any of us had realized.

Let us now have a brief look at some reports showing how difficult it is to come to any conclusion about the numbers involved, mainly because so few incidents are reported. For example, in the 1984 UK Home Office national crime survey of a representative sample of households who were asked about their experience of victimization, it was found that as few as one in ten rapes or sexual assaults on women had been reported to the police (Hough and Mayhew 1985). A 1987 American study by Gene Abel and colleagues showed that 567 abusers, promised freedom from imprisonment under a legal amnesty, admitted to having had almost incredible numbers of victims, far higher than had been expected: on average each non-incest offender against girls averaged twenty victims, while each non-incest offender against boys averaged 150 (Abel *et al.* 1987). No doubt few of these abuses had been reported by the victims.

In a similar vein Ray Wyre of the Gracewell Clinic in Britain remarked at a meeting in 1991:

> At any given time 67 per cent of men who are sent here for abusing within the family have also abused outside the family but nobody knew, so I think that to continually use intrafamiliar and extrafamiliar as a clear-cut definition is actually not what we are finding here in treatment. . . . The men who come here have never been caught for what they've really done. The system in general is not set up to deal with such information. An extreme example, we had one man here who had been sent for abusing two children, but we disovered he'd abused 200, making child pornography with them. If Social Services thought they had a resource problem before they sent him to us, they certainly had one afterwards!

In Russell's study only 2 per cent of all cases of intrafamilial sexual abuse and 6 per cent of all cases of extrafamilial sexual abuse of females under 18 were reported to the police. Only 1 per cent of the abusers were caught and convicted (Russell 1983).

Finkelhor emphasizes that sex offenders in jail are unrepresentative of sex offenders in general, as most sex offenders are never caught and do not get help. Those who do get caught or who end up in treatment are almost certainly very unusual. Also from Finkelhor, 'Authorities on the prevalence of sexual abuse believe that the majority of abuse still goes undisclosed. . . . Such a conclusion can be arrived at by comparing lifetime incidence estimates which come from adult retrospective victimization surveys with the number of cases currently being publicly reported' (Williams and Finkelhor 1988).

However, as I said at the beginning of this chapter, people still want some kind of answer to the question, how common is child sexual abuse? Obviously, after Finkelhor's proviso, no answer can be very meaningful, but it seems from the very mixed figures above that over one-third of women at least have experienced some form of sexual abuse in their childhood sufficiently serious for them still to remember it with concern in later years, and that most of this abuse will have happened before they were 12 years of age. It would also appear probable that, if one were to count minor abuse such as non-touching flashing and obscene telephone calls, then there are few women who will have reached maturity without at least one incidence of this occurring. There are fewer figures available at present concerning boys, but it seems likely that at least a quarter of males will have suffered some form of abuse by the time they are adult, usually at an older age than the girls.

As to the final question, is the incidence of c.s.a. increasing, the only possible answer is, it is impossible to tell. Some, especially the more feminist-inclined, believe it is not, and that the reason we hear more about it now is because of the changed sexual climate which allows people to talk more easily about their earlier experiences, together with a post-Freudian readiness to believe what children tell us (as we noted in Chapter 2, Freud came to believe that reports of childhood sexual abuse were either children's fantasy or that from Oedipal desires the children themselves had seduced their abusers), and that contemporary or retrospective studies are based on truth. Linda Gordon, Professor of History at the University of Wisconsin, points out that in America there have been three waves of public awareness of c.s.a. – in the 1870s and 1880s, again from 1910 to 1920 and since the 1970s – all of them allied to peaks of feminism: this awareness of child abuse was/is a result of women's movements being as concerned with the welfare of children as with women. When feminism ebbs, she suggests, problems such as c.s.a. are pushed back under the carpet (*Independent* 28 April 1990). Other people, however, believe the actual incidence of c.s.a. has increased; they blame in particular the break-up of the family as we have known it, single-parent families with transient partners who lack the 'natural' inhibition of blood relationships, the increase of pornography including pornographic films, the stress caused by unemployment and its resulting excess of free time, and a general lack of moral direction.

Certainly there has been an increase in registrations over the years, at times dramatic, though this seems to be easing off now, but, as the

For many years one of the reasons I couldn't believe all that abuse had actually happened to me was what I now discover is this thing called psychological splits or dissociation. My visual memory of that episode with my father was him standing there by the wall and me right there next to him, except that I was seeing myself about four or five feet in front of me. The same thing happened with my grandfather. I'd go by the bathroom and he would be standing there; he'd ask me to come in and he would unzip himself, out would come his penis, and I could see it getting close to me and then the same thing, he'd be there and I'd be there, but I'd be standing about 5 feet behind myself . . . for many years that was what made me doubt this could ever have happened, because obviously, how could you possibly see *yourself*? . . . I had different names for myself in various flashbacks, with [the other two abusers] too, and for my first day in the loonybin, but my splits aren't alive to the extent they make me a multiple. I've gone over this with the therapist and it seems it's very common, nearly everyone has this.

I have not over-dramatized the after-effects of c.s.a.: in view of the huge numbers of people we have discovered who suffer some form of sexual abuse during their childhood it is obvious that most of those experiencing the milder forms of abuse are able as they grow up to put these aside and proceed with their lives, undoubtedly a little damaged, but few people throughout history have reached adulthood without something having damaged them at some point. There are, however, incalculable numbers of victims who have had to face many years of intense stress and pain before arriving at comparative calm, and many thousands more whose lives have been ruined for ever beyond repair. This is a fact that it is not possible to over-dramatize.

Chapter 9

Outlines of treatment

SOME ASPECTS OF TREATMENT

We must be careful not to negate their experiences as we hurry to blanket victims of child sexual abuse with assurances that they are not in any way to blame for their abuse, lest we make them feel rejected or – as may have occurred in the past – not listened to. They need to be encouraged to talk not only of the pain of their abuse but also about any feelings of guilt or responsibility they may be harbouring for what happened.

This is particularly important if there has been an unsuccessful prosecution and the child has had to return unprotected to an unbelieving family which might scapegoat them and blame them for all the disruption. Even when they have been believed and are safely separated from the abuser they might still have to face another problem, that having been highly sexualized by their past experiences their behaviour in school or with foster families may well cause trouble, which in turn can lead to more rejection and/or a vulnerability to further abuse.

Victims, like the rest of the family, long for the time when the whole business of revelations, accusations and professional interventions can be put behind them; they may insist that they are now better and need no more therapy, when in fact the reverse is true. Loyalty to the abuser and pressure from the family as a whole will increase the likelihood of this happening. In addition, not all professionals are able to deal efficiently with child sexual abuse. Inevitably there will be some who have never been able to come to terms fully with any abuse – physical, emotional or sexual – which they themselves might have suffered when they were children; consequently they find great difficulty in allowing themselves to empathize fully with their victimized clients. This uneasiness can lead to the victim sensing the other's disturbance and desire to have done with the case, and as a result learning to distrust the very person who is supposed to be her/his main ally. Sometimes adults who have been victimized as children report in therapy how in their childhood professionals to whom they tried to talk about their abuse refused to listen at all or did not want to hear any details.

Another possible scenario is that the family, deeply disturbed by all the disruption, would like to have the victim – seen as the evil root of the problem – removed altogether. If the child *is* taken away then such a family will close up and attempt to cut her/him right out of their lives, so that the victim loses not only her family, her previous school acquaintances and any local friends, but also, of course, her abuser who might have been the sole source of any close relationship she has ever known.

A further problem which often has to be faced is that the revelation of the facts of the abuse can bring on a crisis for victims and families who over years of abuse will have formed a pattern of life enabling them to live with the secrecy imposed on them. It sometimes happens at this point that professionals find themselves in danger of slipping into a position whereby they replace the client-victim's secret relationship with the abuser with their own one-to-one confidential relationship. It is equally easy for professionals misguidedly to collude with the entire family's desire for the abuse not to be made public, and to hesitate to call in other protective or legal agencies. In their interaction with the family their loyalties may become attached to the family as a whole, and because of their willing belief in the entire family's protestations that they have reformed they may simply not realize that under this screen of pious innocence the abuser is in fact continuing his abuse. The victim, who is now being even more intensively threatened not only by the father but by all the family who are fearful of family break-up and the arrest of the abuser, colludes in the silence. The worker, pleased at her/his apparent success, allows the case to be closed, and withdraws.

It is essential that all professionals are aware of this danger and, if they have not already done so, they must set about involving a full team of outside support from the first moment it has been accepted that there is an abusive situation. There needs to be much sharing of expertise in an area which has become far too complicated for any one professional to encompass fully alone. But even where a multi-professional network of cooperating workers has been formed it should always be remembered how easy it is for individual workers to become identified with one or other of the members of the family, resulting in clashes between different workers who may be seeing events only from their own particular client's point of view. Close planning with members of other disciplines is very necessary if conflicts which already exist in the family are not to be replicated by those working with them.

The first priority in treatment must always be to make sure the abuse has stopped. This usually means that temporarily at least victim and abuser must be separated, preferably with the child remaining at home. If this first stage of intervention is to be accomplished smoothly and with minimum disturbance the full cooperation of several legal and therapeutic agencies must have been organized right from the beginning so that a temporary legal injunction can be issued immediately, prohibiting the abuser from returning to the house. It is obviously best if the various agencies involved have worked together previously to set up plans for such emergencies so that no time need be wasted in overcoming the reluctance of one or other agency to cooperate in what is almost invariably a rushed and anxious time. The possibility must be borne in mind, though, that a child might be so uncomfortable in the house, perhaps through having particularly bad relations with the mother, that the best results would be achieved if the victim were to be temporarily removed and not the abuser.

The next aim is to help the offender acknowledge that responsibility for the abuse is his and his alone. Other members of the family may have known about it and the victim may have been more or less active in the abuse, but as the initiator and perpetrator the abuser must accept full responsibility; that until he does he cannot return to his proper role as parent, and the child cannot return fully to being a child. Virtually every system of treatment agrees with the importance of this rule, some even refusing to accept the abuser for treatment unless he has made this admission (although an insincere admission, made purely for tactical reasons and likely to be retracted, is useless).

Whenever possible both parents should be present with the child when the abuse is first discussed. This may even happen in a police station but it is important that if, under the first shock of arrest, the father admits to the abuse his wife and victim should not only hear him but also psychologically understand the truth of it, so that any later denials may be rebutted by recalling this initial admission. Where it is the child who is making the first clear disclosure it is generally considered preferable that this takes place in the presence of a social worker and a member of the police force, both of whom have been trained in necessary techniques, with leading questions which would jeopardize prosecution being carefully avoided (see Chapter 4 for details of the use of one-way mirrors, video-recordings, etc., at such interviews).

At the first meeting or as soon afterwards as can be arranged all the family should come together – with or without the abuser, according to circumstances – to establish exactly what happened. This ideal cannot always be achieved and there may already have been many reports made to different agencies, but the secret of the abuse must be opened up as soon as possible and accepted as an acknowledged fact amongst the entire family.

Many therapists feel that the next step should be the building of an understanding between mother and child. This is therapeutic for both and helps to save the child from further abuse if the mother is now able to act in her proper protective role. But before starting to discuss family therapy it may be helpful to look closely at one of the earliest and most influential treatment programmes, the Child Sexual Abuse Treatment Program (CSATP) created by Hank Giarretto in 1971 at San José, California. Based in the community, CSATP works by integrating professional therapists and official workers as well as a considerable number of volunteers and the peer-support of the clients themselves. It took years of effort, dedication and work by its originators for the programme to eventually achieve its acknowledged success. Many people have come from all over the world to study its workings, and more than 152 treatment centres based on the CSATP model have been established in the US, Canada, England and Australia.

The programme was originally targeted at tackling the insensitive handling of cases by police, judges, lawyers and other professionals, which Giarretto believes is still too common in most American states and many other countries. A further difficulty still commonly prevalent is the shortage of therapists trained to deal with the formidable needs of families where, as we have already seen, most parents will themselves have been abused in one way or another as children, and where as a result a variety of mental disorders may be present in the family. The only way to cope with such problems when resources are limited, and possibly the best way overall, is to enlist the mutual help of the clients. In CSATP they themselves raise funds to help run the various groups, help organize presentations to the public, etc., but above all they support each other through their peer groups – Parents United (PU), Daughters and Sons United (DSU) and Adults Molested as Children United (AMACU). Costs are also kept down by using volunteer help and by admitting as interns to CSATP student counsellors and social workers who help in the running of the self-help groups. Giarretto has justifiably pointed out it is a pity that some British professionals seem to consider only his work in family therapy and ignore what he sees as the most important aspect, that of the self-help and volunteer programme.

Believing that a victim is best served if she/he can remain within the eventually reconstituted family, Giarretto obviously disagrees with the assumption of too many police forces that their primary duty is to obtain evidence for committal (I have commented elsewhere on the great advances in the last two or three years in the cooperation in Britain between the police forces and the other child protection agencies). Even in Santa Clara County where it all began not all attorneys agree with the philosophy of CSATP, where an extraordinarily low recidivism rate of around 1 per cent for offenders who have completed the programme is reported, as against 20 per cent for those who have been imprisoned (this last is in itself a much lower rate than experienced professionals such as Ray Wyre expect in general). Admittedly, part of the reason for Giarretto's success is that he is selective in whom he takes on as clients; he accepts only those with a strong motivation, while offenders with a very violent history or with current drug or alcohol addiction are not accepted.

CSATP's preferred method is that when a case is first revealed a police officer and a social worker investigate the family; while not promising immunity from jail, they will assure the abuser he will receive a more favourable court reaction if he accepts full responsibility for what has happened. If he does so, typically a lengthy therapy will be mandated together with a sentence of a few months in jail with work-release privileges so that he can continue to support his family along with time to undertake the all-important therapy. But if one or both parents insist on denying then a former father-offender and mother from Parents United will be called in as sponsers to meet with the family and explain their own earlier difficulties and how they coped with them. The new family will then be invited to PU meetings, and if all goes well the law will collaborate on a recommendation to the court aimed primarily at reconstructive therapy for the whole family, instead of simply extracting retribution from the offender. Hopefully this will be achieved, the given sentence light and therapy mandated for all the family.

Without such a mandate it has been found that offenders soon cease to attend therapy. Indeed, it is known that in Australia and America some offenders start therapy purely in order to achieve a lighter sentence or to avoid jail altogether, and once this aim has been achieved they leave therapy without ever having started to work on underlying problems, such as any abuse done to them in their own childhood or their current alcohol or drug abuse. It is therefore essential to ensure through the courts that the offender undergoes regular therapy for several years at least.

Once admitted into CSATP, fees for treatment are agreed, and the victim is connected with a sponser from DSU if this has not already been done. A therapy programme for the entire family is drawn up and a social worker responsible to the court assigned. The treatment itself consists of a variety of methods such as gestalt techniques, guided imagery, play therapy, self-awareness exercises and personal journal-keeping, all of which aim at changing the too frequent self-concept of clients from self-hatred to a sense of their own worth (Giarretto 1989).

It should be pointed out that, although there are many similarities in various programmes throughout the United States, not all therapists are as sanguine about the final outcome as Giarretto. Lucy Berliner at Harbourview, Seattle, for instance, who sees c.s.a. very much in terms of an imbalance of male–female power, has said, 'We take a more hard-nosed attitude. . . . We believe it is rare a family can be reconstituted when the father or stepfather has molested his daughter.' However, the differences in general are not so great, and one huge advantage America unquestionably has over Britain is the system of 'networking', in which voluntary agencies, self-help groups and clergy work together with professionals in a way that is rarely seen in Britain (Bannister 1986).

Family therapy in general aims to change the entire pattern of maladaptive behaviours in all the members of the family. But in treatment the strengths of the individual members must be valued and used; in talking to me about her work at the Monroe Young Family Centre (which runs in conjunction with the Tavistock Centre and the National Children's Homes and which includes assessment as well as treatment), Suzanne Hood stressed this aspect:

> The day starts with a meeting of all the families; sometimes men turn up but there are no male perpetrators of c.s.a. there at present. They all go into the playroom, meet with the staff who might include volunteers, and for a quarter of an hour we talk about plans for the day – who is going to be seen by whom, and any difficulties or problems are expressed. Each family has a key worker. Then we have group activities with two members of the staff present. The families choose what they want to do with the material available while the staff observe, perhaps making suggestions but not in a heavy way – all the time encouraging the parent to be the person responsible for the child. This is the time they can assess how well the parents are able to do that. We don't separate parents and children during that group time and we don't take over.
>
> Throughout the programme unless they are in a separate part of the building for any reason we make the parent responsible for the child-

ren. Quite often they think because there are experts here the experts will take over, and this may undermine them. We need to show them they have strengths – they all have some – and they may in the long run be able to care for their children. Some of them have difficulty accepting this, though; they think, here is all this staff around and it's a relief not to have to look after the children for once. It's particularly stressful for the parents whose children are currently away in care and who are not used to having them around – most of them do have access, but it's a different kind of contact. There are all sorts of heightened feelings about what's going on, and also about what is going to happen afterwards as a result of our assessment.

After the family group activities the parents are left alone with their children while it's coffee-time, then they may have individual sessions with their key workers. Usually this meeting is just with the adults unless the child can't be left for some reason. Any adults not involved in these sessions would be in the playroom and helping look after all the children. In the adult psychotherapy group the adults meet and work together. The parents bring their own lunches in as we haven't the facilities here, but they can heat food up, and this is a useful time for us to watch and see how they interact and what they do. The key workers maintain contact with the referring agency to make sure that what's agreed within the team is done, and also hold regular meetings with the referrer to look at the progress.

As family therapy proceeds therapists often find that the mother/daughter conflict is becoming the focus of treatment, especially those aspects surrounding the emotional relationship between father and daughter, and the mother's failure to protect her daughter from her partner. It is likely by this stage in treatment that several subgroups within the family will have been formed. Different members will have different needs, and although the overall picture has to be kept in mind it is important that individual therapists, while necessarily sharing many facts with their colleagues, retain the required confidentiality and privacy between the different family members. Furniss suggests that if the abuser is absent his presence should be hypothetically suggested so that issues of responsibility, guilt and blame can be squarely dealt with by the rest of the family, in order that the sexual abuse is seen as a family reality and any lingering secrecy done away with (Furniss 1991).

Varying amounts of work will need to be done with siblings. Sometimes they will have been ignorant of the abuse, but even where this is true they cannot avoid being considerably affected by the legal and protective investigations undertaken by strangers about whom they know nothing. If their father or one or more of their sisters or brothers has been removed from the family they may well be frightened that they too will be taken. It is therefore important that they are present at early family meetings, not only so that they may be reassured as to what is happening but also to prevent the victims themselves from being scapegoated by their siblings out of ignorance as to what actually occurred and blamed for all the disruption. Of course very often the siblings also will have been abused, and it is essential that this possibility is thoroughly explored, but even if this proves not to be so they will need considerable psychological help if they are not to suffer as a result of the considerable disturbance in the family.

Guilt and fear, particularly of re-abuse, are the main two emotions that have to be dealt with before a child can be considered well on the way to health. Guided acting-out of the abuse is necessary for this process, both of what actually did happen and of what the child would have liked to have done in self-protection but was unable to do. Play with dolls, puppets, role play or re-enactment of familiar fairy stories help in this process. It is vital that the victims realize that for survival purposes they had to go along with what was happening and that in those circumstances their decision was reasonable, even strong, and that that same strength may now be used in learning and practising assertive protective behaviours (Bannister 1985b, 1989; Hartman and Burgess 1988).

Another aspect that has to be dealt with is the difficulty the victim has in accepting *without guilt* any physical enjoyment she or he had during the abuse, together with any other positive aspects such as the emotional attention of the abuser. Boys in particular should be taught about the functioning of their bodies so that they may realize that during abuse penile erection or ejaculation can be a psycho-physiological reaction to stimulation over which they have no control.

Alan Fugler, of SOTAP (Sexual Offenders Treatment and Assessment Programme), Adelaide, discussing this aspect with me, pointed out that, although many of the victims' experiences were terrible, as adults they find it difficult to accept their lack of blame because, while in their heads they know the abuse was the perpetrator's fault, in their hearts they still believe they were to blame because of these undeniable positive aspects. As before, this needs to be worked out by helping the victims go back to the time of the abuse:

> You've got to help them reintegrate that part of their personality that is split right off, so I go back with individuals as adult and child

together – in other words the adult has to use visual and transfer work to be able to see themselves in that situation as an adult. The 6- or 7-year-old child in them is standing there and the adult they now are is standing behind them, so that the adult can see the child as she or he was then. Now the child's adult perpetrator will be there as well, and the kind of technique I use is for the adult to relate to that perpetrator and to ask him questions about themselves. I want him to look at the perpetrator and see what kind of person he is – all perpetrators have some kind of problems.

Now people who've been traumatized as children carry a heavy anger, too, and unless you can take that adult back so that he has a look at the person that was abusing them and forgive him – not here [touching his head] but here [touching his heart] – they're not going to be able to move on. They have to be able, as an adult, to take that 6-year-old and give that child a really big hug (I'm being simplistic here, it's a lot more complicated than this) and make sure that kid knows it's really safe. So the adult is able at last to integrate that child into his adult self.

Some people, however, would consider controversial Fugler's comments about the necessity for forgiveness. Anne Bannister told me that she feels forgiveness is a two-way concept and can happen only if the offender is truly repentant, but that in her experience this is very rare. Her worry is that to suggest a survivor cannot 'move on' without achieving this forgiveness is very constricting, and could lead some inexperienced workers to push clients incorrectly down this road. This last is a valid point, but I think one should take Fugler's words as expressing a very real understanding that where bitterness continues to exist it will be difficult for a survivor to work through to peace and happiness.

Children begin to change as therapy progresses and unless work is done to ensure that this change is understood and accepted by the family, especially by the mother, then therapy may be called off and/or much distress caused to the victim. For example, one of the changes that has to be made is an appreciation of the need for modesty by the child if she is not to risk further abuse or rejection by peers and teachers at school, but in chaotic homes such an idea may be sneered at and the child laughed out of it. We may remember how as Barbara grew up she attempted to keep her own bedroom and bed linen clean and how she was mocked for this. It can sometimes be difficult for professionals with a very different lifestyle to appreciate the extent of a problem of this kind.

If the father/abuser has also been receiving therapy at this stage it should now be possible to begin to deal with the relationship between him and the victim. If in later life the victim is to be able to build good relationships with an adult partner it is important that a new trust is established with a father or father figure. But a genuine understanding by all the family, including the abuser, of the abuser's responsibility must be achieved before he is allowed to meet his victim. As we have already seen, sometimes the pressure on the workers involved to complete the case, coming from both the family and the professionals' own needs, can encourage them to attempt rehabilitation of the father too soon. Comprehensive case conferences must be held to ensure that all the family is ready for the next step, whether it be to allow a child who has been in care to return home or the father to meet the victim and/or the family. It is important that the therapist who is looking after the victim is not also responsible for deciding whether or not the abuser is ready for the next move. The abuser will need to be assessed by other professionals whose responsibility it will be to decide whether or not he has changed sufficiently to be allowed ready access to his victim, or indeed to other children. A mere working-out of whatever sentence has been passed will never be enough to ensure this last is so.

GROUPS

'It took me a long time to understand some of what was happening in the group. Often I would go home feeling very torn-up inside. . . . We had feared and fought against self-pity, fended off the indulgence of pain, but the hard accepting silence which had become a lifetime's habit was undermined by others' tears, tears of sorrow, rage, loneliness, meaninglessness, tears which each survivor had held inside, unable to release in any other way. . . . More than anything we had been afraid of losing the innermost grip on our control, of "letting ourselves down", of being swept away in the deluge of our own tears' (Spring 1987). This is a quotation from the book *Cry Hard and Swim* which had been lent to me by Brenda, to whom, it might be remembered, the issue of control was still of great importance. The author was writing about an incest survivors' group which she had joined after therapy and which she, along with all the other members, found very helpful.

Jane also had found her own group immensely helpful, and felt that the women there, all survivors, were able to support and communicate with each other in a way that no professional, however well trained, could. It does seem necessary, however, that at least one facilitator should be available to lead or support a survivors' group: these victims have been severely damaged and the pain and anguish that may be displayed as they open up their wounds may be more than an untrained person can cope with alone.

Furniss considers that group therapy, supported by family work, is usually preferable to individual therapy for children and adolescents. Often believing they are the only ones to whom sexual abuse has happened, they are helped by meeting other group members and ceasing to define themselves simply as dirty, unloved creatures of little value. Instead they discover mutual strengths and potential and lose their previous sense of uniqueness and isolation (Furniss 1991). In their groups children can work on overcoming this sense of isolation and learn how to share with others, building up trusting relationships with their peers which they may not have been able to risk doing before. At the same time it is a good opportunity for them to learn how to relate to other people in a non-sexual way and to become aware of any remaining sexualized behaviour through the reactions of their peers.

Closed groups where a number of children start together and finish at the same time have the advantage of growing together through the same stages of treatment and of knowing each other intimately, but it is often difficult to find sufficient children of similar ages and development to begin a group. An open group has the advantage of being able to be built up gradually, starting with three or four children, and obviously allows for the probability that some children will need longer therapy than others. The disadvantages, though, are that the composition of the group is constantly changing and that it will take time for newcomers to settle in comfortably amongst old members who all know each other well.

For very young children the groups can consist of mixed sexes, but it is generally thought preferable for older children to be placed in single-sex groups. Issues of sexuality need to be discussed in the privacy of one-sex groups; also girls find it much easier to open up in groups than do boys, for whom the intimate sharing of sexual experiences and problems with peers is far more difficult. Already concerned with their worries about sexual identification if they have been abused by other males, they are not helped in this difficulty by having to present themselves, as victims, in a weak non-macho position.

We have already glanced at the groups run by the Giarrettos and their colleagues in San José, where self-help is a most important element. For example, CSATP and other centres dealing with c.s.a., such as the Harbourview Sexual Assault Centre in Seattle, train women who had themselves been abused as children to run therapy groups. In the Seattle group it was stressed it was not a treatment group but was 'educative and supportive' (Bannister 1985a). In Australia groups of various kinds are functioning successfully, and one in particular that could be copied with advantage elsewhere is the Protect All Children Today programme (run by the Child Witness Support Group, 105 Newman Road, Wavell Heights, Queensland 4012), in which trained volunteers prepare children for their involvement in the court process. The volunteers familiarize the children with the court layout, explain the court processes to them, and personally support and accompany them through all the various potentially traumatic occasions that may arise until the completion of the case.

The number of supportive groups is growing in Britain, although as elsewhere financial resources are the continual problem. The NSPCC has run a variety of innovative groups which have proved successful, and their *Working with the Aftermath of Child Sexual Abuse* (NSPCC 1990) is proving invaluable for training purposes. In London the various therapy groups run by the Tavistock Clinic and that invaluable centre of excellence, the Great Ormond Street Hospital for Sick Children, have blazed new paths for everyone working with those who have been sexually abused as children.

Self-help groups assisted by trained facilitators for adolescents, for adults who are still disturbed by their abuse as children, for non-abusive partners, mothers, siblings and abusers are a well-proven, economical way of providing support and growth for all those who in one way or another are affected by c.s.a. In this time of universal shortage of money and an ever-increasing awareness of the size of the problem, surely every effort must be put into increasing the numbers of such groups and those who are trained to organize them.

TREATMENT FOR ABUSERS

Much has been written and many opinions expressed on the subject of the treatment of the perpetrators of child sexual abuse. At the 1990 NSPCC conference on abusers to which I have already referred there were angry cries of 'nonsense!' and 'rubbish!' as Hank Giarretto replied to Dr Tony Baker's comments from the floor regarding children of 6, 8 or 10 years who had been picked up. Baker: 'We do not see "*offenders*" of that age, we see children who have acted in sexual ways with other children, but I refused to call them "sexual offenders".' Giarretto (basically agreeing): 'I would never use the word "offender" with that age. Because if there's no intervention with a 6-year-old he's never going to learn self-enhancement. He'll be just as helpless at 12 and at 35 as he was at 6.

I strongly believe that a person – who is under conscious control, that is – who molests a child will know intellectually it is wrong, but he cannot control it any more than the alcoholic can.' Through several shouts of 'rubbish!', he continued, 'and until he is empowered to make choices he is going to go on doing that. You can arrest him and lock him up but if you don't work with him and give him that capability, he's not going to stop, and the same thing applies to a child.' When a voice from the hall called out, 'They can stop if they want. I know people like that who can, and they still commit abuse because they want to do it', quite a few people applauded loudly.

These opposite attitudes express perfectly the differences that lie between those who basically agree with Giarretto, himself a kind, gentle man of great humanity, and those who, full of righteous anger, have little pity for abusers who have committed what are sometimes almost unimaginably horrendous crimes against children. Admittedly, Giarretto can be a poor presenter at public meetings, but seeing him actually at work with families convinces most watchers of his extremely high quality and success as therapist and teacher. His methods are widely known and copied in many places where resources permit, but for those without his own unresting genius for persuading people in power to support him, or at least not to thwart him, progress is slower than most would like it to be. Dorothy Scott, School of Social Work, Melbourne, told me:

The real success of the Giarretto programme is very early involvement of the offender at the time when he is most vulnerable, that's when he's being charged, and when the buddy system's gone into action – that's the other offender who's been down the track – when he's saying to him, look here, mate, there's light at the end of the tunnel; confess, repent, you can be reborn: it's got to be almost like that. Because of the plea bargaining which the Americans have, and because the treatment programme is reaching out to him at the very crisis point where the police are laying charges, they can often motivate him to plead guilty. I don't think treatment programmes are going to work nearly as effectively if you try to offer them after a conviction's already happened, when there's no carrot, only the stick. The problem with duplicating Giarretto's system in other places is that the charismatic personality, the strong powerful force at inter-organizational level, is missing. What's needed is to pull together treatment and the law, and somehow to try to motivate people for treatment while minimizing the sanctions they will have to suffer legally in a punitive way. There's a lot of suffering in store for them, it's very painful: that's what people who see treatment as a soft option don't understand.

This message is reiterated by everyone who actually works therapeutically with abusers. Bannister writes in her 'The child-centred philosophy', 'Treatment of the abuser then must be confronting. It must seek to remove the scales from the eyes of the abuser, it must enable him to look not only at the pain he has caused but also at the pain he may have suffered himself [as an abused child]. For most abusers this is the most difficult part of any treatment' (Bannister 1988b). Tony Morrison: 'I went to the States and talked with some of these guys and they said the roughest module they faced was not actually going through what they had done to the child but going back and re-experiencing being a victim. If they don't manage this then it's very doubtful they can ever truly empathize with the victims they've assaulted.'

But abusers are not easy people to work with. People find it difficult to cope with the fact that, as we saw elsewhere, the abuse they commit is planned and deliberately organized over time. Morrison again, discussing this aspect of abusers in the workshop he shared with Mai Bentley at the NSPCC Conference: 'There is nothing impulsive, although what they will say on arrest is, "I just found myself in that place, and my hand just there, I got no sexual gratification, I wasn't aroused." When you interview an offender, expect to be controlled. Expect that you will alternately feel sorry, confused, angry, out of control – because that's exactly what they want you to feel, what they are most skilled at.' Later in the workshop as various methods of treatment were discussed Mai Bentley reminded us that in Britain we do not have the resources the Americans have, and that we must take care not to burden ourselves with an over-ambitious set of treatment goals when we have only three hours a week to achieve them as against the perhaps thirty-five hours a week of other more fortunate workers.

Someone in England, though, who does have time is Ray Wyre at the Gracewell Clinic, where all the clients in their much-copied programme are residential. Clients come to the clinic for assessment mainly through referrals from the probation service, from court orders and conditions of parole. Using group and individual therapy, and questionnaires both written and videoed, the therapists work with clients to assess their chance of change and whether or not the prognosis is good enough for them to be offered treatment. After an assessment report is written, it is then decided by the authorities whether the offender goes to prison or, if Gracewell has already agreed to accept him, to be sent there for treatment. The Gracewell system is particularly helpful where there is insufficient evidence to commit a man to prison but where some treatment is very necessary.

Once admitted, the men begin a course of daily and group therapy which is continually adjusted to fit individual needs, which can vary tremendously. There are five key programmes which all clients have to complete: cognitive distortion; victim awareness; sexual fantasy; female and male sexuality; assertiveness. These programmes are organized in blocks of two weeks at a time and by the end of three months the client should have completed the first stage of working on all of the main subjects, both individually and in groups. Where necessary he will continue to work on a particular aspect until it is decided he is ready to move on to the next one; as with most other programmes, however, it is stressed that no offender can ever be 'cured', so that in a sense no client will ever be able to say he has completed his treatment. Although most offenders have themselves been abused, some of them sexually, this particular aspect is not discussed with them in any depth until they have accepted full responsibility for their own abusive behaviour and are able to look at what they have done without distortion or excuse. But it is recognized that unless their own abusive past is dealt with it will remain there 'like an unexploded bomb waiting to go off'.

Where it is appropriate, family work involving couple counselling or family therapy is arranged, during which the client's key worker 'networks' with the family and the other professionals who are working with them. Sometimes family meetings are arranged at Gracewell, and if it is decided that the offender will eventually be able to rejoin his family he has to explain to them exactly how in the past he was able to manipulate them so that they may be armed against any regression, and he also has to detail what he has learned about his cycles of behaviour. Finally, he has to prepare an 'alert' list to help him be aware of the times when he is likely to be most in danger of slipping back into his old ways and which will aid him, when he knows himself to be at risk of committing further abuse, to follow his pre-planned 'escape route'. The contents of this list are then shared with partners and with professionals working with the family.

Thus, before a client leaves Gracewell he must complete his discharge plan and have it approved by his therapist, the group with whom he has worked, his family and the professionals who will be working with him after his phased discharge. If he later should need to return to Gracewell it is possible to do so, provided he has not re-offended, or he can telephone for support and advice. Clients do in fact take advantage of this – as Trevor Price, Director, has said, 'Many other treatment centres have a realize she will deeply miss the presence of the abuser. He is likely to be the only adult in the family apart from herself (though in many cases the man will have made emotional and physical demands on her like the child he still is in many ways, and although she might deny it she would miss this aspect of him as much as she will miss his male company – after all, she chose him as her partner). She dreads having to cope with the reaction of neighbours and relatives and, if she works, with that of her co-workers and employers. In addition, she may have disturbing feelings of jealousy, together with doubts about her own attractiveness. She may feel anger, bitterness towards the child who has stolen her lover and, above all, guilt, guilt that she is so worthless as to put her own feelings before the needs of her child. This process may not be conscious. To voice her suspicions, even to herself, is immensely difficult. To go even further and to break the secret by dragging it out into the public arena is something which – as an abused child she would have been taught must never, ever happen – requires almost unthinkable bravery.

In an interview Adrian Ford, Director of Scarba Family Centre, Sydney, told me:

> If the mothers have been abused they have to avert their gaze because they fear they're being abused again and they're powerless to stop it just as the child is. You have to understand the mother's powerlessness and her collusion because of her powerlessness. They don't always know themselves they are colluding because there are conscious and unconscious processes at work and the experiences they've grown up with is something they're still having to come to terms with. It is incredibly painful for them to face the fact that it's happening again, and I think one way of coping is to not really see, it's a hoping it might go away, just like the sexually abused child herself who hides under the sheets is hoping it's going to go away. . . . Do they acknowledge it to themselves? I don't know. It's very difficult, rarely do you get people who say I know it happened. Much more it's almost a preconscious stage, you get a sense they know the child's been in the room, though they had arranged for the father to look after the girls while they went out – there's also a sense they don't want to know, understandably because it's too horrendous. I think it is too strong to say mothers know, I think people can only know after a great deal of pain themselves and a great deal of very specialized help to be able to get to know.

'Collusion' is not easy to recognize. Mothers in sexually abusing families are often compulsive caretakers. In a practical sense they look after their children competently, frequently appearing caring and close.

But if the victim tells this type of mother that she/he is being abused the mother will probably not accept the accusation but may well 'take token steps to disprove the allegations' (Furniss 1991: 48). We might remember that, after Barbara had assured her local GP she couldn't believe Ted had touched Katie, the doctor told her 'Your home's lovely and clean, your children are well-kept, you've always come across to me as being a very adequate parent.' It must have been obvious she dearly loved her daughter; it is difficult to blame the doctor for not looking closer.

SIBLING INCEST

Sibling incest may easily be taken too lightly. Children exploring together, what can be the harm in that? In fact, over the years I have spoken to a surprising number of women whose lives have been made miserable by incestuous assaults on them by their brothers, mostly much older but not necessarily so. That I have not personally heard from similarly affected men is probably purely due to the continuing reluctance of males to admit they once had to play the 'feminine' part in sex.

Small children sharing a bath in a loving family without secrets are as much a delight to watch as a bundle of kittens romping together. Of course they will be interested in each other's differences although this soon passes with custom, and there is nothing to be worried about in mild sessions of 'playing doctors'. But sensible parents will be alert to any sign of tension among the players, any unexplained change of attitude; the fact is that actual sexual *abuse* by siblings can do as much damage as any other kind.

When sexual exploring, such as looking, exposing, touching, is mutual and appropriate to age, and is a comfortable albeit exciting experience, in 'normal' families this most likely will be a formative, positive experience. But where any force is used, and where difference in age means the older child wants something more advanced and beyond the age-appropriate requirement of the younger, emotional and/or physical pain maybe inflicted – even, in severe cases, life-long trauma.

Diana Russell writes, 'One of the consequences of the myth of mutuality may be that when brother/sister incestuous abuse is discovered or reported, there may be even less support of the victim than in other cases of abuse.' In her retrospective study 78 per cent of women who had sexual experiences as children found their experiences with brothers to be abusive, as did 50 per cent of those whose were with sisters. Eighty-five per cent reported the experience was totally unwanted and only 2 per cent had more or less desired it. Forty-eight per cent had been extremely upset after their brothers' abuse, and 24 per cent somewhat upset. She also reports that 'incestuous brothers may either try to trade on their good relationships with their sisters or, failing this, use force more readily than most other incest perpetrators' (Russell 1986: 49). I am indebted to Jenny Harvey for this information from the Department for Community Welfare, Adelaide.

Brenda, who is now 47, first wrote to me in 1982 telling me of her sexual abuse as a child at the hands of her eldest brother, Donald. She had suffered a breakdown after having her first baby and although she later worked with a counsellor she was still very disturbed, one of the worst problems being her sexual relations with her husband. She explained she had one sister and four brothers: 'My sister had asked me on numerous occasions if Donald had abused me but I always denied it. . . . I have lived with this for so long it just pulls me apart. . . . I feel so tired, I can't keep fighting. I realize many others suffer, poor souls, it is the worst thing anyone could do to another human being. . . . My work involves maladjusted children and I do have understanding of many emotional disturbances and reasoning with the outcome. . . . I am all happy and easy going on the exterior, but the interior is a different matter.'

She kindly agreed to meet me when I was preparing this new book, having meanwhile undergone therapy with a famous London clinic. She is clearer now as to what had happened, but she still has some way to go. When she talks she flits apparently aimlessly from subject to subject, while admitting being terrified of losing control. It is as though she cannot bear to let her mind settle for fear of arriving at the subject ever-present in her mind, possibly culminating in a total breakdown. What should be especially noted in this story is the family setting: abuse is so rarely a single occurrence just happening to take place between two people.

(For the sake of clarity I have adjusted the order of what she says and edited more heavily than usual.)

Yes, my sister was assaulted. There were six of us at home, and I was the last born. The age gap with me and my eldest brother Donald was twelve years, but the gap with my sister and him was four or perhaps five years, and she's four or five years older than me – I'm hopeless with figures – anyway she was old enough to refuse. I don't know how far he went with her, I never asked her. She only told me when she split up with her husband. I've no idea how long it went on for, either, but at one time she told me he did interfere with her, at another time she said he hadn't gone that far. But something must have happened for her to be so protective of me.

Donald was conscripted, and went into the Korean war. He got malaria, and had terrible nightmares when he came home. My next brother might have tried it on, but I was old enough to say don't be silly. But Donald, he was older, a sort of father figure. Looking back, I was getting double messages all the time at home. My mother must have known what was going on, this was our *home*, she *must* have known. But we were all so private. I never undressed in front of my sister, I never bathed with anybody, not even my sister, we didn't discuss anything, not sex, not anything. My mother never told me the facts of life – I'd started my period about a couple of years before she had any idea. I just think we were all very private, it's peculiar. [The girls were unusually isolated because they both went to private school, with ballet, dancing, and other subjects.] It was a very inferior school, but we were dressed up as dolls, I mean everything was immaculate, we never mixed with the children in the road.

Later after I talked to my sister about what Donald had done she told mother and all my mother said was, 'If that's what happened, then you asked for it.' My mother was one of these women that says boys will always take it, so it's up to girls to say 'no'. That's what was always instilled in us all through our life. I think my sexual hang-ups were a lot to do with what happened to me with Donald, but also what was being said around us all the time. There was something about the family. . . . Well, mum's brother had committed suicide when he was a young man, and she herself ran away from home at 15 after her mother died and got married early. . . . She must have wondered at the pattern when both my sister and me had breakdowns when we had babies.

Sex was taboo in our house, really, my father was very narrow-minded. You didn't tell jokes. I mean we were a happy family, but, underneath, no one was listening. My parents quarrelled over mum's extravagance with money and dad worked all hours, they even had physical fights, and I'd sit under the table or out on the porch crying, and my brothers would be laughing. It was a way of life. No, my father didn't abuse *her*, it was my mum used to hit him more than anything! Once when I was grown-up my dad came in one night very drunk, and after she told him off he turned to me and my husband and told us what he'd had to put up with all his life. 'Your Mum's not like a woman, she won't, you know . . . sexually she's not that way.' So it all came out. We said to her, 'Oh, come on, you don't get six children by not sleeping in bed with a man', but she turns round and says, 'I was a victim. You don't have to be sexy to have six children. I was a victim.' So that was around all the time I was growing up.

My father was very nice, but . . . I didn't know then, but now I'm sure he knew about Donald. I think he knew about my sister at least. There was a lot of hostility between my dad and Donald. But we were all really spoiled, we all had the best of everything.

I didn't remember properly what happened until I went for therapy, after I wrote to you. I went there with my husband once a month for two years and it had got to the point where I thought it hadn't happened – in spite of all that talking I didn't believe that someone could have done that to me. So they suggested I write to my brother and tell him I needed the answer to some questions. I had to be ever so careful what I wrote because of his wife, so I asked him to ring me. My parents had just died and with all this happening he got an ulcer, and from me contacting him his ulcer flared up and he went into hospital. There it was, all put back on me. I thought, *I've* made him ill, I've done this, I've done that. But in the end he came and talked.

There was a lot I didn't know, like I didn't know he'd started on me as early as 2. That was the worst thing. He was babysitting and it started off as a game, and he said it just got out of control. He said, I'm sorry, it was my fault, and he cried. He made me feel terrible.

What had he done to me? It's still difficult to talk about it. . . . He penetrated me. He had intercourse with me. No! Not at two, I wouldn't think. God!! He wouldn't say exactly what he did, so I don't know. All I can remember is the army bit, being in his bedroom when he was either on leave or home. I can see his kitbag, I can see his uniform, so whether he was in the army then and on leave, or demobbed, I don't know – that's the only time I can actually see him doing it. I was in the Juniors, 7, 8, but it might have been going on longer, that's the only time I can be sure. He wouldn't say anything about what happened when it started, he confirmed it about the army. At therapy they tried to get me to write a diary to help me find out when it happened, but I just couldn't do it. I don't know how old I was when he first penetrated me.

There were six of us altogether, and we used to have a key on a cord behind the door – you'd put your finger through and flip the key through, and I can remember the two of us being in the house on our own, and him winding that key round the door knob so that people couldn't pull it through, and I can see him locking the back door. You know, I have pictures of things. . . . He was always bigger than me, so I can't see him as any special age. He did body-building, weight-training, so even if he was 16 he would still have been much bigger than me. Was he gentle with me? All I can say is he took what he wanted. It didn't matter about *me*. They asked me at the clinic if I'd enjoyed it at all, or the attention, and I said I don't remember, but I hope I bloody well did, 'cos I paid for it! But I didn't need that kind of attention, I got a mum and dad that loved me, I didn't need it. Yes, he hurt me. He frightened me, he hurt me.

Maybe I didn't want to grow up, but I was a very young little girl at 14, I wasn't promiscuous or anything, I was still wearing my ankle socks at 14. I never wore a tight skirt, and I mean, even now, I think lots of things are common, and it's all mixed up with how you see somebody that's slept around or whatever – I can't define it. My husband said sometimes, you're frigid, there's something wrong with you, and there was, wasn't there!'

I met my husband at 17. I'd had one boyfriend before but when he came on a bit I got very frightened and pushed him away. But my husband was very gentle with me, and that's why I chose him. I'd known him about a year when we first made love. No, I was as curious as he was. At first it was all new: we never did it in luxury like, it wasn't regular, just a quick fumble. He didn't know anything, and I never knew anything, and the first time he done it he just penetrated me. But even then I would bleed.

Then when I was 18 I had appendicitis, and the way the doctor examined me, it started off memories. I didn't want to sleep with my fiancé any more, I didn't want to stay engaged. I think that's what started it off, going to hospital. The doctor put his index finger up my back passage, I wasn't expecting it. Had my brother done that? I've no idea, but I don't think he'd have been so sordid.

When we got married the first year was difficult, because I kept bleeding, and I had mastitis. My GP sent me to see a gynaecologist who examined me, and he said, you poor lassie, and he said it would be best to have a baby and breast-feed him.

I had a hysterectomy a year ago and was in hospital for six weeks. I had tubes in me when I came out, and it's taken me a long time to get over it. I mean, even now, we haven't got a sexual relationship as such at the moment, partly because of the operation, and partly because of all this. It's like whenever I'm with my husband, whatever it is triggers off something, you know, like the breathing in my face. I mean, there is a problem, and I can't get rid of it. I get them both confused, what's actually going on.

The treatment's not solved it as yet. I suppose I'm not one of their success stories. They've helped me. But I still can't talk to my husband. He thinks it'll all go away, he says just relax and forget about it. At times, after we've had intercourse or something, I'll come down and I'll cry. I've never ever climaxed. I can't let go. I can't let go in anything. Yes, my husband knows what to do, but when I get there I can't let go. When I had counselling by the Marriage Guidance people I began to get feelings, but when that happens I have to push him away, and I cry, I sob. This is where I am now. That crying comes from the bottom of my boots, it is totally out of control. Instead of getting a climax I shut it off and cry. It devastates me, it makes me feel suicidal. I can't function as a woman.

It all got to a head, my health, everything. I got to the point where I didn't want my life to go on, I was just being tormented. I wish to God I hadn't told my husband about my brother, because it's made it worse – things didn't get better, all I was doing was putting him through pain. He'd already been through it, he'd come from a very disturbed background; his father was a batterer and his three sisters were taken into care because of the home life, so what hurts me is that he needs what I can't give him.

Sometimes I feel like being really violent towards him, I really want to hurt him. But no, I can't tell him that, bless him. I tried, at the clinic, I said I just want to die, and he turned round and said if you feel like that, then I can't help you. That's the problem, it's why I can't let go, because I know that if I fall he's not going to be able to catch me. It's . . . if I let go, what am I letting go to? Where will I end up? He won't be able to help. Like when there was money difficulty, he just turned to me and said, look what you've done to me – that's what he says, he can't help himself. If there's a crisis in the family, he can unload to me, but I can't to him. Although he's good and he's kind, it's *my* problem. And what am I doing to him? In a way, although we're very close, it's a very destructive relationship.

I can't do with any more let-downs in my life. There's been a lot of incompetence in people dealing with me, in hospital and all that, but that's the story of my life. I think, did I create these problems, what is it about me that makes everything go wrong? I can't see myself moving on. I feel like my life's over.

It's very difficult telling people that, because they feel they've got to give me a label, give me drugs, give me this, give me that. Though this new man I'm seeing, he's an obstetrician and a top man in the field of hormones. He's very nice, and when in the end I told him about Donald he confirmed I wasn't going mad, it was the hormone deficiency, and he said no wonder you've had trouble with your waterworks. One of my only memories with Donald is sitting in the toilet crying because it burned . . . whether all the illness I've had is tied up . . . I'm going back to see him and I'll ask him what he meant, and maybe in a year or so I'll get it all sorted out. Right now, like when I'm talking to you, everything's muddled in my head, it's like a piece of string, and until it's all unravelled. . . .

One last thing that's worried me is that at the clinic when my brother came he kept calling me Sally, that's the name of his own daughter. They noticed it too. He's had terrible troubles with her. I only get it through the grapevine, she's grown-up now, but she was seeing child guidance, she didn't want to be a woman, she wanted to be a little girl, and immediately I thought, ooh! That, I'd never forgive. He's ashamed of what he did to me, he says, but he hasn't learned. Admitting doesn't make them better people.

At least my own two boys are fine. They went once with us to the therapy clinic for a family session, and I was glad they could see my children don't have any hang-ups. One's got his degree now and, anyone can see, there's nothing unhealthy about either of them whatsoever.

Incidence of child sexual abuse and how to discover it

HOW WIDESPREAD IS CHILD SEXUAL ABUSE?

'We wholly accept that the true extent of child abuse is, and will necessarily remain, unknown. However, increases ... in the number of cases reported may well reflect a considerable increase in the actual incidence of offences committed', and 'In recent years substantial and apparently unremitting rises in the number of sexual crimes committed against women and children have been recorded' (Pigot Report 1989). 'Given the nature of sexual abuse, its secrecy and sensitivity, it is unlikely that an accurate assessment of its incidence will ever be established' (Steven *et al.* 1988).

One of the first questions I am often asked is, how common is child sexual abuse? When, in 1982, in my first book on incest I gave the figure of one in ten females having been abused (mainly based on Finkelhor's excellent studies) the shock/horror was almost universal, up-to-date workers in the field excepted. Even at the time of Cleveland (1987) MPs, doctors, moralists, were still able to express in the media their appalled horror at the behaviour of the beleaguered Cleveland doctors, virtually presenting them as perverted freaks. In fact, contrary to media myth, of the 121 cases of suspected c.s.a., only twenty-six were eventually judged by the courts to have been wrongly diagnosed (Campbell 1988).

It *is* difficult to accept the huge numbers involved – it seems probable that nearly one in three women have experienced some kind of sexual misuse/abuse in their childhood, as have, Furniss suggests, between 20 and 40 per cent of boys (Furniss 1991) – and we have to move from that understanding to considering how to cope with such a fact.

Reporting of c.s.a. is so sketchy and incomplete that few researchers are prepared to stick their necks out and hazard more than a guess at the actual figures involved. It is helpful to remember that we should not assume all sexually abused children are necessarily psychiatrically disturbed. Quoting a properly structured random study in San Francisco (Russell 1983) which showed that 38 per cent of women had been sexually abused at least once by the time they were 18, Tilman Furniss points out that these numbers were based on 'a normative and not a mental health definition', and that the conclusion cannot be drawn that 38 per cent of San Franciscan women are psychiatrically disturbed by their abusive experience. But, he says rightly, however disturbed or not such women may be, the sexual abuse 'in normative terms [is] still abuse and should not happen', and the abuse must be judged in those terms. Equally it must not be argued that because it is so common – indeed, almost 'normal' – we should cease worrying about it (Furniss 1991).

In 1985 Finkelhor reported that studies done on non-clinical groups suggested that between one-fifth and one-third of all women had been sexually abused as children (Finkelhor 1985). This is a higher rate than that arrived at in his earlier well-known study of 795 New England undergraduates (1978), which showed that 19 per cent of the women and 9 per cent of the men had been sexually victimized, but since these students were psychiatrically fit enough to study it may be assumed the most severely damaged victims of c.s.a. were not among them. This study has been replicated in other parts of the USA and in Canada, Britain and Australia. The Australian study (Goldman and Goldman 1988b) of 991 students showed that around 28 per cent of Australian girls had reported some kind of sexual abuse during childhood and adolescence, the vast majority of abuse happening before the age of 12 years, i.e. pre-pubertal. Again, about 9 per cent of boys were sexually molested, the majority also before the age of 12 years (Goldman in press).

Statistics issued by the New South Wales Department of Education in their *Child Protection, 7–12* (NSW Department of Education 1989a: 113) show that 30 per cent of girls and 10 per cent of boys have been sexually assaulted by the age of 18. Libby DeLacey, head of the Division of Education, Griffith University, Queensland, told me, 'I did a retrospective study over four semesters of what my students judged to be abuse, and 32 per cent of them recorded experiences of abuse, most of these female students, and the bulk of the abuse was sexual abuse. To make sure experiences of the kind one giggled about weren't counted we asked for severity to be marked according to importance. Now, this is the elite in our community, the best protected, the best informed, so one wonders what the results would be if we did a grander scale project.'

The earlier-mentioned study carried out by Professor Donald West (Director of the Institute of Criminology at Cambridge) found that 42 per cent of a mixed social group of women from two health centres and 54 per cent of a group of female students reported at least one sexual experience in childhood, ranging from an obscene phone call to intercourse. Half the total number of women had been under 12 at the time, and fifteen were under 9 (*The Guardian* September 1984). A survey sponsored by the Economic and Social Research Council and carried out by the North London Polytechnic's Child Abuse Study Unit found even higher figures and concluded that 'most women and more than one in four men were sexually abused in some form during childhood', nearly one in three of these being assaulted before the age of 12. Almost none of the incidents were reported. Twenty-seven per cent of the assaults were flashing and 23 per cent touching. One in twenty of the women and one in fifty men had been raped, pressurized into sex or forced to take part in masturbation (*Independent* June 1991).

In May 1986 the women's magazine *Woman's Own* (UK) published a well-planned questionnaire about rape to which 25,000 of their readers responded, this being the largest number of replies on a single subject they had ever received. Of the respondents 12 per cent said they had been raped, 14 per cent of whom had been under 10 at the time, while a further 29 per cent (of the 12 per cent) were aged between 10 and 16 and 41 per cent between 16 and 24. The majority of those aged under 16 were raped by a relative; 39 per cent of these were under 10 years old and 20 per cent were between 10 and 16. Seventy-six per cent of the rape victims had not reported the attacks to the police (*Woman's Own* 1986).

Official figures are much lower. The UK Department of Health's figures from the Child Protection Register for the whole of England up to 31 March 1990 show, out of a total of 22,500 girls *on the register*, 20 per cent were there for sexual abuse; of 21,100 registered boys, 7 per cent were there for the same reason (Department of Health 1991: 13).

The difficulty of finding out the truth about the numbers of sexually abused children is well illustrated by the following extracts from an interview I had with Lewis Anderson, Intermediate Treatment Officer, North London. He has been working for some years with young boys who were skirting perilously close to trouble, and there had been some suggestion that a ring involving adults might be operating in his area. Anderson's comments on how he dicovered a large number of local boys involved show how acute observers need to be:

> For our summer scheme we had sixty or seventy local kids coming in, most of them knew each other from school or the estates, or from hanging around the snooker halls, amusement arcades. The summer

holidays were coming on and every kid in the area was encouraged to come on one of the weekly coach trips we organized down to places like Margate and Great Yarmouth, forty or so at a time. It had become obvious that the ones not involved in the so-called rent boys scene were getting quite hostile to the four who were clearly identified as having been so. Those boys were getting their backs to the wall, really. The only ones they felt comfortable with were each other; although they knew most of the other kids they were fairly ostracized. They got a lot of common abuse, verbal stuff. The kids that knew nothing about it caught on within a few days and in turn would start dishing out this verbal abuse.

The lads I was working with over this, when they were messing around getting into the canoes and so on they were just like normal kids, and it was one of the few times they could relax, particularly when it was only their group and they weren't getting abuse from other kids. But on the long trips the whole thing was getting out of hand. I tried to shelter them as much as possible but it put me in a very difficult situation, it wasn't the sort of thing I could confront the others with without making a whole issue of it and putting the ones who were verbally abusing in a very difficult situation.

Then one of the youngest kids, he was about 13 at that time – up to then he'd shrug his shoulders and say it didn't matter to him – and we'd been coming back from a long trip to the seaside and this whole thing had been building up on the coach. There were a number of other kids leaning over the seat addressing this boy, giving him a lot of verbal, telling him he was a rent boy, he was gay and he had AIDS and all this stuff. I think he was at the point where he'd just had enough basically, and he jumped up and went round the coach saying, 'I don't know what you're talking about, I've seen *you* and *you* up at so-and-so's place!' and the kids he'd spoken to go a bright red, sit down really quick and drop out of this conversation. He went round the coach and he slowly identified around in the region of fifteen or twenty kids in the coach. It was enough for them, they sat down and stayed out of it. The ones he didn't identify continued their verbal. No, he wasn't boasting or anything, just saying it quite calmly, matter of fact. 'I've seen you up at Harry's, I've seen you up at Stan's, you hang around with so and so' and it shut these kids right up.

It absolutely horrified me, because if those four kids hadn't been on the scheme it would have been a normal scheme for us, the normal kids we deal with day in day out, general run of the mill young offenders. I hadn't realized until then that so many of them could be involved in this sort of abuse in some way – it was obviously on a much bigger scale than any of us had realized.

Let us now have a brief look at some reports showing how difficult it is to come to any conclusion about the numbers involved, mainly because so few incidents are reported. For example, in the 1984 UK Home Office national crime survey of a representative sample of households who were asked about their experience of victimization, it was found that as few as one in ten rapes or sexual assaults on women had been reported to the police (Hough and Mayhew 1985). A 1987 American study by Gene Abel and colleagues showed that 567 abusers, promised freedom from imprisonment under a legal amnesty, admitted to having had almost incredible numbers of victims, far higher than had been expected: on average each non-incest offender against girls averaged twenty victims, while each non-incest offender against boys averaged 150 (Abel *et al.* 1987). No doubt few of these abuses had been reported by the victims.

In a similar vein Ray Wyre of the Gracewell Clinic in Britain remarked at a meeting in 1991:

> At any given time 67 per cent of men who are sent here for abusing within the family have also abused outside the family but nobody knew, so I think that to continually use intrafamiliar and extrafamiliar as a clear-cut definition is actually not what we are finding here in treatment. . . . The men who come here have never been caught for what they've really done. The system in general is not set up to deal with such information. An extreme example, we had one man here who had been sent for abusing two children, but we disovered he'd abused 200, making child pornography with them. If Social Services thought they had a resource problem before they sent him to us, they certainly had one afterwards!

In Russell's study only 2 per cent of all cases of intrafamilial sexual abuse and 6 per cent of all cases of extrafamilial sexual abuse of females under 18 were reported to the police. Only 1 per cent of the abusers were caught and convicted (Russell 1983).

Finkelhor emphasizes that sex offenders in jail are unrepresentative of sex offenders in general, as most sex offenders are never caught and do not get help. Those who do get caught or who end up in treatment are almost certainly very unusual. Also from Finkelhor, 'Authorities on the prevalence of sexual abuse believe that the majority of abuse still goes undisclosed. . . . Such a conclusion can be arrived at by comparing lifetime incidence estimates which come from adult retrospective victimization surveys with the number of cases currently being publicly reported' (Williams and Finkelhor 1988).

However, as I said at the beginning of this chapter, people still want some kind of answer to the question, how common is child sexual abuse? Obviously, after Finkelhor's proviso, no answer can be very meaningful, but it seems from the very mixed figures above that over one-third of women at least have experienced some form of sexual abuse in their childhood sufficiently serious for them still to remember it with concern in later years, and that most of this abuse will have happened before they were 12 years of age. It would also appear probable that, if one were to count minor abuse such as non-touching flashing and obscene telephone calls, then there are few women who will have reached maturity without at least one incidence of this occurring. There are fewer figures available at present concerning boys, but it seems likely that at least a quarter of males will have suffered some form of abuse by the time they are adult, usually at an older age than the girls.

As to the final question, is the incidence of c.s.a. increasing, the only possible answer is, it is impossible to tell. Some, especially the more feminist-inclined, believe it is not, and that the reason we hear more about it now is because of the changed sexual climate which allows people to talk more easily about their earlier experiences, together with a post-Freudian readiness to believe what children tell us (as we noted in Chapter 2, Freud came to believe that reports of childhood sexual abuse were either children's fantasy or that from Oedipal desires the children themselves had seduced their abusers), and that contemporary or retrospective studies are based on truth. Linda Gordon, Professor of History at the University of Wisconsin, points out that in America there have been three waves of public awareness of c.s.a. – in the 1870s and 1880s, again from 1910 to 1920 and since the 1970s – all of them allied to peaks of feminism: this awareness of child abuse was/is a result of women's movements being as concerned with the welfare of children as with women. When feminism ebbs, she suggests, problems such as c.s.a. are pushed back under the carpet (*Independent* 28 April 1990). Other people, however, believe the actual incidence of c.s.a. has increased; they blame in particular the break-up of the family as we have known it, single-parent families with transient partners who lack the 'natural' inhibition of blood relationships, the increase of pornography including pornographic films, the stress caused by unemployment and its resulting excess of free time, and a general lack of moral direction.

Certainly there has been an increase in registrations over the years, at times dramatic, though this seems to be easing off now, but, as the

NSPCC points out, this may indicate an increase in public and professional awareness rather than an actual increase in incidence (NSPCC 1989: 6). I personally have my doubts that c.s.a. has increased over the years any more than other kinds of child abuse, though possibly some of the sexual abuse may have altered in type along with the growing openness about sexuality and the considerable increase in easily available soft and hard pornography. However, earlier generations were well supplied with their own pornography, ranging from the crudest of illustrations to the finest of art – indeed, as long as man has handled a bone or a brush there probably never has been a time when this was not so. The human imagination has little need for extra stimulus where sex is concerned.

RECOGNITION AND DISCOVERY

'Sexual abuse is one of the darker aspects of childhood and it has remained largely unrecorded because the very idea of sexual abuse tends to be unthinkable. The secret has been safe because children have either not told or not been believed, or they have told in a way that has not been comprehended' (Harper 1988).

For Juliet Harper (Senior Lecturer in Psychology, Macquarie University, Sydney) a useful way of recognizing young children who have been sexually abused is through their stories, artwork and play. It must be remembered, though, that, while children may attempt to relieve their anxieties in this way, as their primary aim at this stage is not to inform others of their abuse it takes expertise to recognize the signs. The stories may, for example, indicate a desire for privacy and support by telling of large houses, separate bedrooms, protective parents. But as abused children will have been consistently warned to silence they are often verbally unskilled; rather than create new stories they are more likely to adapt the old familiar ones and use these to express their fear and distress. Harper also suggests there is likely to be a lack of variety of themes in the stories, absence of logic, reason or justice, and there will be little interest in the background to the stories or warmth or humour in them.

There is space to make only a few suggestions with regard to recognition of abused children's artwork, but careful note should be taken of drawings where parts of the face or body are obliterated or shaded, or where mouths or arms are omitted at an age where they would be expected to be included, or where part/s of the body are accentuated in a bizarre way, and of course where explicit sexual actions or parts are shown. But, as Harper points out, such amateur analysis is full of pitfalls, and should be attempted only after a series of drawings have been obtained and the environment and background of the child considered. In their actual play abused children may reveal surprisingly sophisticated knowledge of sexual behaviour or there may be masturbatory play, but this is by no means universal; they may be very concerned with cleanliness especially around genitals and anus, there may be recurring themes of protection, while nurturance may be interpreted erotically. The child may refuse to include her/himself and family in play about families, and her/his concealed anxiety is likely to make the watcher uncomfortably aware of something wrong (Harper 1988).

Because conclusive medical evidence is rarely available, workers in this field must familiarize themselves with every possible method of recognition. Many members of the medical profession are reluctant to recognize c.s.a. and often manage not to see it when statistics show that some cases must have been present. To give two examples of this difficulty, a survey of non-specialist medical practitioners in South Australia showed that between them the 193 doctors who responded had seen only an average of 1.2 cases, while 54 per cent of them had never seen a case at all (Winefield and Castell-McGregor 1986). A group practice in a comparatively well-off part of London with about 5000 patients on their list recently reported that they knew of no current cases of child abuse, stating that with such a small number of patients they wouldn't expect to find it. Obviously ways other than relying on medical reports must be found of discovering these children.

It is difficult for a doctor to suspect that her patient whom she has perhaps known for years is abusing or allowing her/his child to be abused. When an abused child goes to see her doctor one of the parents, probably the mother, will almost certainly be present, and unless the parent is actually reporting suspected abuse the child is very unlikely to talk, even if questioned sympathetically by the doctor. But there are several indications of sexual abuse that a doctor should investigate with persistence: if, for example, a child presents with a sexually transmitted disease; if there are scratches, bruises, lacerations or bleeding in the genital or rectal area; if there is pain on urination or defecation or there are frequent unexplained urinary tract infections. Pregnancy in a young adolescent should make the doctor suspicious, especially if she refuses to say who the father is, or she and/or her family deny she is pregnant.

Where abuse is strongly suspected it is probably best if the child is examined without a parent being present and a nurse or colleague introduced, unless it is the parent who has brought forward the suspicion and the child clearly wants that parent to be present. Trauma to the external genitalia must be looked for (great gentleness and tact always being used), the hymen inspected and details recorded. If very recent assault is suspected swabs should be made in case sperm – which can survive for up to seventy-two hours – is present.

A British paper by Chris Hobbs and Jane Wynne in 1989 on the importance of anal examination was the foundation of the actions that led to the controversy of Cleveland. Hobbs and Wynne, as paediatricians, found that, out of 608 children referred from the two health districts of Leeds primarily for suspected sexual abuse, of whom 337 were confirmed or probable cases, 30 per cent involved anal penetration by finger or penis and 42 per cent of the 337 children showed one or more anal findings, rising as high as 60 per cent of the 115 children of 0–5 years of age. Hobbs and Wynne stressed in their paper that 'physical signs alone are rarely sufficient for diagnosis, but their association with sexually inappropriate behaviour or with a number of symptoms or indications known to be associated with sexual abuse raises the probability. In preverbal children, diagnosis has to rest on evidence other than the statement of the child, and here physical signs of genital or anal damage were of paramount importance.' The anal examination is but a small part of the assessment which must include history, general health, growth and development, and any emotional and behavioural problems.

This is not the place to detail how the examination of a child should be conducted, and copies of their invaluable paper need to be obtained for this, but they stress how important it is that the child should not be violated further by over-enthusiastic examination, and they do not recommend routine instrumental examination. They also point out how rapidly evidence can vanish, so children should be examined as soon as possible before bruises and tears have had a chance to heal. That they do this themselves may be why their figures are higher than others, they suggest. In a conversation with Chris Hobbs and Jane Wynne themselves, Hobbs, emphasizing this point, told me, 'The Americans say they don't see all the physical abuse we describe, but here in Leeds we have a different system whereby we tend to see children very quickly – if a social worker sees a report the first thing they do is to get a medical check on it, very often before they've even seen the family. So if a mother is worried and she rings up somebody the chances are she'll be seeing a paediatrician within 24 or 48 hours. But in other places they might go out and do interviews and if they're satisfied something is happening they may have a medical examination, but some weeks later. We have found how quickly children heal up, particularly the younger ones.' Jane Wynne added, 'We had an 18-month girl in a few days ago and already it is all healed up; she was scratched, probably had a couple of fingers in her. If someone was to be asked for a second opinion in a week's time they'd find a perfectly normal bottom.'

In their paper they reported that 58 per cent of the 141 girls had shown physical evidence of trauma or infection, and eleven children had a sexually transmitted disease. Anal dilation or reflex anal dilatation, which is the most dramatic sign found in anally abused children, is normally a strong sign of abuse, though caution should be used where the child has previously undergone much medical examination or use of suppositories or enemas. There is no evidence, as is sometimes suggested, that threadworm, candidal infection or inflammation through poor hygiene could cause the signs, and an observant doctor will not confuse the signs of severe constipation with those of sexual abuse. Their final words on this subject are worth noting: 'Anal abuse of boys and girls of all ages, from babies to teenagers, is one part of the whole spectrum of sexually abusive behaviour towards children. A greater awareness and willingness of doctors to examine and evaluate physical findings of anal examination would be a major step forward in the detection and prevention of this major form of child abuse' (Hobbs and Wynne 1989).

Since, however, medical evidence is unlikely to be immediately available in new suspected cases, and in any event is very rarely sufficient in itself, what are the more general symptoms of sexual abuse that should be looked out for?

Some indications come directly from the abused children themselves, such as children or adolescents being frightened to go home; children who tell a friend, openly or by hinting, they are being abused, or even tell someone in authority (possibly saying 'I know someone who . . .'), but who often try to insist that no one else be told. Children may express their anguish by aggressive behaviour at school, or, as we have seen earlier, in their stories, artwork or play. Their play with other children may be unusually sexual or betray a sexual knowledge well beyond what is to be expected for their age or they may play sexually with animals or toys. On the other hand, Judith Trowell, British Consultant Child Psychiatrist referring to her work with the Monroe Young Family Centre, said, 'But one child, the one who had most obviously been sexually abused, anally, orally and vaginally, has – at least with us – not shown any sexual type of play. When I used the dolls she showed straight down the line what had happened, but in terms of her play what you get is the violence and the high level of disturbance. She'd probably been abused for some time because she's 4, but it only came to light because of the physical soreness,

really – there wasn't any sexual play or drawings or anything she said.'
Little girls also may push small objects into their vaginas or, as we saw
with Barbara's daughter, draw attention to themselves by sitting
suggestively or by touching themselves publicly.

Abuse is likely to cause changes in normal patterns of behaviour:
previously happy children become depressed and discontented,
withdrawn and sullen, their sleep broken by nightmares or they stay
awake because they are frightened to fall asleep in case their abuser
creeps up on them unawares; they might in addition start wetting or
soiling their beds. Some withdraw into fantasy worlds, and may become
so lost to the ordinary world that they are even thought to be retarded (see
Chapter 8 on multi-personalities). Children who had been doing well at
school may become uncooperative and disappoint their teachers by
failing examinations and losing all ability to concentrate (remember
Peter's problems at his public school). They might complain of
stomach-ache, headache, fatigue, or develop obsessions, phobias, tics,
fears of objects or people they were not frightened of before. Their
appetites may change, perhaps becoming non-existent, or on the contrary
they may stuff themselves as though they had not eaten in years. In
adolescence these symptoms may become excessive to the point of
anorexia nervosa or bulimia nervosa.

The incestuously abused girl victim will be having problems in the
home additional to the abuse itself as she tries to adjust to the situation
where she loves/hates/despises her father/abuser/lover. He must be
obeyed, but he is feared and distrusted, as is her mother/rival, who has
failed to protect her. The child is both wife and not-wife, and usually finds
herself taking on spousal duties such as attempting to protect other
members of the family from abuse or from the break-up of the family
should her own abuse become known. Guilty, lonely, isolated (this last
encouraged by the abuser whose greatest fear is that she might reveal the
abuse to someone outside the family), she may have difficulty in mixing
with her peers, or only make friends with those who like herself are under
stress or experiencing problems at home. With both boys and girls, but
especially with boys, this is likely to end in delinquency and/or markedly
aggressive behaviour.

At school they may well refuse to join in social activities, mocking
them, and may avoid physical activities because they are physically sore
and uncomfortable from the abuse, or out of fear of having to undress in
front of others who, they imagine, might sense their 'dirtiness' or notice
physical signs of abuse. They may cut lessons, be picked up for truancy,
or finally drop right out of school, and perhaps even run away from home.

Huge numbers of runaway children have left because of some kind of abuse at home. Unfortunately this is well known and large railway stations are patrolled by men looking for runaway victims who, after a little sham caring, they turn into prostitutes and rent boys.

Drugs, drink, prostitution, suicide attempts – and, of course, the possibility of the beginnings of yet another cycle of abuse. Abusers, themselves abused, sometimes begin to molest others in early childhood, as young as 4 or 5 years of age. Surely the emphasis in the future must be on recognizing this last truly tragic aspect of abuse, and on doing everything possible to halt the process before it is too late.

We will finish this section by noting a breakdown of the behavioural signs and symptoms of 411 children on the local authority sexual abuse registration list for Greater Manchester (311 had been sexually abused and 100 were at risk of sexual abuse), for the period 1 March 1988 to 28 February 1989, which shows the following (some children showed several symptoms):

32 per cent	–	school problems
25 per cent	–	sexualised play
16 per cent	–	aggressive/destructive behaviour
16 per cent	–	withdrawn/compliant behaviour
13 per cent	–	lack of trust
12 per cent	–	social isolation
11 per cent	–	running away
10 per cent	–	excessive masturbation
9 per cent	–	bedwetting
8 per cent	–	sleep disturbances
5 per cent	–	eating problems/disorders
9 per cent	–	others

(NSPCC 1989)

THE USE OF ANATOMICALLY CORRECT DOLLS

The use of anatomically correct dolls in diagnosing child sexual abuse has been very controversial. My own reaction when I saw them for the first time in Britain at a meeting at Great Ormond Street with Dr Arnon Bentovim and others when they were first introduced was – after mild shock – straightforward gladness that such a clever and obviously useful aid had been invented. Basically my opinion has not changed: the use that Judith Trowell found for them (see p. 74, 'when I used the dolls she showed straight down the line what had happened'), was exactly what they had been invented for, a useful aid to diagnosis.

One major criticism has been that, because of the way they are designed, they are inevitably suggestive and some think them also unethical and in themselves an abuse to the child. Against this criticism is the approval of a number of highly experienced sources (Westcott *et al*. 1989). The dolls themselves come in different types, sizes, races and all ages. Although the males always have penises, the adult females have breasts and all adults have pubic hair, not all vaginal, anal and mouth representations have actual openings, a disadvantage since without them children cannot demonstrate clearly what has happened to them.

When I asked Judith Trowell how she used them, she explained:

I always have them under the desk to bring out as and when it feels they might be helpful. Dolls have their limitations but they are a kind of distancing manoeuvre, so that sometimes, if it's very difficult for the child to talk about the abuse, it can be easier with the dolls. Some may find it easier with pipe cleaner dolls, some that it's easier to draw pictures. I remember a boy of 12 – he couldn't bring himself to talk about his abuse by a man – but when I said, 'Do you think this might make it easier?', thinking a 12-year-old boy might freak out about dolls, he was actually very relieved to show me what had happened. With little children especially it can be very helpful. But sometimes when you produce them some of the children are terribly upset at the sight of genitals, or when you start to take the trousers down – then I'd not necessarily persist with that. Yes, the very fact they behave like that *is* indicative, but standing up in court and saying that will not get you very far. But the balance between finding out the truth to help the child and re-abusing it as a professional. . . . Yes, I'd try again later, and certainly with some of them the second time around . . .

I asked her whether, if you set the right part next to the right place, an unabused child wouldn't make the connection?

There's something about the excitement of an abused child even when they're terrified, and there's the quality of doing it almost without a thought – whereas ordinary little kids may or may not undress some of the dolls or sit them around and have a tea party and pour cups of tea, they may experiment and fiddle around with them and look at the holes and say what's this bit? or isn't this rude? kind of thing, but with abused kids there is a quality of immediately zapping into the sexual position. Yes, an ordinary child might eventually get it right, fiddling around, but then you can say, what's happening? and has it happened to you and has anyone ever touched you?

But that distancing of doing it with the dolls first is a way in. One child was terribly freaked out because our dolls don't have fingers and that was very indicative, sort of saying – I can't show you what Daddy did to me – because she wanted to put fingers inside the vagina. If fingers aren't there and they pick that up, it's pretty clear. Another child – the dolls don't have proper ears – said, 'They don't have proper ears, he did it in my ear, I can't show you.' I took that as pretty definite that the child knew what she was talking about.

They're not magic, though. I think there was a feeling among field workers at first, well, we've got the magic dolls, we can crack it now. For a while it was felt this was the answer, this was the diagnostic test. But it's not, it's another piece of the jigsaw.

Surveys conducted in several countries into the success of the use of dolls for diagnostic purposes have shown varying results. White *et al.* (1986), studying 50 suspected-abused and non-abused children, found significant differences between them in the way they played with the dolls, but other researchers did not. Westcott and her colleagues, having examined many studies on this subject, call for information on 'valid and reliable norms of baseline behaviours that could serve to differentiate between victimised and non-victimised children', necessary because in addition to professional groups having differing views as to what constitutes convincing evidence of abuse through the use of dolls, they also do not agree as to what is normal exploratory or play behaviour. Research is also needed, they point out, on the differences between the reactions of children who have directly suffered sexual abuse and those who have been exposed only vicariously, such as, for example, those who have been made to watch pornographic material. These points are particularly important from the legal point of view (Westcott *et al.* 1989).

People have also worried about the possibility of an unsettling, almost abusive effect on unmolested children by the showing of such explicit dolls, but it does not seem that children are affected or upset by them. Danya Glaser, Consultant Psychiatrist at Guy's Hospital, London, and Carole Collins conducted a carefully controlled study to isolate 'the specific responses which the dolls might encourage' in non-abused children. Ninety-one children, split almost equally between boys and girls, with an age range of 3–6 years, were observed. The rag dolls that were used had satin-lined openings (large enough to admit a child's finger) for mouth and anus, and vaginal openings for the female dolls. Male dolls had penises and scrotums, the adult dolls pubic and axillary hair, the females breasts. All had embroidered faces, nipples and navels.

Great care was taken to make sure the children were comfortable, in familiar surroundings and with familiar people, and a broad range of appropriate toys such as pushchairs, baths, beds, etc., were available to help them play freely. There was a limited amount of directed play where children were asked to name the various parts of the body, for example, and where they were encouraged to undress the dolls, and to dress them again at the finish. Only five children showed any explicit sexual play and in three of these exposure to previous explicit sexual activity was identified.

As a result of these observations Glaser and Collins concluded that at present there is not enough information to allow play with dolls to provide a 'clinically reliable screening test for sexual abuse', but nevertheless they feel it is unlikely that 'young children's explicit sexual play with the dolls arises innately or that the dolls lead the children to sexual play'. Where such play occurs, they suggest the 'learning source' should be looked for. Since in the course of play so many of the children in the study touched the genitalia of the dolls it is suggested that this should be considered a normal response, and is not in itself indicative of previous sexual abuse. Interestingly, not one of the children inserted their finger into the vaginal or anal slits. Glaser and Collins finally state that, while unabused children clearly noted the difference between ordinary dolls and the special dolls, they were not at all traumatized by them; that the overwhelming majority did not show any sexually explicit play; and while absence of such play does not reliably exclude the possiblity of abuse, 'it appears that explicit sexual play with the dolls may well arise from the child's preoccupations which are based on previous exposure to explicit sexual information or activity' (Glaser and Collins 1989).

Tilman Furniss calls the dolls 'the icing on the cake' of solid knowledge, warning that without the existence of the cake the icing can be dangerously misleading. He stresses the dolls should be provided only as part of a carefully organized setting and can be successful only where the interviewer emotionally links up with the child, who must discover the dolls in her own time and way. The interviewer must observe the child tactfully but continuously once she/he comes into contact with the dolls, but the lead in 'playing' with them must come from the child, not the professional. An important point too often ignored is made, that professionals themselves can be embarrassed or upset both by the use of the dolls and by the revelation of the child's abuse, and they, and mothers if present, must be properly prepared in advance if the child is not to be alarmed and put off by the adults' behaviour.

The very first reaction of the children on discovery of the dolls' sex organs when they undress them may give vital evidence: they may become tearful, look frightened, even to the point of becoming frozen with fear, or talk or play openly in a sexually knowledgeable way. On the other hand, they may show by their first reactions that it is unlikely they have been abused. If a child shows strong anxiety or avoidance this should be dealt with sympathetically first before the dolls are returned to, even though this may take more than one session. The use of the dolls is not intended as a short cut to a disclosure, although their use 'can be extremely helpful . . . the dolls are only one tool amongst others and . . . they can only be used in an overall context of communicating appropriately with the child. Other ways and alleys of communication may have to be explored as well' (Furniss 1991).

I feel there is little doubt that properly, i.e. expertly, used dolls are a helpful adjunct to the professional's armoury, although more research needs to be done to help convince legal minds of their usefulness when used in this manner. With the dolls' help a preverbal or a learning disabled child may well be able to demonstrate what has happened to her/him, as will older children who find using words like vagina or erection embarrassing. But, as has been repeatedly stressed, anatomically correct dolls are only an aid, not a final proof in themselves.

THE ART OF INTERVIEWING, INCLUDING 'DO CHILDREN LIE?'

Anne Bannister, referring to the Cleveland Report, expresses unhappiness with its statement about believing children. She writes, 'The recommendation is that "professionals should always listen carefully to what the child has to say and take seriously what is said". Most experienced workers would make a clearer statement: "The child should be believed." This does not mean that a careful assessment of all the facts, including the child's statement, is not made, after the interview. It does mean, however, that the interviewer does not treat the child with scepticism' (Bannister 1988a).

Hank Giarretto, at a NSPCC conference in London, 1990, discussing false allegations in custody cases, feels similarly: 'We've certainly treated over 10,000 kids and I can count on one hand the false allegations – very rarely does a child tell a lie, especially in such cases.' However, the British Law Society Local Government Group and the National Children's Bureau's report, detailing their joint national conference on the Cleveland Inquiry Report, expressed a caveat worth bearing in mind: 'Within the court processes, lawyers should be advising on representation of evidence and performance as a witness. . . . The phrases, expressions and jargon employed within meetings and discussions with colleagues who fully understand the nature and meanings of these terms *are not necessarily appropriate for use within the court* [my italics]. For example, how often have we heard . . . the phrase, "Children do not lie." This is not helpful in presenting evidence to magistrates or members of the judiciary who, drawing on their own experience, know that children certainly do lie. They also fantasise, exaggerate, minimise and misunderstand' (Davie and Smith 1988).

A comparatively new problem, the one Giarretto was discussing when he made the above comment, has been the rise in allegations of sexual abuse in divorce cases when custody battles are being fought, particularly where the couple is already separated and the child makes unsupervised visits to the other parent. A child who is being fought over is likely to be put under a different kind of pressure from that in normal c.s.a. cases – pressure from the opposing parent, from both parents' lawyers, and from social workers and other professionals dragged into the case. There are those who believe that children can be manipulated into saying what is wanted, and it is probably true that in some cases a child being dragged in various directions may end up confused, and may, through a desire to please or to be left alone, give evasive, misleading or even untruthful answers. But properly trained investigators, given opportunity and time, should be able to unravel the truth – children describing experiences they have actually been through will often use phrases so unexpected (like Barbara's daughter's telling phrase, 'he put a gun in my bottom and put glue all over me') that there can be little doubt of their veracity.

The investigator's first tenet, then, should be that the child is almost certainly telling the truth. Her prime duty, the care of the child and attention to her/his needs, should not however blind her to the necessity for providing evidence that will stand up in court if it is decided to take legal proceedings against the abuser. Wherever possible the interview should be recorded on video, the child having been informed of this beforehand.

It is considered by many that the most useful procedure is to have joint interviews (which must always be child-focused) with fully trained therapist/social worker/interviewer and police officer working together, a method which overcomes the problem of the child having to give repeated interviews and which also ensures that the police have the opportunity to ask about and confirm the details they need for legal purposes at the time of the first interview. Preferably the two professionals will have worked together before and developed mutual trust and an understanding of each other's methods. It is often found that one of the two interviewers gets better results than the other, or that one is better at working with one sex while the other is best at working with the opposite sex, in which case the interviewers should decide among themselves who will conduct the interview and who will stay quietly in the room listening, or possibly retire to an adjoining room where she/he can observe and hear the interview through a one-way mirror and an audio link (the child having been previously told what is happening).

Major advances in collaboration have allowed for courses to be successfully arranged between police and social services, the attitudes of both sides having changed extraordinarily in the past few years. The theory of Statement Validity Analysis (SVA), developed by American and Canadian psychologists from Professor Udo Undeutsch's work in West Germany in the 1950s (showing in essence that truthful accounts can be distinguished from lies by their richer quality), has moved on to become the basis of what is known as the 'Step-Wise Interview'. After Detective Inspector K. Lawrance and Roy Jackson (NSPCC) attended a training course in SVA at the University of British Columbia organized by Professor John Yuille earlier in the year, the West Yorkshire Police Authority invited Professor Yuille to lead a 5-day workshop in Wakefield in June 1989, the first of its kind in the UK. Police from Domestic Violence and Child Abuse units, training officers from Social Services departments, and senior members of the NSPCC attended. It was interesting that the average length of service of those attending was over ten years, but, while the child protection workers had been involved in child abuse for nearly seven years nine months on average, the police officers had been involved on average for only one year two months. The workshop, which was voted a great success, included interviewing and video-taping school children from a local school and later reviewing these taped interviews.

John Yuille's Protocol for interviewing starts with the *location*: if possible a specifically designed quiet room should be provided with comfortable furniture suitable for children, but not a play room, i.e. interview aids such as dolls, drawing materials, should be kept out of sight. Built-in audio- and video-taping facilities should be provided if possible, and a separate entrance if the room is in a police station, for example. *Participants*: preferably only the interviewer, sitting comfortably close to the child, but where inter-agency cooperation demands both a social worker and a police officer then it should be arranged in advance who will conduct the SVA interview; the non-interviewer, sitting apart, should ask questions only when the SVA interview has ended. Parents or others should not be present, but allowed to watch the video-tape or see events through a one-way mirror. If no video equipment is available an audio-recording must be made.

The Step-Wise Interview: always proceed from the general to the specific. The steps are: a. rapport building, b. discussion of truth, c. introducing topic of concern, d. free narrative, e. open questions, f. specific questions (if necessary), g. interview aids (if necessary) – each step to be made when appropriate. The interviewer must patiently allow the child to tell with as little prompting as possible. Interview aids are to be used only when unassisted interviewing has failed to draw out facts from the child, and non-suggestive methods such as the child making drawings should be used first. Anatomically correct dolls should be used only as last resort for fear of compromising any arising legal case. Language problems between adult and child must be borne in mind and a common sexual language established. Children's attention span is limited – this and their bodily needs should be remembered.

In more detail, the steps are:

A The child must be helped to relax, gentle general questioning (not about the abuse) helping develop rapport and an understanding of the child's way of talking.

B The importance of truth should be established.

C Gently introduce the subject of the abuse, as indirectly as is necessary. Leave all specific issues to the child. Only be more probing as a last resort.

D The free narrative phase is the most important part of the interview. Move from the more general aspects of the abuse to the more specific. Do not interrupt or challenge the child, and allow her/him to move at her/his own pace.

E Questions will probably now be necessary for clarification purposes. It will help in sorting out times and places if different incidents are given simple identification names the child can use. If there is something the child does not wish to talk about at this stage, this should be respected and a signal such as a raised hand arranged in advance.

F More specific answers may now be sought and inconsistencies ironed out, but care must be taken not to feed the child information obtained from other sources.

G It is at this point that it may be decided that aids such as drawings are needed, but anatomically correct dolls should be used only as a last resort to help the child describe a sexual act. They should never be used to obtain a disclosure.

Finally, where a child has consistently refused to disclose, direct leading questions may have to be asked for the sake of the child's future safety, but this can only be done at the risk of jeopardizing the chance of a successful prosecution (Lawrance 1989).

Anne Bannister and Bobbie Print in their own *A Model for Assessment Interviews in Suspected Cases of Child Sexual Abuse* (1988) stress the need for the interviewer to be seen by the courts to be neutral and as not pressurizing the child in any way. If a child denies abuse it may in fact merely mean she/he is not yet ready to disclose, but the court may regard further questioning as pressure. To combat this problem Bannister and Print have produced their model to help overcome the possibility of faulty techniques, a programme which in many ways is similar to the Step-Wise programme we have just been looking at. Leading questions, they say, should be used only when no other method has worked, even though necessary evidence needed to protect the child may then be destroyed; previous information, apart from details such as who they live with, family nicknames, the child's developmental level, etc., should be ignored as far as possible during the interview; questions must not be loaded and should be as open-ended as possible, including the possibility of a neutral reply, such as 'Can you tell me how that felt?' which allows, for example, 'Was it a bad feeling or a good one, or was it neither?'.

Interviewers should not indicate approval or disapproval of answers, and it is helpful where possible (and if the child is safe) to have three sessions with the child over two or three weeks. The purpose of the interview/s is to give therapeutic support; to validate or otherwise the allegations of c.s.a.; to help the child give sufficient information for legal purposes; and finally to assess the child's needs. Location suggestions are similar to those above, with the addition that it is best if interviewers can be on the same physical level as the child – large floor cushions are suggested. Also Bannister and Print prefer play things to be openly on show, with a selection of puppets suitable for use as 'good' and 'bad' toys, such as soft cuddly animals and sharks or witches; an equipped doll's house with open rooms; paper, crayons and modelling clay; a toy telephone to whisper secrets into, and they positively recommend anatomically correct dolls to be present, although with the cautions detailed earlier.

They also recommend that all interviews be video-recorded, as, even if the tapes are not allowed in criminal proceedings (although they almost certainly soon will be), they can be very useful in civil courts where permitted – in addition to spoken words the child's body movements and gestures add enormously to interpretation. Importantly, it saves children from having to repeat their stories to others such as lawyers, police, etc., a process which in the past has been thought to cause extra trauma. They also prefer one person at a time to interview the child, but joint interviews are preferable to repeated interviews, although only one person should lead – who this should be being settled as suggested above. The parent/s or accompanying friend should not be present at the interview although when the interviewer first introduces her/himself this is a useful opportunity for the child to witness the cooperative attitude of the parent/ friend who has brought her/him and also to be assured they will soon be reunited. If the child is still nervous at being left, the parent/friend can leave her coat in the room to show she is not far away, and the toys can be resorted to immediately as a distraction.

During this introductory play the interviewer can learn much about the child, and the interview will follow much as in the Step-Wise programme nos A–F, except that play material is used from the beginning and not kept for reluctant use at a later stage. If the child begins to disclose, then details should be sought, but great care must always be taken that leading questions are not asked. The child should be reassured and praised and made to feel confident and comfortable, though he/she must not be allowed to take control, the interviewer keeping a gentle but firm approach. Play with puppets and dolls' houses will disclose many details about who used what rooms, where is safe and who is hurtful. At this point interviewers must be careful not to over-reassure a hurting child, stopping her expressing fear or anger. She/he needs to be helped to act out what has happened, both for investigative and therapeutic purposes.

At the end of the interview/s it is important to leave the child understanding that the abusive behaviour can be stopped with the support of other people, and the child's future must be discussed with her/him. The paper finishes, 'An interview conducted along the lines we have suggested, watched by a consultant or video-recorded, will provide much useful information about the child and his/her behaviour. This should help to provide a firm base for future therapeutic work since this interview is the first step in therapy' (Bannister and Print 1988).

By the time *Innocence Destroyed* is published the British Home Office's new Code of Practice for Joint Interviews, at the time of writing still in draft stage, should be issued. I understand it will incorporate the phased approach supported by both Yuille and Bannister, and a more open use of play materials as recommended by Bannister. Anatomically correct dolls will also be recommended for use at a later stage when thought necessary, but with caution, a view Bannister particularly endorses as she informs me she has too often seen them used badly by ill-trained people. The Code will also make it clear that the video-taping of interviews is essential.

Finally, one problem that occasionally occurs in interviewing arises from differences of religious and cultural beliefs between the interviewer and the child's family. As I found myself when in India, Indians 'don't have' child sexual abuse (see Chapter 2). Immigrant Asian families in this country would like the same to be 'true' here, so that if a case of c.s.a. is confirmed the family closes up tight. Clint Brannigan, a London police-man, told me of an Asian family he had worked with where the grandfather had abused: 'The shame of the family is intense, they don't want relatives to know, especially back over in India, because no one would have anything to do with them any more. . . . The main thing they were worried about was whether the girl was still a virgin, and marriageable – she was. They were very westernized, but because of the shame they were adamant they didn't want a social worker or anyone at all from the Asian community to work with them. No, that situation's not uncommon.'

Cath Laws, talking of teaching child protection in New South Wales, said, 'With migrants I guess the only problems we've had is with Muslims because of the issue of girls and sex education. When that happens we send someone to see them or have them up to the school, and once they realize that it's not sex education or about having relationships with boys, it's about protecting themselves, even the Muslim groups have been quite happy for their daughters to do it. So for them we have all-boy and all-girl classes as it's against their religion to discuss sex in front of males.' Muslims I have talked with in Britain have insisted that women are so looked after and respected in their communities that c.s.a. could not possibly happen.

At the time of writing a court case against two Jewish men from an extremely tight-knit community of Hasidic Jews in north London is in progress. The head of the local Child Protection Team, Detective Inspector Compton, told me 'until the press got hold of the case a wide section of the community didn't know what was going on because some members of the rabbinical court wouldn't deal with the issue, wouldn't even acknowledge that that type of behaviour could exist within their community. We tried to have meetings with various rabbis but they wouldn't meet us or talk to us. The family have suffered tremendously, and the children went through hell in the trial – the tactics used by the defence were legally right, but I thought very bad. I've never known a case conducted like this; if I'd known the defence was going to be so vindictive against the family I don't think I'd have recommended bringing the case. The father, a chartered accountant, has lost 75 per cent of his business. It wouldn't surprise me if at the end of the day they move away out of it to Israel or America.' The family have been ostracized in their own community, the children forced to change schools and verbal abuse inflicted on the entire family.

Such refusual to admit the possibility of c.s.a. in your own community is unfortunately still common all over the world, not least in our own villages and towns, but closed communities whose religious and cultural practices are different from those of surrounding folk are more susceptible to this blindness than most of us. Breaking through an abused child's pain and enforced silence is difficult enough as it is, and interviewers – through their own embarrassment or fear of seeming to show racial prejudice – must not permit themselves to be misled by the self-deception of those who dare not allow themselves to face the truth that their own community, too, has human faults.

Chapter 5

The victims

This chapter looks at various facts about the victims; the after-effects of their abuse are examined in Chapter 8.

HANDICAPPED/LEARNING DISABLED AND DEAF CHILDREN

Children who need other people to care for their more intimate needs or who, for one reason or another, depend on the attention of others more than is usual for ordinary children are especially open to the risk of sexual abuse. This is particularly so for children with learning disabilities, or mentally handicapped children as they are still sometimes called. Article 6 of the United Nations Declaration on the Rights of Mentally Retarded Persons states that 'the mentally retarded person has a right to protection from exploitation, abuse and degrading treatment'. But rights are one thing; reality is another.

Few statistics on the sexual abuse of children and adults with learning disabilities are available, but although it is a criminal offence to have sexual intercourse with a 'mental defective' (UK Sexual Offences Act 1956), accumulating evidence indicates that the learning disabled person is highly vulnerable. Figures from the Seattle Rape Relief and Sexual Assault Centre show that between 1977 and 1983 over 700 local developmentally disabled children and adults were sexually abused, defining sexual abuse as cases of rape, attempted rape, incest and indecent exposure. Ninety-nine per cent of the victims were abused by relatives – fathers, foster fathers, uncles, brothers, grandfathers, or by caregivers, such as residential staff, bus drivers, volunteers, etc. A stranger was the abuser in only 1 per cent of the cases (Ryerson 1984). Chamberlain and colleagues, working in a Cincinnati adolescent clinic, found that of eighty-seven learning disabled girls aged between 11 and 23, twenty-two (i.e. 25 per cent) had suffered attempted or successful coerced intercourse. Nine were victims of incest. It was found that those with a mild learning disability were most at risk (Chamberlain *et al.* 1984).

As Hilary Brown and Ann Craft, editors of *Thinking the Unthinkable* – an invaluable publication from which I have drawn much of the following – state in their introduction: 'Those with milder handicaps often have a good understanding of cultural and group norms, but have difficulties in achieving age-appropriate goals, which can heighten a sense of frustration or despair. Previous rejections and isolation may increase their desire to please and their responsiveness to attention and affection. . . . Individuals with severe and profound handicaps may find it difficult to distinguish between different sorts of touch when most or all body care is attended to by other people' (Brown and Craft 1989: 3).

Learning disabled people who have a need for other people to perform many activities for them, some intensely personal, are very vulnerable to exploitation and abuse by anyone who comes into contact with them. They are likely to have poor social skills and because of their need for the help of others they learn to be accommodating, rarely challenging those who care for them. Choices that most of us take for granted – how to live, what to eat, what clothes to wear – are usually not available to them, and unlike most of us they do not learn as a normal part of growing-up to be aware of the dangers of sex and the need for self-protection. They may not have fully taken in, for example, that they should not sit carelessly so that their underwear shows or that touching or rubbing their 'private' parts is not appropriate behaviour in public. They may in time grasp a superficial knowledge of sex, but unfortunately this may make them appear dangerously less innocent than they really are.

In a world which places emphasis on intelligence and physical attractiveness, the learning disabled person's sense of self-worth and pride is likely to be too fragile to protect them against those who ruthlessly take advantage of their vulnerability (Walmsley 1989). Previously abused children can unwittingly send out signals that abusers, who are expert at recognizing potential victims, do not miss. This is particularly so with learning disabled children who may have few, if any, inhibitions about behaving in a sexualized and provocative manner once they have been sexually aroused, thus increasing their danger of further abuse.

As with all c.s.a., most of the abuse takes place within the family or is committed by those who are familiar with the victim. This is not only equally true for children who have learning disabilities, but remains so as they become adults with the IQ of children. The Pigot Report on video evidence, remarking on these special needs, states, 'failure to include mentally disordered [adult] witnesses with children under 14 as persons eligible to use the live television link has been presented to us as a serious omission . . . special consideration should be given to the needs of this group, members of which seem, sadly, to be particularly subject to sexual and violent crime' (Pigot Report 1989).

A major problem is that carers looking after the learning disabled may not be trained in recognizing or dealing with sexual abuse, so that overtly sexual behaviour such as excessive public masturbation or highly sexualized approaches to other children or carers, or symptoms such as bed-wetting and withdrawal, may be assumed to be merely part of the natural behaviour of a learning disabled child. Physical signs may be thought to have been caused by the child abusing itself, and even the existence of venereal disease such as gonorrhoea is occasionally explained away as having non-sexual origins by doctors who would never accept such an explanation from adult sufferers. I recall one case where a small baby was supposed to have caught a venereal disease simply from sleeping on the contaminated sheets of its parents' bed.

Recently both in the UK and in America there has been a spate of horrific cases of long-standing sexual abuse taking place in residential children's homes and child-care institutions: where the people in charge of these homes and institutions are the abusers it is impossible for the staff to protest without risking their jobs, and years can and do pass before the world outside learns the truth. Any institution containing children who for one reason or another have difficulty in speaking up for themselves *should have regular inspection by outside bodies trained to recognize sexual abuse.* In addition, key workers responsible for individual children need to meet regularly with other staff members when the progress or otherwise of each child can be openly discussed. Where a child's behaviour has changed or an observant worker has noticed symptoms, queries about the possibility of abuse can be voiced and the child closely watched. Where speech is limited or virtually non-existent investigation is difficult – as Jane Wynne put it to me, 'without speech you have a big chunk of your jigsaw missing. Anatomically correct dolls are especially helpful here, though these children can show their aggression very clearly – a while back one of us had the penis bitten off his doll by a very angry handicapped boy!'

Where a child spends most or all of its day alone with family members or visiting carers the situation is more difficult to watch. Difficulty in communication will be enhanced by an abuser's prohibition on telling. As we saw earlier, even ordinary children may become uncommunicative and confused under these circumstances, and in some cases what is thought to be retardation may in fact be the result of sexual abuse. British Consultant Child and Adolescent Psychiatrist Eileen Vizard has suggested that this prohibition against communication may lead to lack of curiosity (questioning of adults being outlawed) and consequent under-achievement at school (Vizard 1988). This situation would of course be exacerbated where learning disability is present and 'low self-esteem, cognitive confusion, emotional dependence and a great fear of the consequences of disclosing sexual abuse may all combine with the child's learning difficulties to keep the victim silent or, possibly more correctly, wordless about his or her plight' (Vizard 1989).

People often dislike the idea of teaching 'innocent' children, with or without disabilities, about sex. But, as we have seen, because of their acceptance of adult direction children with learning difficulties are particularly open to abuse, and it is essential that within the bounds of their own understanding they are taught about good and bad sexuality, learning sufficient self-assertiveness to be able to say 'no!' to potential abusers. They must also learn about their rights over their own bodies, and where possible how to care for their 'private' parts themselves; in doing so they will learn how to distinguish between appropriate and inappropriate touching by others. It is important they learn terms for all parts of the body, especially the sexual parts, to enable them to talk about any abuse they may have experienced and to help arm them for the future. They also need to be taught appropriate social behaviour, in fact what used to be called modesty. Such words can raise a laugh in today's free climate, but nevertheless such ways of behaving have become second nature to most children before they reach their teens. The learning disabled must be helped to achieve the same self-protection.

In teaching self-protection, since students with learning disabilities are likely to have poor concentration, only one target should be aimed for at a time and if necessary returned to again and again, varying the approach as seems appropriate. They may have already picked up the need to beware of strangers, but may not have learned, or been taught, of the greater possibility of abuse from those nearest to them. This last is particularly important for these children and they must be taught to understand that reporting such incidents is the right and proper thing for them to do.

Sex education and assertiveness training for the learning disabled may be considered out of the question in areas where funds and staff are short, or where such ideas are dismissed as ludicrous, but their importance can hardly be over-stressed. Learning how to say No/Stop/Go away! convincingly is even more essential for a disabled person than for the rest of us (Craft and Hitching 1989; NSW Department of Education 1989c). Ann Craft, in addition to several publications, has prepared an excellent series of teaching slides for use in sex education programmes for the learning disabled, entitled *Educating Mentally Handicapped People*, and these are available for sale or hire from Camera Talks Ltd, 197 Botley Road, Oxford, OX2 0HE.

Deafness is another disability that may put children more at risk than has been previously realized. Anne Bannister, in a 1985 article prepared after a trip to America, wrote about a training group led by Diana Eckhaus in Washington DC in which four residential workers who worked solely with deaf children revealed that the children they looked after 'seemed to have suffered an unusually high incidence of sexual abuse'. No statistics were available at the time to support the claim, but there seems to be no question about their vulnerability. One particular problem in working with deaf children is, as Jane Wynne pointed out to me, the difficulty of communicating with severely impaired children who can neither talk nor sign. This means that behavioural symptoms have to be relied on if there are no medical ones, though again the use of anatomically correct dolls can be very helpful.

An important project started in Britain by Margaret Kennedy, the Keep Deaf Children Safe Project (KDCS), is now run by the National Deaf Children's Society (at Carlton House, Family Service Centre, 24 Wakefield Road, Rothwell Haigh, Leeds, LS26 0SF). The Society, responsible for 65,000 hearing impaired children in the UK, in developing its child protection programme has produced an illustrated multi-racial protection aid booklet with open-up flaps, *You Choose*, which has sign language illustrations as well as English wording. The book is not only extremely helpful to adults working with deaf children in discussing the possibililily of abuse and how and from whom they could get help should they need it, but, because of its simplicity and clarity, has also proved popular with teachers of developmentally disabled children.

THE ABUSE OF BOYS

It is only comparatively recently that it has been realized how frequently boys are sexually abused. Because of a combination of fears, including fear of the loss of the 'macho' image, of being thought homosexual and latterly of having AIDS, boys are even more wary of admitting having been assaulted than girls. The suggested percentage of boy victims to girl victims varies. Fifteen per cent of the victims in the NSPCC Greater

Manchester Report on c.s.a. registrations were male (a ratio of 1 boy to 5.6 girls), while other studies show ratios of between 1:2.5 to 1:6 (NSPCC 1989). As we saw in the last chapter, Furniss writes that research shows between 20 and 40 per cent of sexually abused children are boys (Furniss 1991).

It seems that the more recent the study, the closer the figures between boys and girls become. Finkelhor, who finds a high percentage of boy victims, suggested in an early study that when boys are abused within the family it is likely to be in tandem with the abuse of their sisters. But when boys are abused alone (apart from any girls) they were two and a half times more likely than girls to be abused by a non-family member. Abused boys are also more likely to come from poor or single-parent families than girls, and are more likely to have been physically abused. But, as with girls, their abusers are usually male (Finkelhor 1981a). Finkelhor also suggests (1984) that hospitals and child protection agencies see proportionately fewer boys compared to girls than the police, which may account for the difference in the ratios reported.

AT WHAT AGE DOES CHILD SEXUAL ABUSE BEGIN?

It used to be believed sexual abuse usually began slowly and gently, with a small child first being patted and stroked in a comparatively innocent way. Then gradually the attention would become more sexualized until by the child's early adolescence the abuse might, in fairly rare instances, develop into partial or full intercourse. This approach is now known to be untrue: although it is still a fact that most abusers carefully 'groom' their young victims into acceptance, much abuse begins horrifyingly early, sometimes starting in babyhood, and is likely to be much more severe than was thought earlier.

More research is being conducted into the age at which abuse begins than into many other aspects of c.s.a. and a number of statistics are becoming available, some more precise than others. For instance, it is reported that in 1988–9 in Queensland 55 per cent of all the substantiated cases of c.s.a. involved children aged 0–9 (Queensland Centre for Prevention of Child Abuse 1989). The Department of Health figures for Child Protection Registers for the whole of England (not Wales or Scotland) for the year ending March 1990 are more detailed but they illustrate the difficulties of selecting which facts to use. For a start, the Registers themselves, which are intended to register all children considered to be at risk of *any type* of abuse, record only 'approximately 43,600 children and young persons', which, at the rate of four children per thousand of the population under 18, is certainly a severe under-representation of the total number of abused children in England (this same fact will apply to most registers of children at risk anywhere). Then the Department of Health tables show figures both for Category A, a 'snapshot' view, i.e. a total of figures on the registers on one particular day, 31 March 1990, and for Category B, a total of the numbers registered during the course of the year ending 1990. These figures differ surprisingly, so which to choose for my summary? The figures in the two tables below show *sexual abuse* percentages for boys and girls out of the *total* number of boys and girls registered for a *variety of abusive reasons* under each separate age group, so that, for example, the first figure of 3 per cent shows the percentage of boys under 1 year old (out of a total of 1400 variously abused boys and girls under 1) who were sexually abused. The second line shows that 4 per cent of boys between 1 and 4 (out of a total of 7300 boys and girls between 1 and 4) were sexually abused.

In Category A the Department of Health figures show:

3 per cent boys and 3 per cent girls were under 1   (total 1400)
4 per cent boys and 10 per cent girls were between 1–4   (total 7300)
10 per cent boys and 21 per cent girls were between 5–9   (total 7100)
13 per cent boys and 34 per cent girls were between 10–15   (total 4700)
22 per cent boys and 50 per cent girls were between 16–18   (total 500)

In Category B:

2 per cent boys and 3 per cent girls were under 1   (total 1800)
5 per cent boys and 12 per cent girls were between 1–4   (total 4500)
10 per cent boys and 21 per cent girls were between 5–9   (total 3800)
13 per cent boys and 37 per cent girls were between 10–15   (total 2500)
20 per cent boys and 49 per cent girls were between 16–18   (total 200)

(Department of Health 1991)

A further difficulty is that various sources use different criteria by which to judge ages. Some, for instance, select the age at which the child was first *registered* as being in danger, although the actual abuse may have *commenced* several, or even many, years previously. Also, the difference in the minimum and the maximum ages being recorded in any particular survey can make a considerable difference to the final figures. The very useful NSPCC profile of Greater Manchester c.s.a. registrations shows the mean age of abused males was 8.6, the minimum age being 2 years and the maximum 17, while for female children the mean age was 10.08, the minimum age being 1 year, the maximum 17. The profile does not show any figures for babies under 1. Fifty-one per cent of the children were under 10, and the youngest victim actually abused was a girl of 1 year and 3 months (NSPCC 1989). But Hobbs and Wynne's British study, which included babies but excluded children over 15 years old, showed a mean age for both boys and girls of only 8.8 years in 1985 and 7.4 years in 1986, The general distribution was:

9 per cent of boys and 27 per cent of girls were between 0–5
11 per cent of boys and 25 per cent of girls were between 5–10
7 per cent of boys and 21 per cent of girls were between 10–15

(Hobbs and Wynne 1989)

Tilelli and colleagues in a Minnesota study of 130 abused children found that the mean age of the eighty-three who knew their abusers was eight, and that of the other forty-seven who did not know their abusers was 13.2 (Tilelli *et al.* 1980).

Goldman and Goldman (1988b), in Australia, give the mean ages of 10.3 for boys and 9.8 for girls; general distribution was:

10 per cent of boys and 15 per cent of girls between 4–6
23 per cent of boys and 28 per cent of girls between 7–9
62 per cent of boys and 41 per cent of girls between 10–12
5 per cent of boys and 16 per cent of girls between 13–16
(but note that *4 years* is the earliest age recorded).

In his hospital-based study of 104 sexually abused victims Chris Goddard (Victoria) found that almost 65 per cent were 8 years old or less, and 49 per cent were under 7. Thirty-five per cent were under 5, and the most common ages were 3–4 – then, in descending order, 7–8, followed by 10–11 (Law Reform Commission of Victoria 1988). Goddard remarked in a personal interview, 'The most common age of the sexually abused children at the Children's Hospital was 3. We followed it up with two more studies in which again the most common age was 3 or 4. Getting the necessary evidence from children who are barely verbal is one of the most extraordinarily difficult legal questions.'

Clearly, there is no question that a great deal of abuse begins at a horrifyingly early age, from a few days old onwards, and when this youngest section of abused children is fully taken into account we will find that the mean age for the total is much lower than used to be thought. At present, though, figures are too confused for me to be able to present a clearer summary than that.

VICTIMS AND THEIR ABUSERS

It is now generally accepted that the majority of child sexual abusers are well known to their victims. Where the child is familiar with the abuser she/he might cooperate out of fondness or trust, not realizing she is being exploited, whereas similar approaches from a stranger are more likely to be resisted (Finkelhor 1981b). Mrazek, Lynch and Bentovim found in a study that 74 per cent of victims already knew their abuser and of those 58 per cent were abused by a family member (Mrazek *et al.* 1983). An abusive close relationship, particularly where the father is the molester, makes recovery even more difficult than it might be otherwise. Trust in adults may be destroyed and the self-confidence of the child weakened to the point of non-existence.

The father, for instance, may have told the victim that the mother will believe him rather than the child because he is older, or the child may come to believe she must be to blame otherwise her father wouldn't have treated her like that. Perhaps she would almost rather be the one who is in the wrong, because if that is not so and it is all his fault, then she will be left with no one in whom she can believe (Burgess *et al.* 1990). Because of their imagined guilt these children sometimes punish themselves physically, and may continue to do so in adult life (see Jane's story in Chapter 7).

The most difficult age to persuade children to disclose their abuse, Wynne says, is when they are past very early childhood and not yet arrived at an age where independence is beginning to grow:

> If at 7 or 8 the parents are in the next room and they've been told to keep quiet they will. Children at nursery school might just blab away, but at 6 or 7 they understand threats. If you say I'll cut you up into little pieces if you tell, or I'll kill the rabbit if you tell, it's quite easy to keep them quiet. The difficult ones can be very difficult. We had this girl, she sat between both her parents, and she drew all the things about herself – in a cage with tears running down, all kinds of symbolic material, but she wouldn't say a word. It was so symbolic of how she was sitting, silent, between Mum and Dad, and there she was with bruises on her upper arms, places where she'd pinched herself, scratched herself, horrible! There's another girl on the wards I've just seen, pinch marks all over her chest, and we know something horrible is happening to her – she is 8 and she's sitting smiling at me.
>
> (personal communication)

As a result of such threats, or out of misplaced family loyalty, children will sometimes deny that sexual abuse has happened, a lie far more likely than the false accusation they are occasionally suspected of. Another effect of the abuse itself which is difficult for all of us to accept is that the sexual arousal deliberately induced by the perpetrator can in itself contribute to the loyalty of some victims (Furniss 1991). In addition, the mother is often perceived as, or actually is, emotionally cold or distant. Perhaps she has refused to believe the child's assertions, so the victim now turns to the father/abuser for the comfort she/he needs, when he is actually the cause of that need. Although when the abuse is finally revealed the victim may express intense hate for the abuser, in cases of long-term abuse the attachment between the two may still be very powerful. A natural yearning for a trusted father figure remains, even when the child has been so consistently betrayed, and she will continue to seek one.

Because the victims feel dirty, of little worth, it is very important for their eventual recuperation that the abuser can be brought to admit his guilt and *in front of the victim* accept the blame for what has happened. This will help the abused children not only to realize fully their own lack of blame, but also it will go some way to allowing them (in their own minds at least) to fulfil their longing to restore the father to his proper place as protector. This last may seem almost an obscene suggestion, but one must remember that in some cases the abuser's attention might have been the only 'caring' the victim has ever received. There are a few victims who never want to see the perpetrator again, but, as Professor Kim Oates (Camperdown Children's Hospital, Sydney) remarked to me in an interview, 'most of the children say something like, "I really love my father, I just wish he'd stop doing this to me on Thursday nights." '

If the child is left to think the blame is entirely hers she is likely to develop the self-abusive behaviour mentioned earlier which will probably increase in type and severity, and she may 'face a life blighted by self-inflicted dissociative disorders' (Giarretto 1989). Burgess and her colleagues suggest that 'children, to survive molestation, dissociate complex units of personal behaviour. When there is no clinical intervention, these units of behaviour are not only blocked but contribute to further developmental lags . . . [the children] also demonstrate they are dissociated from self-assertiveness behaviours' (Burgess *et al.* 1987). This dissociation, and a blocking out of the abusive events, frequently noted by those working with abused children, may be the only way the victim can survive in everyday life. Sometimes the child appears to be frozen emotionally, and in her/his defensive silence may be extremely difficult for professionals to get through to. Long-term therapy is probably the only answer in these cases.

WHO SHOULD LEAVE – ABUSER OR VICTIM?

As we have seen, in the majority of cases of c.s.a. the abuser is already known to the victim, and is likely to be a family member. Therefore, a vital question that arises on discovery is, who should leave the family home – abuser or victim? Since very frequently the perpetrator is the father/father figure this question is fraught with difficulties. He is probably the main breadwinner, the handyman around the house, an adult male presence the mother does not want to lose. Quite apart from any emotions involved, to make the decision to become an unsupported single parent – at least for a lengthy period of time – is something that many mothers, after the first shock of learning of the abuse, refuse to do. Too often they reject the child's accusations out of hand rather than have to make the unwanted decision, even when they are assured by professionals that the victim truly has been assaulted. Sometimes the result of disclosure is that the family closes up, everything is denied, even by the victim, and in the end because of lack of any proof there is no choice but to let the family go on as before.

But there can be no question that wherever possible the abuser and the victim should be separated, at least temporarily. Most professionals today agree that for the child's sake it is the father who should leave. However, there is not quite the same immediate urgency in cases of c.s.a. as there is in physical abuse, where a short delay may mean the death of a child. If removal of the abuser can be organized before the family has had a chance to draw together again after the initial shock of disclosure then measured plans for treatment can be acted on, but, as mentioned earlier, over-hasty moves before basic plans have been made can result in a lost case. Above all, the child must be made safe and, if all the professionals concerned have cooperated efficiently in advance, obtaining a legal injunction to remove the father from the house should present no difficulties. There will be, of course, some cases where the child would actually prefer to leave home her/himself, as may perhaps be the case with an older, more independent child, or where the victim has been scapegoated or totally rejected by the rest of the family. If this last problem cannot be sorted out, considerable work may have to be done with the victim to help her to realize the blame is not hers, but her abuser's.

The reaction of the mother during the crisis of disclosure is of vital importance, but inevitably her loyalties will be torn between partner and child, and nothing can be taken for granted here. We saw in Barbara's story the lengthy struggle she had with herself before she could accept the truth of her daughter's abuse and finally take action. A mother's needs and courage in these circumstances must not be underestimated. Furniss writes of one family where the child's brothers and her mother missed the abusive father so bitterly and were so hostile to her it was decided it would be less traumatic for the victim to be removed than for her to continue to live in such an angry family (Furniss 1991).

The victim can end up traumatized almost as much by the eventual outcome of the revelation of her abuse as by the abuse itself. Libby DeLacy, Division of Education, Griffith University, Brisbane, had kindly convened a meeting with several colleagues to discuss c.s.a. with me, at which Liz Drew, Social Worker in Charge at the Royal Children's Hospital, said:

> I remember a 14-year-old girl who gave really explicit evidence of violent abuse by her father. It was the sort of middle-class family where people would say this can't be happening – she was a beautiful girl who gave really convincing evidence, and she said she didn't want to go home. There was a police interview but the father consistently denied it and he couldn't be charged because there was no corroborating evidence. We went to court with an application and the family came, saying they consented to the application. They just said to us, 'She's been a problem in recent years, if that's how she feels and she says she doesn't want the family any more, that's fine by us, you can have her.' So OK, we have this girl who up until that point had a solid family, and suddenly she's ours, she's had her whole family just drop off the face of the earth – I mean, that is a dreadful situation for us, let alone for the girl. Suddenly we are all this girl has got.

Libby De Lacy: 'That's institutional abuse, which is dreadful.' Liz Drew: 'That's right, that's what burns the social workers out more than anything else – they start personalizing it, say to me what are we doing?, as though I created this problem!'

The Cleveland Report implying that care should be taken before victims are removed from their homes, was welcomed by Anne Bannister in her 'Conclusions from Cleveland': 'it is difficult to explain to a child they are being removed for their own safety. To the child it feels like punishment and to a sexually abused child, who is already suffering from guilt, it seems to confirm those feelings. The recommendation that consideration should be given to removing abusers is most welcome' (Bannister 1988a). The British Children Act of 1989, in operation since October 1991, has changed procedures. Money may be available to move offenders under Section 2 (5) of this Act, and if it is possible to arrange this then for the sake of the children no efforts should be spared.

There is an urgent need, Furniss states, for the creation of 'men's houses' to which abusers can be sent in the first stages of the disclosure where therapy can be initiated (Furniss 1991). And Tony Morrison points out, in an article on treating offenders, that one of the most dramatic effects of Cleveland 'was the removal of huge numbers of children instead of offenders ... [because of] the absence of effective treatment facilities and limited alternative accommodation for offenders to live in the community but out of their homes' (Morrison 1989).

As we have seen, if the child is taken into care or separated from the family she/he will feel they are being punished and abandoned. Sometimes, when a prosecution has failed or not been attempted and there are no bail provisions, this argument can be used to persuade a father to move out of the family. In Western Australia, for example, SAIF (Sexual Assault in Families), a non-statutory programme aimed at persuading people to seek treatment under conditions of confidentiality, has been set up. Contracts are made which, among other child-protective conditions, require offenders to live away from home during the period of treatment (Harrison 1990). Since so few offenders are discovered anyway, it does seem that voluntary schemes, which encourage extended as well as close family members to 'twist the arm' of the abuser to seek help without courts being involved, may be the only way of picking up some of the many cases which would otherwise continue to be hidden away.

The hope that the family may eventually be able to come together again is one that most offenders hold, as do their families. But before there can be any chance of this happening there has to be a great deal of devoted work and therapy for all the family by social workers, therapists, psychiatrists and not least by those involved on the legal side. Hank Giarretto's innovative work in San José has shown that this can sometimes be achieved, but there seem to be few other places where success on his scale has resulted. Even in San José, I understand there are no long-term follow-ups for the mass of the clients, but at the very least the outcome for all concerned has to be improved by the use of the Giarretto system of group work for all the family, including the abusers, from the very first moment of disclosure.

Chapter 6

The abusers

WHO ARE THE ABUSERS?

Professionals who have worked with child sex abusers agree that abuse is not a result of a sudden loss of control but is the result of careful planning with full intent of abuse (Bannister 1988a). So who are these people who are prepared cold-bloodedly to plan the abuse of their own and other people's children? Given the vast amount of abuse that is committed, they are obviously not rarities but the man (or woman) in the street, your next-door neighbour.

We have already seen in earlier chapters that most child sex abusers are known to their victims, being either family members, close to the family or in contact with the child. The size of the incidence of stranger abuse is suggested as ranging from 26 per cent (Goldman and Goldman 1988a) to Goddard's statement in his Report for the Law Reform Commission of Victoria that strangers make up only 3.8 per cent of the perpetrators. He found that the most common perpetrators were natural fathers at 35.5 per cent of cases. He added that other studies have similar results, but refers to Russell's (1984) study as an exception which shows stepfathers to be 'far more commonly the perpetrators'. He calculated that 54.4 per cent of victims were abused by blood relatives, and as many as 67.1 per cent if 'reconstituted relatives' were counted. Mothers accounted for 3.8 per cent of known cases. He adds that Russell (1984) 'reports intrafamilial offenders outnumbered extrafamilial by a ratio of almost 2:1, very similar figures to those in the current study' (Law Reform Commission of Victoria 1988).

A major reporting problem is that at present there are too few statistics based on sufficiently similar criteria for any firm figures as to the identity of the perpetrators to be given. For example, Mrazek *et al.* (1983) show 48 per cent of perpetrators to be the natural father, step-parents 28 per cent and 5 per cent the natural mother – but these figures relate only to cases of abuse *carried out by a family member* (Steven *et al*. 1988). An NSPCC report from their register research (Research Briefing No. 11 – Child Abuse in 1989) reports natural fathers as suspected in 25 per cent of cases, 'followed by brothers and other relatives in 23 per cent and father substitutes in 20 per cent ... natural mothers in 2 per cent and both parents in 3 per cent'. But the authors go on to point out that no allowances are made for where and with whom the child was living, and that if you control for this, then these figures change to 43 per cent for natural fathers and 54 per cent for father substitutes.

Finkelhor (1979b) stated that children from reconstructed families are between two and five times more likely to suffer c.s.a. than those living with their natural fathers. In their vast study of 991 Australian first-year social science students (based on Finkelhor's earlier study), the Goldmans confirmed that, in spite of the undoubtedly high numbers of paternal incest, students with an absent natural father were at greater risk of abuse than those with their own father at home – 39 per cent of the girls in single parent or remarriage families had been sexually abused as children, 8 per cent of these girls having had 'an experience with a grandfather' (Goldman and Goldman 1988a). Incidentally, Furniss, while reaffirming that children in reconstituted families are 'part of a high-risk group', warns that in such circumstances accusations from adolescent girls should be treated with some caution lest this be one of the rare cases of a child lying in order to remove someone she sees as an unwanted family intruder (Furniss 1991).

The NSPCC regional profile of c.s.a. registrations in Greater Manchester also bears out these findings. Of the 281 families in the profile (with 311 registered children) only eighty-six (30.5 per cent) contained two natural parents, the fathers being the abusers in forty-six (53 per cent) *of these cases*. In the ninety-eight families where the mother lived with the stepfather or cohabitee, the father figure was the abuser in sixty-two (63 per cent) cases. Further figures of interest are that in fifty-nine (21 per cent) families the abused children lived with the mother alone, in eleven (4 per cent) with the father alone, and in seven (2.5 per cent) with their grandparents. (Twelve per cent of the non-abusing mothers were known to be survivors of sexual abuse and a further 3 per cent were thought to be undisclosed survivors, although, as the authors of the report rightly point out, given the current statistics on the number of abused women in general such figures may show no more than a chance link.)

Fifty-two per cent of the victims were abused by a male relative, and if we include the victims' stepfathers, male cohabitees and stepbrothers in this figure, as I feel we should because of the similarity of the betrayal of trust and emotional disturbance to the child, then it rises to 78.1 per cent, which compares with Goddard's figure (above) of 67.1 for reconstituted families. To be more precise, 29 per cent of the abusers were the child's natural father, 16 per cent the stepfather, 9 per cent an uncle, 8 per cent the male cohabitee, 7 per cent a brother, 6.7 per cent the victim's grandfather, 2 per cent the mother's boyfriend, 1.7 per cent a stepbrother and 0.7 per cent a male cousin. Finally, outside the family, 4.7 per cent of the abusers were babysitters, 1.7 per cent were neighbours and 1.7 per cent family friends.

The five female abusers were mainly involved in multiple perpetrator situations, where there was a total of twenty-two perpetrators – three females and nineteen males. Eleven children were abused in this way, nine of them by two people. Two of these last victims were abused by the natural father and mother, and one by the stepfather and mother. Other combinations of pairs of abusers were natural father and brother-in-law, natural father and uncle; grandfather and brother, grandfather and family friend; and stepfather and neighbour. In the two remaining cases the victims were abused by three perpetrators – one triad was composed of stepfather, brother, family friend, and the other of two stepbrothers and family friend. In this last case the victim, at 5½ years old, was the youngest boy to be multiply abused. Most of these multiple abuse victims were female, the youngest girl (abused by her grandfather together with a family friend), being only 3½ years old. Of the two lone women abusers, one unrelated female digitally penetrated a 3-year-old boy's anus, while the other genitally fondled her own 2-year-old daughter (NSPCC 1989).

In this final case the mother confessed the abuse. Although adults undergoing therapy are increasingly disclosing retrospective childhood abuse by females, since such abuse is so rarely reported contemporaneously to the authorities one can only wonder how frequently it occurs but goes unreported. By the very nature of the caring relationship of mother and child, and also of other female carers, detection of such abuse must remain problematical except where physical symptoms are picked up (see the section of this chapter on female abusers).

It can be seen, then, from these assorted figures that natural or step/cohab-fathers between them probably commit from one-third to over a half of the total of childhood sex abuse, but which of these two groups commits the greater amount remains unclear. It should be noted that in the cases discussed by the NSPCC (Research Briefing No. 11, 1989), as many as 12 per cent of the parents and parent substitutes were not living with the victim, the abusive incidents usually happening on access visits to or from the child. Altogether it seems probable that around half the abuse is committed by blood relatives, which figure, when all members of the reconstituted family are included, increases to around three-quarters. Much of the remainder of the abuse is committed by family friends, neighbours, carers such as teachers, social workers and ministers, etc., with total strangers accounting for only a comparatively small proportion of the abuse.

Although some recent research is reporting that there is far more female abuse than was previously thought (see below), most workers agree that the large majority of abusers are male, with suggested figures ranging from a minimum of 90 per cent (Furniss 1991; Goldman and Goldman 1986) to even higher. The NSPCC regional profile of the registration of sexually abused children in Greater Manchester shows that as many as 98 per cent of the 294 abusers were male, the remaining 2 per cent being female (NSPCC 1989).

Finkelhor in 1985 put forward three reasons for this dichotomy. Firstly, that as potential child carers women are taught about non-sexual affection from early childhood, whereas overt physical affection is withdrawn from men early on, only to be regained through sexual relationships in later years. Secondly, men are socialized to separate sex and affection, whereas women focus more on the relationship on which the sex is based. As far as a male is concerned, a 'child has the right set of orifices to provide sexual gratification', but in most cases women are too distracted by the inappropriateness of sex with children to be able to fantasize or be aroused. Thirdly, men are trained to be attracted to smaller, younger, less powerful people than themselves, and women exactly the opposite. The hurdle to be leapt by men is therefore lower than for women (Finkelhor 1985).

As we saw earlier (Chapter 3), child sexual abuse happens in all classes and also, it seems, with offenders of virtually all ages. However, according to a 1979 Home Office study in Britain, it seems that perpetrators under 30 are most frequently involved with post-pubertal females aged 13 and above, while older abusers aged 30 or more are more often involved with victims under 13. 'This seems to support the widespread opinion that many molesters of very young girls were middle-aged or elderly' (West 1987). The NSPCC sexual abuse regional profile for Greater Manchester showed the ages of the abusers on the reviewed registers as being between 5 and 70, with a mean age of 34.6. Nine and a half per cent were under 17, 4 per cent between 18 and 20, 17 per cent between 21 and 30 and the largest percentage, 27.5, were between 31 and 40. The numbers then fell to 11 per cent of abusers being between the ages of 41 and 50, 7 per cent between 51 and 60 and 4 per cent 60 or older. In 20 per cent of the cases the ages were not known. The youngest 'abuser', himself abused, that I have heard of was a 4-year-old who was supported over his 2½-year-old sister as he was encouraged by both his parents to attempt to penetrate her: at such an age it clearly becomes absurd to use the word 'abuser'. Semantics apart, I want to stress here that age is no barrier, either for the abuser or for his victim.

The abuse of children by a grandparent is not uncommon, as we have already seen from the case histories of Peter and his sister and of Barbara's mother. It should not be thought that I searched for such cases, indeed chance had it that my problem rather was finding suitable cases where grandparents were not involved. In Chapter 7 we will look at multi-generational abuse, beginning with the story of Jane, a grandfather-abused girl, now adult, which horrified me more than any I had been told before, probably because of the charm and natural sweetness of the victim and the unquestioned selfishness and brutality of the grandfather. But first we will look more closely at what we know of the characters of the abusers.

SOME ASPECTS OF THE CHARACTERS OF CHILD SEXUAL ABUSERS

Williams and Finkelhor, in their 'The characteristics of incestuous fathers: a review of recent studies' (1988), write 'the evidence [is] against a simple single factor hypothesis. . . . The idea that all or nearly all incestuous fathers were themselves molested as children was not supported. . . . There are characteristics that seem relatively common[:] many . . . appear to be passive, dependent, isolated, somewhat paranoid, and lacking a core masculine identification.' Between a fifth and a third show signs of general sexual arousal to children, but more widespread 'is a pattern of low sexual arousal to or even disgust with normal adult sexual objects'. They go on to say that many have been mistreated in their families of origin, particularly through rejection by their fathers, many have poor marriages with low levels of sexual satisfaction and difficulty in feeling empathy, but few of these characteristics apply to the majority of offenders. Indeed, there are many abusers who have little in common with this list.

They put forward a framework of four possible factors which probably have to be combined before sexual abuse occurs. The first factor is emotional need (including the abuser's need to feel powerful and dominant, especially if he himself has been victimized), which may be satisfied by a relationship with children. The second is sexual arousal. Only a minority of incestuous fathers have a deviant attraction towards children in general, so does the deviance of the majority of child abusers lie in the fact that, while still showing normal arousal to customary sex objects, they feel arousal for their own children? In other words, the authors ask, would 'normal' men be able to interact sexually with their daughters if the usual inhibitions could be removed? The third factor, blockage, raises many questions. What stops these men from satisfying themselves sexually and emotionally as most 'normal' men do? Are the blockages, which might be connected, for example, with introversion, poor marriages or isolation, sufficient to push them into relationships with their own daughters, even if they don't feel positive sexual arousal to them? Wouldn't the opposite be more likely? Fourthly, what causes the disinhibition which allows the father to act as he does? Some studies suggest psychopathy, mental illness, low intelligence, alcohol, or subcultural acceptance. More recent studies also suggest impaired empathy and bonding, causing lack of concern for or awareness of the effect on their daughters, but whether this lack is specific to their own children or is general is undecided at present (Williams and Finkelhor 1988).

Joan Thompson, Senior Child Advocate at the Children's Interests Bureau, Adelaide, agrees with much of what they say. She told me when I asked her about her experiences:

I've been to many conferences and listened to people talking about offenders but I've never felt that people have got to grips with the dynamics of what makes a person a child abuser or a paedophile. I don't think the profiles I've seen are very useful: I've found abusers to be infinitely various. The ones I've met have come from the pits of society to highly respectable establishment. I don't know what the dynamic is, I can't see a link between a person who comes from an old-established family and someone who's tattered from his head to his toes – except that both have been capable of sexually abusing their own children.

There's only one characteristic I've found the men have and that is that they're usually very pleasant superficially; some of them have been overtly sickeningly charming, you know, quite over-the-top charming, and they've got this propensity to suddenly change from that to being very nasty indeed. Yes, I feel the majority are like that, in fact I've got to the stage where I wait for it to happen. They can be trying to give a good impression but then they turn on you. It's almost as though they don't like adult women – now, that is impressionistic, but I do feel that has something to do with it. It's really interesting the way their behaviour changes and you see in them the person who will threaten the child, and quite often they will threaten you. When I used to supervise the Department's Custody and Access Service as Senior Social Worker I found time and time again that they'd turn on you – very angry. They can be extremely unpleasant, even harassing you in the street. One person I knew had very bad persecution that went on for a couple of years, all sorts of things thrown all over her house, the whole neighbourbood leafletted with wild stories about her lesbian lifestyle and her lesbian lovers who'd committed suicide – you know, 'Do you realize who's living here!' kind of thing. . . .

It can happen like – I was talking to someone, not accusing him, and he suddenly said to me, 'I don't think you're going to help me, Joan, you're not going to help me, are you!' – there was real menace in his voice – and I was really frightened because I was in his house on my own. Yes, his manner was terribly menacing, and there I was trapped, trying to think of ways how I could get to the door before he jumped on me. . . . I've been abused and sworn at over the phone, and often there's this sense the man's getting pleasure out of abusing a woman. It's totally impressionistic, but it adds up to a total picture, I've come to expect it.

Many people, perhaps most, feel that abusers themselves must have been through some kind of abuse in their own childhoods – neglect, emotional, physical or sexual – for them to act as they do, but it appears that the majority were not actually sexually abused. Thirty-eight per cent of the perpetrators in the Greater Manchester profile were found to have been victims of c.s.a. themselves, and most studies show rates of well below 50 per cent (NSPCC 1989). Ray Wyre at the Gracewell Clinic, while finding that many of the offenders in their care had themselves been victims of c.s.a., says that the clinic tries to deal with this at a later rather than an early stage in treatment. As long as the abuser is still deep into his feelings about himself his thinking about the abuse he has committed is distorted, so that he justifies and minimizes it rather than genuinely attempting to empathize with his victim/s.

Hank Giarretto, who believes that many of the mothers also have suffered some form of abuse, says that, because of the resulting deep-rooted emotional problems, therapy for the family as a whole must include therapy for the parents as abused children 'before they can become effective parents' (Giarretto 1989). A psychiatrist experienced in working with abusers, who had been listening to Giarretto speaking at a conference on child sexual abuse, commented during the following discussion that, while she agreed with him that many abusers have powerful drives beyond their conscious control, 'at the same time we must be very careful not to fall into the trap they lay for us, that they are victims of their own circumstances.... In everyday life and in the treatment situation we've got to treat them as adults.' Giarretto's reply was, 'Child abuse is a self-destructive device – there is nothing a person can do to harm himself, deprecate himself, more than abusing a child. No man, no woman – using the common language – in his right mind would abuse a child. It's not volitional, it's a dissociative disorder.'

Another highly experienced psychiatrist entered the discussion, arguing:

> I think it's a developmental disorder. If we look at their social and sexual development, their cognitive and emotional development, we'll find the reason offenders are not just one entity is that there is a whole continuum of ranges of offences and depths or ranges of offending behaviour, with different mental components coming into play. If we address the assessment issues in terms of the different developmental strands of this person who's before us, we aren't going to be able to expect adult behaviour from him until these developmental needs are addressed. That isn't to condone; I think people do quite consciously sexually abuse children for reasons that they may well be in touch with. There may also be unconscious drives but I don't think we do people any favours by saying, you are out of control. It may well be that their impulse control is a result of their developmental disorder, but we mustn't deny people their conscious motivation to abuse, and it seems to me that if you use the idea of disease rather than developmental disorder I think you are allowing people a sidetrack to escape into.

There is no question that most sexual offenders know what they are up to. They know what pleases a child, how to make them trust them, initially, at least. Outside the family they will look for needy children and befriend them, much as Barbara's own abuser did. Once they have won the potential victim's trust they will gradually desensitize them to sexual advances, so that the child, who may have no or little sexual knowledge, may at first even enjoy the sensations produced. But very soon these pass beyond any age-appropriate enjoyment, causing confusion and fear. It is probably at this point that intimidation, if it has not already occurred, begins. This process of grooming, followed – once the child is submissive – by threats, is the same method adopted by abusers within the family.

Surveys of offenders have shown that they will frequently admit targeting children who seem vulnerable, trusting or withdrawn, children who are not assertive or outgoing, and especially those who have been victimized before. A child who feels unloved and isolated is a sitting target for a man who knows what he wants and has no qualms about using his charm and his clear understanding of such a child's doubts and uncertainties (he understands them well enough – he himself has never been without them).

It is now becoming commonplace to refer to the abuser as an addict, even to accept that, like an alcoholic, he can never be fully cured. He may sometimes, with expert treatment, be helped to lead a trouble-free life, but, again like an alcoholic, for the rest of that life he must remain consciously aware of his own susceptibility (see Chapter 9 on treatment). Ray Wyre said recently when discussing his work at the Gracewell Clinic, 'sex offending never just happens, it's always deliberate. Lawyers claim something "just happened". To me that's the highest of risks – if he just happened to do it once, why can't he just happen to do it again?' One of the difficulties of discussing the characteristics of child sexual abusers is that, as we have already seen, the great majority are never discovered, and therefore those that are questioned are in the main the rare exceptions who perhaps through carelessness, lack of intelligence or drink, have been caught. (As far as alcohol itself is concerned, although it is sometimes cited as one of the causes of c.s.a., and it certainly can act as a disinhibiting factor, it does not seem to be a significant one, only a frequent 'accompanying feature' (Goldman and Goldman 1988a).)

The sheer numbers of abuses that some men are known to have committed raise yet more questions about their characters and motivations. For example, French (1990) reports eighteen imprisoned offenders in Western Australia as having admitted to 1070 assaults on 328 children, and Abel et al. (1987) showed that 567 non-imprisoned abusers admitted non-incest offences at the rate of an average of twenty victims for each man whose offence was against girls, and 150 victims where the abuse was against boys.

In one of his studies Professor D.J. West commented that paedophiles – as opposed to assaultative offenders who tend to be aggressive and uninhibitedly impulsive – are often reported as being shy, gentle, timid, unassertive, with feelings of inadequacy and insecurity. He then compared these findings with his own from research among ex-members of the Paedophile Information Exchange (now banned), men who had not been charged with any offences. They turned out to be very different from c.s.a. offenders who were interviewed in prison. They were more confident, assertive, better-educated, and were not only over-representative of professional men, but particularly so in jobs where their work might bring them into contact with children, such as in teaching or social work (West 1987).

Indeed, as I wrote earlier, more and more cases are coming to light about abuse by the very people who should be spending their working lives caring for the children they abuse: professionals in children's homes, institutions, boarding schools, even in day nurseries. In Britain, at the time of writing, a long-drawn out case has only just been concluded where Frank Beck, social worker and officer in charge of three children's homes in Leicestershire, and two of his senior staff have been convicted of repeatedly buggering, sexually assaulting and beating children under their care over a period of thirteen years. Young social workers working in the homes were also assaulted and forced or persuaded into performing sexual acts against their will. In another current case the headteacher of a special boarding school for boys is presently on trial accused of abusing boys under his care over a period of five years. It seems that, although he had been previously accused on different occasions of sexual assault by three of his pupils, he had been able to avoid conviction by discrediting them on the grounds that he was 'unable to perform sexually'. Finally, after a fourth complaint from yet another boy, the police opened a full investigation, including interviewing past pupils, and were able to collect sufficient evidence to bring charges. A particularly outrageous aspect of this case is that the victims, whose fees were paid by local authorities, had been sent to the school as being in need of special attention because of social and/or behavioural problems. What is going to be the future of these boys, and others like them, when public 'caring' has proved to be such a mockery, and adults so painfully untrustworthy?

JUVENILE OFFENDERS

'Boys will be boys' was an excuse often made when an adolescent was found having some kind of sexual experience with another, but it is heard less often in today's climate of a wider understanding of the effects on the victims of sexual abuse. Nevertheless it is not always easy to draw a line between what may be considered as permissible experimentation or play and what is definite abuse. Perhaps one of the first considerations should be to ask whether or not the incident being considered was appropriate to the developmental age of the less dominant child. If not, should the last be considered a victim, and if so might the incident, now properly called abuse, be repeated.

Ronald and Juliette Goldman in their book, *Show Me Yours* (1988a), based on their previously mentioned study of 991 social science students, report that 64 per cent of the male students and 58 per cent of the females had had some sort of sexual experience with other children before the age of 12, typically as children of around the same age exploring each other or playing mild sex games such as mothers and fathers or doctors and nurses. A child being coerced against her/his desire to do something they didn't want to do was the exception. About 11 per cent of the incidents reported by those who had had experiences with other children before 12 was with siblings. Most of these consisted of the children showing their sex organs to each other, perhaps touching, and occasionally a certain amount of sexual fondling. The Goldmans write that since so many children have such experiences these should be considered normal, or natural if that definition is preferred: they add, 'sex curiosity is not artificial; in most cases it . . . arises from the child's need to know and understand reality.'

Nevertheless a great deal of sexual interaction between children goes well beyond mutually enjoyed experimentation and becomes straightforward abuse, involving exploitation, lack of consent and/or inequality in age, physical or mental power. A study by the Department for Community Welfare in Adelaide (from a 1990 unpublished memorandum loaned to me) on 200 child and adolescent perpetrators of child abuse over a period of three years showed that the most common category of offence was indecent assault (ninety) followed by indecent exposure (forty), the most common age of young males charged being 13 (forty). There were only nine female offenders, a ratio similar to those in many other studies of adult offenders (see the next section, on female abusers). The NSPCC Greater Manchester profile gave the mean age of their twenty-eight child/adolescent perpetrators as being 14.3 years. All were male, and 79 per cent were related to the victim, sixteen being brothers (NSPCC 1989). One child was abused by a babysitter, an occurrence that probably happens more often than most parents are aware.

I discussed some of the above points with Jenny Harvey, at the time Senior Social Worker at the Family and Community Services Centre (FACS), Adelaide. She told me:

> We went through a period where most child or adolescent perpetrators were immediately regarded as victims, but now we no longer make that automatic assumption. If the child is under 10, then yes, it is very likely, but if they are the same age and what is done is done by consent, then is either one of them a perpetrator? But we have to make sure there was consent – it's still abuse if the partner doesn't want it to hap-

pen. I would certainly have a problem with thinking a 6-year-old would be able to consent to sex with a 12-year-old. With, say, two 11-year-olds or two 6-year-olds exploring each other, it's probably OK, but if there's a large difference in intellectual ability, or understanding of the process. . . .

We recently had a case there was a lot of debate about, where a 6-year-old girl was performing oral sex on three 8-year-olds. Now in that case she was being seen as the victim because clearly she didn't want to do it, although there didn't seem to have been any coercion. We found that the boys had been looking at a pornographic magazine one of them had got from his home. That was probably all there was to it, but in a case like that there still is a need for intervention – the problem is that once they establish patterns like that they can go on doing it. It doesn't necessarily follow they will become long-term abusers, of course, but that's how some adult offenders can end up having 300 odd offences.

If force is used then there's no question it's abuse. Or sometimes a younger girl might feel she has to do what her elder brother says, so even though there isn't physical force there's a power difference. I'd say that if there is an age gap of more than two years it's enough to make a difference. For instance, there was a boy of 14 who looked at and touched a 6-year-old girl he met at a swimming pool. Force wasn't involved, but yes, I do call it abuse because of the power differential. That boy needed sessions with a counsellor because he hadn't learned in his own family setting about not having the same rights over another person's body as one has over one's own. I mean, you don't steal into another person's house to find out what their videos are like because you haven't got one yourself. Work needed to be done with the parents, too, in that particular case.

We have not been addressing the problem of juvenile abusers early enough; we say 'boys will be boys', they're just experimenting and it's all OK, but then when it comes to they're adult and they've established that pattern and are committing numerous offences, then we say we must do something. So now we are trying to take action during adolescence and move in before the pattern has been established.

Most workers are now concurring with this final analysis, that treatment must be undertaken *before* the abusive behaviour patterns have become ingrained and less amenable to treatment. I can think of few changes more likely to improve the current horrifyingly high incidence of child sexual abuse. Finkelhor writes of the 'evidence showing the very impressive correlation between the age at which someone starts their assaultive behaviour and the likelihood that they will be a high-frequency chronic offender sometime in the future' (Finkelhor 1986b). Since we know that in some cases a child can begin his first abusive acts at early as 4 or 5, it is clear that future intensive abusers-to-be must be trawled for not only amongst young teenagers but also amongst those just beginning school, even in kindergarten.

Because this is an aspect of c.s.a. that people have been unwilling to think about, few realize just how many offences are committed by child/adolescent abusers: various studies show that the numbers of child molestations committed by offenders under 18 years of age against children mostly younger than themselves range from a minimum of over 20 per cent to 50 per cent of the total abuse committed by all offenders (Fehrenbach *et al.* 1986; Finkelhor 1986b; Davis and Leitenberg 1987; Cavanagh 1988).

Davis and Leitenberg (1987) report that, against earlier assumptions that adolescent sex abusers were experimenting out of curiosity or lack of sexual experience, research showed that in fact they were reported to have had more sexual experiences, including consenting ones, than other groups of adolescents. But agreement on this last point is not general. Furniss, for example, suggests that if a boy has suffered homosexual abuse by his father or another male he may find himself unable to experiment with girls as other boys do and will be more likely to relieve his tensions in compulsive masturbation and sexual activities, possibly leading to sexual abuse with younger boys (Furniss 1991). The worry, as we have seen, is that such adolescent behaviour which is deviant and not experimental can become established and lead to repeated sexual offences.

Many recent studies have shown that a significant number of adult offenders have begun deviant sexual patterns before they have reached 18, a significant number committing their first offence between 12 and 15, and some even earlier (Becker *et al.* 1985; Bonner 1990). Finkelhor writes that Judith Becker showed in her New York study that 'about 90 percent of the high volume molesters against boys have gotten into this pattern by age 18, something like half of them by age of 14' (Finkelhor 1986b). It seems that markedly similar patterns of offences are found in adult and adolescent offenders, 'such as similar victims, thought patterns and sexual acts' (Bonner 1990; NSPCC 1989).

Where sexual abuse is already being committed by adult/s in the family there is an increased danger of sexual abuse occurring among the children themselves. Furniss suggests that boys growing up in families where siblings have been abused, even if they have not been abused themselves, may know about it or have witnessed it, and out of identification with the abusing father are at risk of themselves becoming abusers. Older brothers may see themselves or be seen by younger siblings as being in an authority/ father position and thus able to do as they want (this of course can and does happen without father/child incest already being present), but the abuse of one sibling by another very close in age in an abusive family is more likely to mean that both children, in need of comfort, are giving each other the caring they crave in the only way they know, i.e. sexually. In such cases or where children close in age who are emotionally or otherwise deprived act sexually, the effect on the 'victim' will be very different from cases where there is a large age or power gap. In any event, Furniss along with many other workers in the field considers that any sexual abuser under 15 should be considered as having potentially been abused him/herself (Furniss 1991).

As with the studies of adult offenders referred to at the beginning of this chapter, it is now thought that juvenile offenders are a very diverse group with a continuum of severity of psychopathology. Kavoussi *et al.* (1988) found that 'many sex offenses committed by adolescents are part of a pattern of poor impulse control and antisocial behaviours'. They added that other psychiatric disorders were much less severe than was suggested by earlier studies as these had given misleading results due to their having been conducted on in-patients who already had a history of repeated nonsexual violent behaviour and had been arrested for violent sexual assaults.

At present many adolescent abusers are not charged with their offences, sometimes because the parents of the victim do not want them to be, and sometimes because of differing opinions about the nature of the offence (was it experimentation or genuine abuse?). But it is increasingly being felt that it is important they are charged with a criminal offence in order to ensure they undergo non-voluntary treatment, one of the main objects of which will be to teach them to learn responsibility towards and empathy with victims. Because of the long-term view this aspect of the legal impact on juvenile offenders is even more important than in the case of adult abusers, which we will explore in Chapter 9.

FEMALE ABUSERS

One of the newest aspects of child sexual abuse to come under the searching eye of research is the involvement of women. Until very recently studies suggested that between 2 and 10 per cent of all abusers were women, with around 5 per cent being the most typical number suggested (Davis and Leitenberg 1987). In a 1983 paper Finkelhor and Russell, already coming to believe that there was a severe under-estimation of the amount of abuse committed by females, suggested that probably 5 per cent of girls and 20 per cent of boys were abused by women (Finkelhor and Russell 1983). His current estimation is significantly higher. West (1987) writes that his researches on retrospective 'recollections of young males suggest that some 12 per cent may have had sexual experiences with older females when they were under 16, most of them being recalled as non-traumatic or pleasurable.' Furniss in his 1991 book writes that very few mothers are involved actively, and 'not many' know consciously and allow it to happen openly. He finds, however, that during therapy in cases of long-term abuse it emerges that many of the mothers have at some point been told by their children or known in other ways of the abuse, and it seems now that he too suspects a much higher rate of female abuse than has previously been acknowledged.

Thus, although most of the material presently available shows that comparatively few females are involved, and when they are it is mostly as 'accomplices' to a male abuser, it seems likely that the truth about female abuse may be very different. Just as in the late 1960s when Henry Kempe wrote about what was then called 'baby battering' and no one wanted to accept that mothers – gentle Madonna figures that they were – could possibly ever deliberately harm their own children, so today there is the same reluctance to believe that mothers could sexually abuse their own offspring. Of all people, women, particularly mothers, should be caring, protective. The fact is that women can and do commit any type of abuse that a man commits; the only thing a woman cannot do is to penetrate a child with a penis. The more anti-male feminists, outraged from the very beginning at these slurs on women, finally had no choice but to accept the evidence that women as well as men physically hurt, mutilate and torture children, and that it is a fact that not all children's suffering is caused by men. Now, many years on, it seems possible that they and the rest of us may have to accept that perhaps as much as 25 per cent of sexual abuse is directly committed by women.

As yet the evidence is thin on the ground, and proper analytical research has hardly begun, but those working in the field who have forced themselves to open their eyes and see what is in front of them have been shocked by their discoveries. Madge Bray of SACCS, Sex Abuse Child Consultancy Service, Shropshire, UK, says that – like most other people – until comparatively recently when a man was arrested for sexually abusing a child she did not necessarily work from the perspective that the mother may have played a part in the abuse. But gradually over the years, observing the play and the reactions of the children being treated by herself and her colleagues, and listening with an open mind to what they had to say, she began to realize that many of the mothers involved had not only ignored what their children were telling them about their abuse by fathers or father figures, but in a significant proportion of cases they were themselves directly involved.

Bray is sure there are some women who are genuinely unaware that abuse is taking place, and some who are what she calls 'pre-consciously aware' – they have a sense, for example, when they come into the house that the man has just come down from the bedroom, but they don't ask questions or put themselves into a position where they might discover something they do not want to know (we remember Barbara at this early stage, and how she managed to forget the smell of sperm). Higher up the scale, she suggests, is the mother who knows something is happening, but for whatever reason is unable or unwilling to do anything at all to stop it. Beyond her is the mother who passively facilitates the abuse, for example by doing the child's hair and making up her face when she comes in from school, perhaps even dressing her up in adult clothes, making a game of 'getting ready for Daddy coming home', and then disappearing into another room or leaving the house when he does arrive. Beyond that again is the mother who actively joins in the sexual abuse, perhaps by holding the child down to enable a man and/or others such as neighbours or friends to abuse the child, or even actually sexually assaulting the victim herself.

Possibly even more difficult to take in is that some mothers will abuse their own children on their own initiative for their own sexual gratification, without any support or instigation from others. Bray, who together with colleague Mary Walsh has established a treatment facility for a number of grossly abused children under 9 years whose current behavioural difficulties preclude adoption, finds a significant proportion of children as young as 5 years whose behaviour is so grossly eroticized that their interactions with adults, peers and even younger children are dominated by their sexual preoccupation. There are boys, for example, who have been sexually abused by their mothers from birth who have great difficulty in discriminating between sex and love. They literally do not know the difference. We have seen in the previous section the future danger this attitude represents, and the most careful and intense treatment is necessary for such victims if they are ever to enter into normal life. There are some, Bray regrets, who may never do so.

Madge Bray reckons that 25 to 30 per cent of abusers are women who are directly involved, i.e. women who actively facilitate the abuse of children or who actually themselves commit the abuse – she does not count in this total those who profess not to know what is happening or who absent themselves from the house at the time of the abuse. Interestingly, although when these findings were first discussed in training groups feminists would react angrily, she now finds that an awareness of the problem has developed so that the issue of the mothers as perpetrators is no longer challenged.

I have been writing mainly about mothers committing sexual abuse. This breaking of trust and betrayal, as many victims see it, has particularly destructive and long-lasting effects on children, as we will see in Chapter 9, but there are many female abusers other than mothers, such as sisters, aunts, grandmothers or women who are employed in a caring relationship to their victims, such as babysitters, nannies, teachers. Other women, such as neighbours or friends of the family, are sometimes involved, either abusing directly or as part of a multiply abusing group. One commentator on an extensive case in Kent, UK, that came to court recently wrote, 'It seemed that this was routine, almost casual abuse of children by father, mother, relatives, friends and neighbours in the same way that other families might entertain people for a drink or a game of cards' (*The Guardian* 22 December 1990).

As with male paedophiles who, as we saw earlier, may choose to work where children are to be found, as teachers, caretakers of schools or flats, social workers, doctors or scoutmasters, so we must assume that women with a sexual interest in children may choose similarly to become nannies, nurses, social workers, etc. Because of social expectations in their upbringing I think it probable that women are more likely than men to disguise their true motivations even from themselves, and that therefore it must be even more difficult to check female applicants for jobs involving vulnerable children than it is to check males. But at least with the growing awareness of female abuse it may now be hoped that in future more care will be taken in their selection processes by parents and by those in charge of organizations actively concerned with children.

CHILD SEXUAL ABUSE OUTSIDE THE FAMILY

We have already glanced at several types of abuse which fall into this category: some paedophilia, families sexually sharing each other's children as in the Kent case mentioned above, teachers and others in a caring position who take advantage of their opportunities to abuse their charges. This is a brief additional section indicating other types of sexual abuse such as satanic or ritual abuse, paedophilic rings and pornography. I cannot ignore these perversions as though they did not exist, although many would like to do so, for exist they do and in far greater numbers than most imagine. There is nothing new about any of them, but so keen are we to retain in our minds a delightful picture of innocent childhood – perhaps it is psychologically necessary for our peace of mind, even sanity – that with each revelation of a new horror a loud denial springs up that such things can ever take place. There is space here to make only a few brief points about the above list; for further study more specialized books should be consulted.

Satanic and ritual abuse are only recently beginning to be researched and we face the problem of a severe lack of positive evidence. Many people who have dealt directly with victims – such as psychiatrists, social workers, the NSPCC and some police – have no doubt of its occurrence, but others are equally certain it is myth and equate prosecutions with the Salem witch trials. Facts, however, are beginning to emerge. For instance, Ann Burgess, highly respected Professor of Psychiatric Mental Health Nursing, reports that a study has shown that children suffering ritualized sexual abuse had undergone significantly more physical abuse, a greater number of different sexual acts and more offenders per child, and also presented a higher total symptom score – especially internalized ones – than a control group of non-ritually sexually abused children (Burgess *et al.* 1990). My own feeling is that there are undoubtedly a number of abusers who, at the very least, use satanic ritual as a useful tool with which to subjugate young children. The mysticism, pseudo or otherwise, helps impose total secrecy and, combined with sexual, physical and emotional abuse, it helps to terrify children into compliance. So forward-reaching are the threats of what would happen if secrecy were to be broken that far into the future many victims cannot and will not tell the truth, even if they are capable in their terror of knowing what the truth is or was.

What Detective Inspector Dave Compton (then head of Southgate Child Protection Team, North London, and very concerned with all aspects of c.s.a.) told me during a long interview about a particular case he was working on suggests the manner in which many, perhaps most, of the less outrageous cases coming to the notice of the police may be dealt with:

We've got a case of that kind at the moment. No, I'm not charging it as satanic abuse, I jokingly say the parents are not satanic, I say they're doing their GCSE in demonology – they read Denis Wheatley novels, it's not a family of high intellect. It's a way of . . . not even terrorizing, but a sort of *mystique* for the children. We've prosecuted, we've charged the mother and father with indecent assaults and rape, charges like that, but not with satanic abuse. There were things like the pentangle in the floor and the children were made to stand in that, but it was all stuff from Denis Wheatley books, that was the type of book they had in the house. In this case I think it was just a way of pressurizing the children into it, they weren't practising satanists.

In the more serious Epping Forest case in England which collapsed in November 1991 (the judge commenting that the younger girl's evidence had been 'uncertain, inconsistent and improbable'), two young sisters were so accustomed to the satanic ritual abuse to which a group of adults, including their parents and godparents, had subjected them that they believed such behaviour was normal adult behaviour. It was alleged that the abuse had taken place ever since the youngest girl, now 10 years old, was a baby. The girls had allegedly been abused at their home and had been taken also to a stone gypsy monument in the Forest which was covered in black cloth and bore candles, stars and horns. While incense burned and adults dressed in black danced and chanted or sang, their godparents, called king and queen, conducted a ceremony during which the girls would be given a drugged drink from a chalice with two handles. Strange words were used and references made to Lucifer and Beelzebub. The eldest girl, called princess, then had to mount the stone while her godfather followed by other males would vaginally, orally or anally abuse her, sometimes more than one at a time. Then the younger girl would be similarly abused on the ground.

The case broke down partly because the distressed condition of the girls after being questioned in court for days on end resulted in unclear evidence, and partly because they had talked to each other about what had happened before eventually telling their grandmother with whom they had been living ever since their unmarried parents had separated. There has been much criticism of the way the children were forced to be present in court, although admittedly screened, without even being allowed the benefit of live video-links. Because the case has been dismissed I cannot discuss whether or not the abuse happened, but two doctors who thoroughly examined the girls decided their condition suggested 'long penetrative anal and vaginal abuse', and it is agreed by social workers and others who dealt with them that the children are deeply disturbed and frighteningly knowledgeable about sex. The girls had also talked of the ritual slaughter of babies, including the eating of the babies' flesh, both at the stone in Epping Forest and at their home, but no police evidence of this last has been found. It is possible, of course, that in their drugged confusion they would not have known if animal substitutes and life-size baby dolls were being used. Such accusations have been made in many other cases, but no evidence has yet been discovered proving the validity of this practice.

Many cases of satanic and/or ritualized abuse are surfacing world-wide. In America, Canada and in Holland similar cases have been reported. In Perth, Australia, a cult involving 300 boys involved in devil worship was recently revealed by the police, the alleged leader of the cult having joined scout groups and befriended single mothers in order to find victims (*Independent* 13 October 1990). At a conference in Melbourne a forensic pathologist spoke of aborted foetuses and unregistered children born to child victims being used as human sacrifices, and added that a main obstacle in successfully prosecuting these abusers, who were 'often well placed in society', was that the details were so bizarre people had difficulty believing them (*Sydney Morning Herald* 26 November 1990).

Because of the extreme secrecy enforced on victims in these cases and peer-group pressure, together with loyalty to the abuser, evidence which will stand up in court is very hard to come by, but the NSPCC has no doubt of the existence of satanic abuse. In 1990 seven of its sixty-six child protection teams were actually working with victims of ritualistic abuse, abuse which, as well as physical and sexual abuse, involved calling on supernatural powers, the use of masks and costumes, animal sacrifices, the drinking of blood and urine and smearing of faeces on the victims. The terror these victims show and their pathological disturbance have amazed and horrified social workers and foster parents and others working with them, accustomed as they are to 'ordinary' c.s.a. There have been many cases where abusers have been accused of satanic and/or ritual abuse which have not hit the headlines, but nevertheless in a disturbingly short time there have been a number of notorious cases such as that in Orkney, Scotland, where nine children were removed from four families after allegations of ritual sexual abuse involving a priest as part of a paedophilic ring. At the time of writing, many months after the case broke down, an official inquiry into the conduct of the case is still continuing.

Rochdale, Manchester, Nottingham – for those involved in any way with c.s.a. these are no longer merely names on a map, but places where accusations of satanic/ritual abuse were made and where huge uncertainties about what exactly happened remain and will probably continue to remain.

CHILD PORNOGRAPHY

Child pornography ranges from sexy postcards of children displayed in newsagents and stationers all over the country to hardcore sex videos available by mail order from Holland. The last show children being raped and buggered. Of course such videos are universally banned, but the law has never yet stopped the majority of paedophiles from getting their hands on the material they want, one way or another, in one form or another. International links allow sexual perverts from all over the world to buy and sell the bodies of children, alive or on film. Arguments continue as to whether or not watching pornography encourages violence against women and children, but people who deal with abusers have little doubt what use they make of it. In prison, prosecution documents detailing various assaults are passed around among the prisoners, although attempts are being made to ensure such material is no longer available. A strict control will be kept on videos made by professionals of children telling of their abuse, so that these do not become objects of entertainment for those so inclined.

As for the cards mentioned above, apparently known in the trade as 'cute', they mostly show sweet little things of either sex saying or implying they want sex. Athena, a stationery publisher, produces some greetings cards that are – to those who have dealt professionally with child abuse – explicit, though Athena deny it. The problem is that paedophiles will jump at any chance to convince themselves and others that what they are doing to children is educational, good for them and desired by them. The kind of picture showing babies, children or young adolescents in sexy adult-type clothing, slipping shoulder straps and all, looking out at the camera with suggestive sexual intent, can only encourage potential and actual abusers to kid themselves that sex is what these children really want, even if they say they don't. Sexually provocative clothes specifically for children are now available in popular high street stores – even the British Marks & Spencer have slinky underwear for girls from 5 upwards, and make-up and scents for little girls may be bought from such respectable emporia as the John Lewis group. The line between being pruriently prudish (*News of the World* style) and sensibly conscious of the need to retain the childishness of children is clear. Children have fun dressing up in *adult's* clothes for the childish fun of it; encouraging them to wear lace-trimmed bikini underpants and matching bra specially designed for a 5-year-old is another matter altogether.

Meanwhile, according to the British Campaign against Pornography and Censorship, pornography available on top shelves in newsagents is now carrying titles like *Shaving Special* and *Shaven Ravers* which show flat-chested young adult women in gingham dresses and ankle socks, pubic hair shaved off to make them look like children. The intention is clear; the researchers note 'close-up shots of genitals stretched, gaping or with inner labia pulled out. Woman on her knees like an animal . . .' etc. (*Independent* 17 April 1989). No comment.

PAEDOPHILIA AND CHILD SEXUAL ABUSE RINGS

Detective Inspector Compton, commenting on rings, said, 'Rings do exist. We know there are a number of paedophiles in this country, computer linked; they've got their own intelligence system, and yes, there have been rings broken into, but it's very difficult.' Linda Jones, now working for Howard House, a child abuse therapy centre in North London, told me, 'When I was working as a social worker in Enfield, we came very close to a ring that we knew was very active, then it disappeared. It works in cells like terrorist cells. No paedophile who's linked knows of more than one other, so they'll use the child then tell him to go to someone else – there are huge rings, with children passed from one to another to another.'

According to West, many paedophiles are brought up in 'the classic constellation of domineering, over-protective mother and weak or absent father . . . in a sexually repressive, puritanical atmosphere.' Paedophiles claim they are helping boys by befriending and advising them and by gradually introducing them to sexual experimentation, much as the early Greeks used to. Violence to boys by paedophiles is rare, most of the sex being masturbatory, anal intercourse being very minor, West writes. In most cases the boys are not expected to become homosexual. Homosexually orientated men who are interested only in young boys are considered true paedophiles, and are rarely interested in adult males. The boys, often isolated or from unloving families, are glad of the attention and gentleness they are likely to receive (West 1987).

This benign representation may be correct in some cases, but a more vicious picture is emerging. We may remember Barbara's abuser who was abusing boys before he was introduced to her through her brother. He was almost always gentle, kind and friendly, giving love and attention which the children did not receive in their own families. Nevertheless the damage he caused was tremendous. Every so often one reads of horrifying cases where young boy/s have been murdered in the course of what the press usually calls a homosexual orgy. A recent case where four men were jailed for killing a teenage boy is still being pursued, as one of the men was later found guilty of also having killed a 6-year-old boy. The police suspect that as many as eleven other boys could have been murdered by members of the same ring of which the arrested men were members. In most cases murder is probably not intended, but events progress and what may sometimes begin consensually with a boy prostituting himself to a group of men for money can get totally out of control and end in homicide.

Trevor Price, Gracewell Institute, talking of paedophiles they had been treating, said:

There are lots of ways to help these men begin to see the harm, the pain and the damage they are causing. Bill, 73; it's two and a half years since he left but he's still involved with us and there's been no re-conviction – without our treatment a man like that would not have survived two weeks without going back to prison. Without the right sort of treatment the prognosis for paedophiles who abuse boys is probably the poorest of all, especially because of arousement fantasy. If a homosexual paedophile feels able to move into a relationship with an adult man we encourage it, but some can't cope with that until you start moving on to their victim experience, because going with a man reminds them of their powerlessness when they themselves were abused.

Giarretto, at a conference in 1990, said, 'If they have a history as a marauder of children, stalking children since they were young teenagers, and they show no evidence of being able to develop true adult relations, then we classify them as paedophilic and we wouldn't take them on. I don't know of any progress with paedophiles. Sure as hell such a man will have been abused as a child.' On the other hand, clinical psychologist Alan Fugler, Director of the Sexual Offenders Treatment and Assessment Programme, South Australia, who thinks Giarretto has done marvellous work but feels his model is limited, told me in an interview, 'the evidence shows that the people who respond best to these programmes I have been telling you about are long-term paedophiles. So it seems much more sensible to employ therapists' time in treating a predatory paedophile who has had 400 to 500 victims – I've had some with over a thousand! – than Joe Smith down the road who's put his hand down his daughter's pants once that you know of, and save forty to fifty children from being abused. Now most programmes won't go along with that, for the wrong moral reason in my opinion, because people find predatory paedophiles very distasteful.'

Ray Wyre, commenting that prison without treatment is useless, estimated that 'fixated paedophiles' on average abused another 100 children after they had been released. Fifty-five per cent of child sexual abusers were re-convicted, and he estimated that almost all paedophiles offended again within three years of being freed. Probation Officer David Murray writes, 'Paedophiles [in prison] in particular tend to congregate in groups. They often swap addresses and units can be the breeding-ground for sex rings. Usually they don't think there is anything wrong with what they've done – they think it is society's attitudes which are wrong' (Prison Reform Trust 1990).

Unexpectedly I learned of a 'ring' that turned out to have been started by the boys themselves. Intermediate Treatment Officer Lewis Anderson, whose dealings with a group of 'rent boys' I wrote about in Chapter 4, explained:

The impression the Department had before I started working with them was that a lot of local kids appeared to be involved in a paedo-phile ring. With these two lads in particular – they'd been in all sorts of minor trouble, petty offences, kept running away from school, from home, sleeping rough, severe problems at home, that sort of thing – it struck me both the boys were desperate, it was like a dam just waiting to break. They weren't the hardened criminal type we occasionally get in, they didn't strike me as being the kind who'd work themselves right up the system. They'd got to the point where everything was meaning-less, but they didn't know how to change what was happening. The one I first talked to started crying and it was like a dam breaking, it all came out at once. He gave me names and addresses of men he was seeing and who were paying him for his sexual services. The other boy did the same. By that time their lives were totally in chaos, they'd really gone down the tubes pretty fast.

What became clear was that the adults involved mostly didn't know each other and certainly didn't introduce each other to young people. It seems to have started with a couple of older cousins of one of the boys – they had a relationship with a bloke they were working for on a fruit stall in the market, and he'd seen this little blonde 10-year-old hanging around and he'd asked them to bring him up to his flat. That was the kid's first experience, and after that it opened up for him with other blokes. He involved some other kids he knew – it was easy money – and it spread out from there. The organized bit was from the kids themselves. Each kid would have a small network of adults they visited when they wanted money – basically as prostitution – and they'd put other kids in touch with these adults and take friends along with them. Then some other kids who knew what they were involved in would introduce them to new adults, or they'd do a bit of cruising around the local shopping area and the market, waiting to be picked up, basically. They didn't have anywhere to go, anyway, if they'd bunked off school. They knew what to watch out for, could quickly identify an adult showing undue interest in them and were becoming quite sophisticated at naming their price – ten, twenty pounds, it varied depending how desperately the kid wanted the money.

I suspect there was a whole gamut of offences against these kids, I don't think there was anything they hadn't come across – initially all they would admit to was they'd been masturbated by these men although it was obvious there was more to it than that. I got the impression what these kids were saying was they don't enjoy it but it doesn't hurt, they get paid well for it. Quite often they'd go up to the man's room or flat as a group, stay in the front room or whatever, and go off one at a time to the bedroom with this bloke. Now all the lads in the room know what's going on in the bedroom but they don't talk about it. The flats were pretty squalid, I gathered, some of these blokes were pigs, basically, and with some of them – one in particular, they'd sussed he was a bit soft in the head – they'd smash up the place, throw dishes and mess him around and he'd put up with anything because he wanted the kids there in his flat.

What would happen was these men would have open house, they'd encourage the kids to come up and hang around, and ten to one there'd be other kids there. They'd be allowed to drink, smoke dope, whatever, and obviously that's an attraction for a lot of these kids, they'd scrounge a couple of fags, be given a couple of quid. The unspoken contract was that if they were in this bloke's flat they were open to abuse by him and were not going to refuse.

After I'd been working with some of them for a while they'd try to come off it. They'd tell me they didn't want to do it any more, they'd walk in off the streets for a cup of tea looking a bit upset, they'd say I just saw so-and-so outside, he keeps trying to get me to come round his house, he's following me about. Because the kids were withdrawing from the scene the adults were trying to get back in, you know – they'd say, 'Why haven't you been up for ages . . . ? come round I've just been paid', and all this sort of bit, 'Bring your mates, come round tomorrow . . .'.

I got the picture of a group of unhappy little boys who didn't see their way out of it. Everywhere they went they'd be approached by blokes left, right and centre, in the toilets, at the market. By that time part of it was a number of blokes going to the area specially to look for boys and part of it was a number of boys going there looking for men. Yes, it was both ways by then. Other kids had gradually drifted into it and in the end it didn't seem such an out of order thing to do. It comes to a situation where you want something and you haven't got the money and you know you can go up there and get 5 or 10 quid in 20 minutes, it's dead easy. It puts a lot of pressure on these kids, it's difficult for them to resist it.

I'd say when they told me, 'You've done the right thing, stay out of the market for the day, I'll give you a lift back to school' – it was just keeping going from one day to the next. . . . Making up your mind you want to get your life sorted out, getting your act together is one thing, but sticking with it. . . . And other young people would put pressure on them, 'Why haven't you been up to so-and-so's house recently?'

Chapter 7

Families

JANE'S STORY

Jane, 33, a qualified librarian, is an attractive, rather small woman, with the tender, particularly sweet appeal I have noticed in some victims. She came to our interview with her partner. Phil, a social worker and eleven years older, has a comfortable physical appearance; he is of middle height and well-built, bearded, very gentle and kind with a soft voice. I was very drawn to both of them. As Jane's story emerged I became more angered than I have ever been before at the sheer brutality and, as Phil calls it, the evil of the grandfather who not only sexually abuses his tiny grand-daughter but also verbally abuses her so that when she is grown-up she cuts abusive names on herself with knives. The reader may be surprised to read that we all laughed as she told of this last – but this often seems to happen at the most intense moments when people tell of such things – perhaps they would not be bearable otherwise: the mutual laughter could not have been more warm or loving.

I first came across Jane at the end of 1989 through her highly literate protest published in the *Independent*'s letter columns about reports of a book which had just been rejected for a book prize as it dealt with the 'repellent' subject of incest. 'As a victim', she wrote, 'I sincerely hope it was not the subject matter that was considered so "repellent", for that would reflect on me, dragging me back through all the feelings of degradation, shame and humiliation that I am fighting so hard to escape. . . . Child sexual abuse may not be a "nice" subject to think about, but it is a horrendous experience to live through and with, and any attempt, however explicit, whether sympathetic or not, to bring it out into the open is to be applauded.' It was a brave letter, signed with her own name (I have not used real names here, however), and when I met with her I thought her story well worth telling as it illustrates many aspects of abuse within families.

Currently Jane is working with an incest survivor group which she eventually found through the help of her local radio station in Bristol. 'I phoned them up in desperation,' she told me, 'I'd got to the stage where I was phoning anybody who might help, and they said they didn't know of any groups in Bristol but they'd find out for me, and a couple of days later they phoned back with the name of this one some miles away in Gloucester. The NSPCC officer I spoke to in Bristol offered me help if I wanted to start a group there, but I'm not quite ready to do that yet. At some time, perhaps – but I need to get a couple of counselling workshops under my belt to train me up a bit first. As well as the group I go together with Phil to joint therapy sessions, because it's affected him as well.'

Phil's comment on this is a sad reflection on how little, even today, is still known about c.s.a. among too many of the very people who ought to be most familiar with it: 'I didn't know anything at all about incest before I met Jane. I just knew the meaning of the word. Anything more I picked up along the way. I must have been dealing, in fact, with quite a lot of incest survivors in my work and not knowing it.'

Jane: I'd had what I suppose some people would call a breakdown about four years ago – I spent a week in a psychiatric hospital, but that was when my marriage was breaking up, and I just didn't meet anyone there who asked the right questions, they just didn't touch on it. I saw a psychiatric nurse on a one-to-one basis for about three months after I left the hospital – once a week for between one and two hours, and she never once brought up the possibility of sex abuse, not once. Nobody ever asks the question, was there any trouble with father or grandfather or uncles or brothers? Everyone just treats the symptoms – they'll treat you for depression or anxiety or any other problems you have, but nobody seems to have the courage to ask the questions that might put an end to it.

Phil: I think they're afraid to open up the can of worms – what the hell do you do with it then? It's much easier to treat people symptomatically. . . . It's my opinion the training we get is totally inadequate for today's society.

Jane: I felt that if someone asked the right questions I'd be more than willing to tell them, but nobody asked. Though to be honest, I was frightened somebody would ask. Yes, I remembered most things even before I started going to my group.

I . . . it was my grandfather, my father's father, who abused me. He'd had four sons, and he'd always wanted a daughter. I was the first grandchild, a girl, and his favourite. Last year, after it had come out openly in the family for the first time, my sister came over and admitted he'd tried it a couple of times on her when she was older. I'm not really sure how old I was when it started, but I know it was before I began school, so I was probably about 3 or 4, maybe younger. It started off more as a game than anything, and there were chocolates and sweets afterwards . . . and 'it's got to be our little secret'. At that stage it was just messing around, I think, because I remember when he actually started intercourse. Yes, full intercourse. I was 6, or 7 at the most – I remember because it was before I was in junior school. By the time I was 9 I could have made a fortune on the streets.

He was a big man, very heavy. No, he wasn't gentle with me, certainly not by the time I was 8 or 9, which was the time I began to remember things very clearly. By then it was just intercourse, and oral and anal sex as well – no more presents or anything like that, just the threat if I told people of what they'd do if they found out. But my parents weren't the sort of parents you could confide in, anyway – they sent out the wrong sort of messages, basically I felt we just came from different planets. If I'd tried to tell them I don't think they'd have believed me. Their attitude was children should be seen and not heard. This lasted until I was 18. It was easier for the others, both of whom lived with partners before they were married, whereas I wasn't even allowed to hold hands with boyfriends! . . . According to my mother I was born bad. When I left my husband and children she turned round and said to me, 'You've been trouble since the day you were born.'

I don't know if when it began I was even old enough to know it was wrong. But I knew after a while it was, because if it wasn't wrong then there wouldn't have been any need to keep it secret. I remember the chocolates at first, and 'it's our little secret' – maybe I did know it wasn't right, but I didn't know just how wrong it was.

Phil: And being the oldest child Jane didn't pick up . . . she was very ignorant at first.

Jane: He began threatening me after intercourse started. I knew that that was wrong because it hurt. He used threats like, 'there are places for *girls* like you'. Oh yes, he verbally abused me. Called me whore, slut, I was a disgrace to the family, things like that. Perhaps he got a kick out of it, I don't know, I think he enjoyed calling me names.

Phil: From what I've heard you say, there was a personality change when he was with you – while people were around he was a nice, kind, well-meaning sort of person, but once you were alone together he would change. I knew about all this before I met him but. . . .

Jane: He wasn't the ogre you were expecting.

Phil: No, he's not an ogre.

Jane: At home I wasn't very popular, I was 'too much trouble'. For the first couple of years my mother and I had lived with her parents because my father was away in the Navy six, nine months at a time. I spent as much time as possible with them, even when we moved away from them. My parents didn't have what you'd call a good relationship; there were rows, and they were very different from each other. He enjoyed the social life in the Navy, whereas my mother was very stay-at-home, wanted lots of children. She had three: I was the eldest, then was my brother, then my sister – eighteen months between us all. Both of them I dislike intensely. For a time I thought I must have been adopted because I didn't get on with any members of my family except my maternal grandparents. My brother was the one I objected to most of all, I apparently made it very obvious I didn't want a baby brother.

I saw my paternal grandparents fairly regularly – they were living in the Midlands but they had a car and they used to visit us often. Then when they acquired a new car they gave my father the old one and after that we took it in turns to visit, about twice a month. Mostly it was only for a day, it was rarely an overnight stay. Oh, they were very respectable people. My grandfather was a churchgoer, high C of E, belonged to the local golf club, played in a local brass band, was what you'd call middle class. My other grandparents were definitely working class, my mother is too.

Usually a visit to my grandparents in the Midlands meant, if the weather was good enough, a walk in the Malvern Hills or a drive out somewhere to admire the scenery, so the whole family went except if my grandfather said he didn't feel like going then he'd keep me at home to keep him company. My parents were very strict, we had to do what we were told and no questioning. Nobody ever questioned when my grandfather said, 'Oh, I'll just take Jane out for a walk', or 'We'll just go out for a drive.' If the family were going out nobody questioned it if he said, 'I'll keep

Jane here to keep me company.' Nobody ever asked *me*. It was just accepted. I was Grandad's little girl. Looking back, it seems as if it was almost a conspiracy. I'm sure nobody knew what was happening, at least I'm 99 per cent sure. I'm not sure about my grandmother, my paternal grandmother – she never liked me very much. So we'd go out for a walk and he'd find a place to do it, or in the car, or in his home when we were visiting them.

But when I was older I'd try to find excuses to be out when my grandparents were coming, or not going up to visit them – that was when it stopped. I say stopped, but even now I wouldn't want to be in the same room with him. When it all blew up last year I wouldn't see them any more. Till then if he had a chance he'd still try another quick grope. I'm 33 now, and he's in his eighties, but it doesn't make any difference. I wouldn't leave any of my sons with him, not for a minute.

But I survived. I found myself lots of escape routes. Not so much while it was going on, but by the time I was 13 I was hanging around with a skinhead gang – we'd moved to a rougher area in Bristol. We indulged in the usual shop-lifting, breaking windows, that sort of thing, but at the same time, during the day, I was a good little girl at school. Sexually there was nothing, I was very plain, very much the tomboy, so I was regarded more as one of the young lads. The girls of all ages used to stand there with make-up, fluttering their eyelids at the boys, the young men, but that wasn't me at all. I didn't have my first serious boyfriend until I was 16 – I didn't think men were much fun! – it was a long time before we slept together. I was fairly indifferent to sex, but I knew sooner or later I'd have to say yes or we'd split up. Looking back, I'm glad – I can't say I enjoyed it, but he was very gentle and it was . . . fun. It was quite a shock to find it could be fun.

Well, I got pregnant at 17, although I was on the pill and very careful, and he wanted to marry me but I didn't want that, I wasn't ready. I wanted to go on doing my A' levels at school, and I did – I got three – then I had the baby and I had her adopted. It had been very difficult at home, my parents finally noticed I was pregnant when I was about seven months. They were furious. My father called me all the names that my grandfather had used that I didn't understand at the time but I understood perfectly well by then. I must have been very naive not to have known them as a child, but we did have a very strict upbringing – my father was almost Victorian, even though he's not that old – he's still in his fifties. We couldn't go out to play on Sundays unless we went to Sunday School first, for instance. I'd meant before I had the baby to go on to university, but after that I decided to take a year out and work before I decided what I was going to do. But then I met my husband-to-be, and it seemed like a good idea at the time . . . .

That pregnancy with the boyfriend wasn't the first time. My grandad had got me pregnant when I was 13. And I didn't even know what sex was, because we had no sex education at school, and not at home, either. I didn't think it was what happened with my grandfather. My periods had started when I was 12, and when they stopped about a year later one of the older skinheads sussed out what was going on – sometimes we just talked, and I suppose he guessed. There was a woman on the estate and he'd probably used her a lot of times before – it was a very large, very rough council estate – and everybody knew she'd get rid of unwanted babies for a fiver, a tenner, a bottle of whisky, cigarettes – it didn't take much.

I was trying to avoid my grandfather by then so it wasn't so often I saw him. When he came I'd get out of the house if I could. Officially I was going round to friends' houses to do homework, but once I was there I'd borrow some of their clothes, because the clothes my parents bought me certainly weren't something I could go out with my friends in, and I'd just scribble off the homework when I got home.

It was in my early teens when I started using drugs, mostly acid or dope on and off for almost . . . twenty years. I started cutting myself, too. No, not attempted suicide, though I've done that a couple of times as well – just general mutilation.

Phil: It wasn't typical mutilation – I've seen a lot of people who mutilate – generally they go whoosh, whoosh, whoosh (he makes cutting gestures) – Jane cuts names, or used to. . . .

Jane: I cut the word (she laughs self-consciously) . . . 'whore' (we all laugh in recognition), 'unclean' (more laughter). . . . Funnily enough, it made me feel better. I don't cut words any more, but if things aren't going well I still cut occasionally – it's something I haven't got rid of entirely yet. Where I do it depends on whom I'm living with at the time. With my husband I could have cut them on my face and he wouldn't have noticed. I don't think my parents would have either, but Phil's much more switched on. He knows when I've been cutting so I wear a nightdress in bed!

Phil: At the time when it was most acute her arms would be covered with words, and various other things. Yes, you're right, it's grossly unfair. It's absolutely evil. It's also indicative of her grandfather's attitude towards her.

Jane: Anyway, I got married, though I don't think we ever did know each other very well. It sounds callous, but I married him to get out of my parents' house more than anything. I've got three boys now, but they live with their dad. When I was having that first breakdown I told you about – I hate that word – when my marriage was finishing, he didn't know about everything. I was drinking very, very heavily at that time – a bottle of vodka a day, a couple of large bottles of sherry, whatever I could get my hands on. And taking drugs and cutting myself, like I told you. And from as far back as I can remember I've had eating disorders, either bingeing then making myself sick, or starving for days on end. Even now I'm not sure what it is to eat normally – I'm working on it. But last year, when I was in the psychiatric hospital and access arrangements got messed up, I told him. Apparently he'd said to his new partner when they were visiting my grandparents what a nice man my grandfather was. We'd had some awkward times since we split up, he's been very sticky over access arrangements – I only see the boys once a fortnight, occasionally I have them to sleep overnight for special occasions – so I was quite surprised he accepted what I told him without questioning.

My father? No, my father never abused me. Certainly not. Was my mother abused? Ask Phil. He talked to her when I was in hospital.

Phil: Mum kept ringing when Jane was in hospital and wanting to know the whys and wherefores, and all Jane would say was that it was something that had happened ages ago. So I went over there to try to keep them off Jane's back. Jane's sister was there and she said, 'Yes, Grandad tried that on with me'; and Mum came out with her own brother had had incest with her, and also that her father, Jane's *maternal* grandfather that is, had tried it on with Jane's aunt, his daughter. Now how far that went we don't know.

Jane: Those were the grandparents I spent my first two years with and every school holiday with after that until I was nine, but nothing like that ever happened.

Phil:　She was very safe there, I think from what Jane says partly because there were only two people who really loved her in her childhood and that was her maternal grandparents.

Jane:　I don't know if Grandad ever touched my father. He refuses to talk about it, even acknowledge it. The strange thing is my father is one of four sons, all of whom have daughters, but none of them keep in touch with my paternal grandparents. One of them has actually disassociated himself and his family completely from his parents. Everyone wondered why, but now I think perhaps my grandfather had abused my uncle's daughter as well, and rather than have a big family row he chose to do it that way. My father doesn't want to know about me *at all*. My mother insists on calling my trouble 'depression', and when I actually used the word 'incest' with her a few weeks ago, she asked what it meant! So I told her. After we told them what had happened, there was silence from them, we didn't hear from them for weeks, and during that time I just didn't want to know them. Now I talk to her sometimes, but not about the incest, there isn't any point. We haven't communicated for thirty-three years and I don't think we can start now.

　　As for my grandfather, I don't feel I want to see him ever again. I haven't seen him since last summer. I don't even read the letters that my grandmother sends.

　　If it hadn't have been for Phil I don't know what would have happened. I'd told him in October 1988. We were sitting in a pub and he was telling me about a problem he'd been having with a client and it just slipped out. . . .

Phil:　That opened the door for you. . . .

Jane:　I was very tired. I'd had to run the library alone for three months which I enjoyed immensely, but quite often I was exhausted. It coincided with the start of my Open University course, which takes about fifteen hours a week, plus an evening tutorial. Plus I was having problems with my husband over access arrangements, and at home the kitchen was being rebuilt, the cat was having kittens, etc., etc. There was more and more pressure. It finally got to a stage where I couldn't take any more, and so I took to my bed and told the whole world to go away and leave me alone.

Phil:　Jane talks in her sleep, and once she'd opened up to me she used to talk about it a great deal and things came out in dribs and drabs, to an extent that I know more about some things than perhaps even Jane does. She not only talked rationally in her sleep, but she'd talk as if she was a child and it was happening. It was as if she was in a hypnotic state; at times I could converse with her. I was careful though not to talk to her about it when she was awake; things were falling apart for her, and my objective at the time was to keep her together. It's been very, very painful for her. (He holds her hand all through this and they obviously love each other deeply.) I think if she hadn't been able to open up by now she would have entered the mainstream of psychiatric treatment.

Because of the closeness of our interaction I was able to help her open the doors and support her all through it. And unlike the first time when she was ill, not only was she lucky with the nursing staff that second time, she was also lucky with her GP. He was a lovely chap.

Jane: . . . but he was also a trainee, he hadn't had time to get hardened. I hate GPs.

Phil: In the caring professions we've always treated people who cut, take drugs, alcohol abuse and so on, as plain straightforward personality disorders, and we've given benzodiazepams, Valium, that sort of thing. . . .

Jane: There are lots of people in the group who have been taking tranquillizers, sedatives for years.

What had happened was that I'd sat down to write my last-but-one assignment for the Open University course, and I wrote pages and pages and, when I looked at it, it was rubbish, it wasn't even coherent; pages of nonsense.

Phil: It had been brewing up for several months. At night she'd go into a semi-asleep, semi-awake state – this was when we used to find out about it all. I'd be awake to 2 or 3 o'clock, cuddling her, holding her, trying to reassure her, and she would be very, very agitated. . . .

Jane: When I woke up I'd know I'd had a bad night, and I was more tired than when I went to bed.

Phil: When Jane's agitated she has the habit of scratching herself with her nails, sometimes when it was bad her arms and chest would be covered in scratches which she never knew she'd done. Finally it escalated until she took to her bed, just lying there like a zombie.

Jane: In the end I managed to get myself to the doctor's and he was very sympathetic, supportive.

Phil: He got you in to see the consultant. I did all the talking – all you remember of him was his feet! She was becoming very, very withdrawn. And I pushed. Partly because I couldn't take it any longer – the lack of sleep and the strain was affecting me as well. I actually gave Jane an ultimatum to disclose at this point, and said either you do something about it or we split. If I hadn't I don't think she would have. (He turns to her.) Isn't that true? If you're honest?

Jane: If I'm honest, I think that's true.

J.R.:   Since we're being honest, *would* you have split?

Phil: (He shakes his head, smiles and hugs her.) Perhaps I'd have disappeared for a few days, but if Jane had turned round and packed her bags I'd have chased after her.

Jane: The future? I'm back at work after nearly seven months at home, and I've started the Open University course, and *nothing's* going to beat me this time.

Phil: That's right. And although the incest was so nasty, so vindictive, so sadistic, eventually the memories will fade, or they'll find their proper place in Jane's life so she can live with them at peace. I think it will take some considerable time, though. . . . People everywhere have got to learn to face up to this cancer that is in society and to try to deal with it.

(See also Chapter 8 on 'psychological splits'.)

MULTI-GENERATIONAL CHILD SEXUAL ABUSE AND MULTI-PROBLEM FAMILIES

I had originally intended, after writing about multi-generational c.s.a., to discuss – under its own heading – the subject of multi-problem families where sexual abuse was just one of the problems. But I now think there is little point in attempting to separate them out since when c.s.a. has occurred over generations it is highly unlikely there will not also be other problems in the family. Whether the reverse is true is beyond my brief.

Reviewing a national survey of American adult men and women, Finkelhor found that the most powerful risk factor for abuse appeared to be growing up in an unhappy family, the likelihood of abuse being more than twice as high. Even after controlling for the possibility that the families were unhappy *because* of the abuse, it was still found that an unhappy family life was a strong risk factor, both within the family and outside it. The reason for the last, they suggest, is that in such families the children are likely to have poor supervision, and additionally their needs for affection and caring make them particularly vulnerable (Finkelhor *et al*. 1990).

In Jane's story we saw many of the factors that are frequently present in families where sexual abuse has taken place over several or many generations. Jane's mother had had incestuous relations with her own brother (how very harmful that can be the reader will remember from Brenda's story in Chapter 3), and the *maternal* grandfather had at the very least attempted to abuse one of his daughters (Jane's aunt) although he never touched his granddaughter, Jane. Endless questions occur which in this particular family will probably never be explored. Why didn't that grandfather try to abuse Jane as well as his daughter? Did he realize she was already being abused and pitied her or loved her too much to add to the abuse? Or was it that picking up the depth of her distress he could not bring himself to acknowledge her pain to himself, since it would have intensified any guilt he might have felt about his behaviour to his own daughter? Did his wife know at the time it was happening that one of her daughters had suffered at least attempted abuse by her husband and the other daughter actual abuse by her son, and did she later realize what was being done to her granddaughter by the other grandfather? Imagine the hidden pain of the silence in this family, with all of this happening and no one ever saying a word to anyone. And how many generations back did it all go?

In tandem to that family is Jane's father's highly respectable family. Jane's sister was able, it seems, to prevent the paternal grandfather from abusing her (or perhaps to prevent it continuing, we don't know much about it) but Jane's father's four brothers – all of whom had daughters – went so far as to break contact with their father, one of them completely, which Jane thought probably meant he had at least attempted to abuse that granddaughter too. From the general pattern of behaviour in similar families it is likely he had also attempted the same with the other granddaughters. And since Jane's father, a strict uncommunicative man, the only son to keep in contact with his father, absolutely refused to discuss the matter with her it seems possible that he too had been abused, as perhaps had one or more of his brothers. Otherwise a more normal reaction of fury towards the man who had molested his daughter might have been expected. The result of these complicated interactions in both families was that Jane's mother refused to notice her daughter's distress, merely commented she'd been trouble since the day she was born, and now refers to Jane's breakdown as her 'depression', while Jane's father will not even acknowledge what had happened. The amount of distress locked up in these two families and others like them is one of the reasons professionals working with them suffer from burn-out if they cannot be given adequate support.

Tilman Furniss refers to the problems faced by abused mothers of abused children as the 'circle of avoidance'. To deal as a mother with the abuse of their child forces them to face their own abuse; similarly they are unwilling to deal with their own victimization because then they would have to face the suffering of their child. It is important, he stresses, to deal with these two roles separately in treatment – mother as abused child and mother as mother of abused child – or the double trauma to the mother may cause the case to be lost through the mother withdrawing, unable to face the resultant guilt and anxiety. When all of this is happening she may show increased open hostility to the child; in instances where the mother's background is unknown and such hostility occurs the possibility that she herself was abused should always be considered (Furniss 1991).

Another aspect that is part of the background of c.s.a. far more often than people care to accept is that children from abusive families subconsciously sense abusive backgrounds in others whom they only too frequently marry, although unaware in any conscious sense of the other's past, and once again an abusive pattern is likely to be set up. This happens with all types of abuse, the kind of abuse which was in the parent's background not necessarily leading to the same type of abuse to their children – I frequently saw this pattern of like searching out like in battered women, for example (Renvoize 1978). Class is irrelevant; I have met the smoothest, most charming men who in private terrorized their wives and/or families, and whose background turned out to be abusive, and the same can be true for sexual abusers. We only have to recall Peter's Russian grandfather, a charmer of royal blood, who, like Jane's church-going, golf-playing grandfather, treated his grandchild as a sexual plaything of little value.

Judith Trowell, child psychiatrist, in an interview about her work with the British Monroe Young Family Centre, said, 'If you just focus on sexual abuse you lose sight of the child and the family which may have been very chaotic or neglectful. So we're trying to think about the individuals as people and to look at the neglect and all the dysfunction that's been going on in the family alongside the child sexual abuse. I think it's the emotional abuse which is the most destructive component of sexual abuse anyway. We want to think about the whole child and the whole family and all the dimensions, not just about child sexual abuse. It may be that in a family which has been chaotic and neglectful this could turn out to be much more damaging than the sexual abuse itself.' Bannister (1988b), looking at assessment issues in cases of suspected c.s.a., writes, 'It is important to remember that child sexual abuse is one reason for a child's problematic behaviour. There are many others. In some cases child sexual abuse can be a small or transient part of long-standing emotional abuse or neglect.'

These views are confirmed by other research. In Goddard's hospital-based study for the Law Reform Commission of Victoria, it was found that in the families of abused children nearly 70 per cent of parents/substitutes reported a history of abuse and/or neglect, over a third reported domestic violence, 39.3 per cent drug or alcohol abuse, and nearly 39 per cent had psychiatric problems (Law Reform Commission of Victoria 1988). We saw earlier that a minority of child sex abusers had themselves been sexually abused, but perhaps twice as many had suffered from some form of physical abuse or other maltreatment as had suffered sexual abuse (Finkelhor 1988).

West, looking at suicide and severe problems as a result of incest, writes, 'The observation that the perpetrators in incest or the wives of incest offenders have often been victims of sexual abuse in their own childhood is too easily taken as a direct cause and effect. Unfavourable environmental factors and personal inadequacies are often perpetuated in families through social deprivation, selective mating and genetic transmission, resulting in a multiplicity of behavioural problems occuring in successive generations, of which child abuse, physical or sexual, is but one possibility' (West 1987).

Most workers in the field agree that sexually abusive fathers tend to be emotionally immature, and – although they may appear to others to be aggressive or independent heads of family, while their wives are weak and compliant – the mothers in fact are more likely to be emotionally stronger than their partners who are probably dependent on them for emotional caring. Very often the entire family will have created its own set of myths by which they all live. Each individual may have made up their own story which justifies the way they live – the offender to allow him/herself to continue the offences, the victim to help her/him to survive the abuse, the partner, usually the mother, to ignore or rationalize the other partner's abuse. These myths are their reality, and it is very difficult for involved professionals not to be drawn into going along with the myths. Furniss (1991) finds it useful to divide families into what he calls 'conflict-avoiding' (or organized) and 'conflict-regulating' (disorganized) patterns, though, he writes, 'They are the extremes of a continuum. . . . In the complexity of the organization of families no typology could ever do justice to the uniqueness of real families.'

Comparing these two basic types Furniss suggests that the first, strictly moralistic type, who appear to outsiders to function well as a family, nevertheless do not begin to live up to their own imagined self-image in actual reality. In the second type, the disorganized family, the conflict is in the open and there is little discrepancy between the way they see themselves and true reality. In the first the father is often successful and highly thought of in the community, but the disorganized or 'conflict-regulating' family may well already have social workers and other professionals deeply involved in their everyday life, people who have become, indeed, 'uncles' and 'aunts' like members of an extended family. These 'conflict-regulating' families often play these last off one against the other – large case conferences are held which may be attended by as many as ten to twenty professionals – effectively preventing any progress from taking place. Sometimes different professionals will find themselves siding with different members of the family, forming, as it were, opposing teams. This pattern reflects the way in which the family also controls its own members.

In the first type of family, although sexual relations between the spouses are likely to be strained, the marriage remains idealized, with problems denied; the incest is kept secret among family members, all of whom collude to avoid any acknowledgement of what, in that tight family atmosphere, would apparently be totally unthinkable. In the second, conflict and sometimes violent aggression are open, and the victim is surrendered to the abuser in order to keep the family together. This last may not be overtly acknowledged, but the collusion between all the family members helps to keep the father – emotionally and otherwise dependent on his wife and family – safely tethered. Both types, of course, do everything they can to keep the sexual abuse totally secret from the world. A major difference between the two is that in the first usually only one child is involved in a very special relationship. In the second several children of both sexes may be abused, consecutively or even simultaneously.

The reactions of the two types are very different when the sexual abuse becomes known to outsiders. In the first the family is in danger of immediate breakdown; the gap between the standards the family has apparently upheld and the reality is too huge to be coped with. Mothers often immediately seek a divorce and fathers may run away, become ill or even threaten suicide; at all costs the real issues have to be avoided. But after a while the wife often, perhaps secretly, returns to the husband, talk of divorce is dropped and family therapy at last becomes possible. Eventually such families may through treatment be able to face the truth about themselves, and sometimes (though the future welfare of the victim/s must remain of primary importance) the family can be reconstituted.

In the second type of family the crisis will not be so climactic when the sexual abuse is revealed. There has been less secrecy within the family all along and the gap between their self-image and reality is not so great. But when their professional helpers cease being controlled by them and become able to organize their network of help efficiently, the family, rather than lose control of their lives and be forced into change, may well break off therapy and as far as they are able will return to their old patterns. As a result of these reactions to discovery, the first type, the organized family, stands a much better chance of eventual rehabilitation than the second (Furniss 1991; Kaye and Winefield 1988).

One aspect of c.s.a. which is causing concern is that allegations of sexual abuse are sometimes being used in divorce and custody cases, more so in the USA (where a divorce lawyer described such claims as 'the nuclear weapon of marital custody battles') than in Britain, though the incidence is also growing in the UK and Australia. In custody cases in America the men's pressure groups which accuse mothers of inventing stories of abuse in order to win their cases are so strong that there has been a growing backlash against women. We saw earlier that children are particularly at risk of abuse during access visits; it is very important, therefore, that any hitherto unreported accusations of c.s.a. are taken seriously and not dismissed as tactical lies to assist a divorce and/or custody case.

One aspect of family life not always sufficently considered is that feelings do not necessarily change because one member is absent. Ray Wyre and his colleagues in Birmingham point out in their Gracewell Assessment and Treatment Programme, for example, that while the abuser is away, perhaps in prison, he may still be controlling and manipulating the victim through 'loving' letters. He may have isolated her/him from the rest of the family by their 'special relationship' and his apologies and protestations to the child – concerned solely with his own needs – of how worthless he feels and how he did what he did out of love may serve to make the lonely child sorry for him and insist in reply, 'It's all right, I'm OK.' In families where the victim has been isolated and scapegoated the other members may be glad to have the child removed, seeing her/him as a 'core of moral evil' (Furniss 1991). Remember how Jane's mother said to her, 'You've been trouble since the day you were born.'

Another type of abusive father will have been careful to build up an image of himself as a 'good family man', and the danger here is that he will often try to insist that the family be reunited before therapy is attempted. Then, if he succeeds in this demand, he will insist there are no longer any problems since he and his family know he will never ever again repeat the abuse. In this type of family the members, even the victim, will probably concur and back him up.

Trevor Price, Director of the Gracewell Institute which is very concerned about the offenders' families as part of its work with them, talked about the way offenders deliberately manipulate the different family members: 'One mother, for example, full of guilt that she had not known about the abuse but had kept herself occupied with her outside interests, was not aware that these had actually been encouraged by her husband. She had not remembered that years before he had said how they ought to have their own interests – "you go and join the badminton club and I'll do this, that and the other" – and so grooming the situation that years later when the abuse came out into the open she considered she had voluntarily done those things. Now she sees it was a grooming process to establish the environment in which the abuse could take place. Yes, we discovered this in treatment and we fed it back to those working with the family.' It is sometimes difficult to credit these complicated and far-reaching stories of deliberate grooming, but I have heard of too many now not to be convinced of the reality of these manipulative patterns.

As we saw at the beginning of this section, interactions between family members contain so much hidden material that it is often difficult for outsiders to make any sense of the confusion that results. Peter, whose full story we read in Chapter 3, tells us what happened when, quite recently, he was finally able to confront his father and mother about his grandfather's abuse.

My father's reaction was very interesting. I drove him over to my therapist's office. That afternoon my sister had not only told him what had happened to her and also what our cook's son and Raymond [Peter's earlier abusers] had tried to do to her, but that as a result of our grandfather's urination fetish she used to get sore because of his moustache on her vagina. So he knew the ball game. He came into the therapist's office, and sat down, and she told him I was going to explain to him what had happened to me. I did, I said I was very angry about it, about how badly he had handled my obvious problems when I was growing up, and that he should have done a much better job. I explained I was sexually abused, and then I said, 'I will tell you who did it: the first man was —— . . .'. My father's response was, 'Oh yes, an interesting lad and his father was a pillar of the church, nice person.'

I was a little bit taken aback by that, so I tried the next one. 'Raymond ...', I said. 'Oh yes, a nice lad, always very reliable, etc.' So then I went on to my grandfather. He wasn't quite as positive about him, but he said, 'Well, of course, your grandfather was such a nice social person, very charming, etc. etc.' and the gist of it was he just hasn't got a clue, I don't know what universe he is living in, I don't know whether it's the Milky Way.

My mother's comments when I told her was quote interesting un-quote, and 'Well, that's fine, now get on with your life.' In group I tell them how when I told my parents all I got out of my mother was – who cares; and out of my father – how wonderful all these molesters had been.

Peter's bitterness and obvious disbelief, still active after all these years, that his family could possibly be as uncaring and emotionally abusive as he had thought, is clear.

Finally a reminder that, while it is true c.s.a. occurs in every class, it is a fact worth repeating that poverty increases the likelihood of general abuse in a family. Don Edgar in his report to the Australian Parliament of Victoria in an *Inquiry into . . . Community Violence* (child abuse being included as an aspect of family violence) writes, 'The terrible fact is that family life is the source of our greatest warmth and support yet is, at the same time, the most violence-prone setting in society. It is in the family that children learn whether violence is a "normal" and acceptable way of handling differences or conflicts and it is in the family that most violence actually takes place. . . . Over 50 per cent of family law clients are victims of family violence because of the male assertion of power over other family members as "property" and their learned assumption of unequal rights to control.' Deeply concerned with the still existing profound effects of social differences, he finishes, 'The removal of poverty, unemployment, poor living conditions which exacerbate family stress lies at the base of any attempt to reduce community violence' (Edgar 1988a).

Chapter 8

The after-effects of child sexual abuse

Some victims of child sexual abuse will recover completely, some will seem to have put their experiences completely behind them, only to find themselves overwhelmed by painful memories later; for many others their lives will be dogged by a variety of ills, such as anxiety, depression, low self-esteem, self-destructive behaviour, a tendency to substance abuse and revictimization, and difficulties in allowing themselves to trust anyone. At the far end of this continuum of damage lies total psychiatric breakdown, or suicide. Browne and Finkelhor (1986) suggest, conservatively, that less than one-fifth of survivors show evidence of serious pathology.

In West's retrospective study (detailed earlier), firstly of general patients in two health clinics and secondly of students, 14 per cent of the health clinic patients who had been sexually abused in their childhood considered themselves to be still affected by their experiences, as did 22 per cent of the students who had been victimized as children. Significantly more abused women (23 out of 68 women) than women in the control group of non-abused women (3 out of 31) reported current negative attitudes to sex. In line with this finding, a much higher percentage of the abused women were without male partners – 28 per cent as against 7 per cent of the non-abused women. West did not find the promiscuity noticed by many other researchers, although he did find that the abused women tended to greater extremes than the non-abused women, either having become sexually active at a very early age or withdrawing from adult sex. 'Ultimately', he writes, 'it is the individual child's assessment of any sexual contact with an adult and her reaction to it (whether extreme or not) which determines whether or not the event will affect her adversely' (West 1985).

The damage may not be seen for years. Where victims have been deliberately 'groomed' to accept what was happening to them they may appear to be among the fortunate ones with no after-effects, but these are likely to be the very survivors in whom triggers in later life awake old skeletons which break through into consciousness, causing devastation. The extent of trauma to the child will depend on a variety of factors, such as the relationship of the abuser to the victim, whether or not the assault was a one-off by a stranger or multiple abuse by many, whether physical force was used, how frequently the abuse happened, what type of abuse was committed, whether there was treatment – successful or otherwise, etc. The more serious forms of abuse not surprisingly tend to cause the more serious long-term disturbances, as does a large difference in age – thirty or more years – between abuser and victim.

Victims who came to respond sexually to their abusers often feel immensely guilty, believing that since they had positive reactions to the sex and sometimes even enjoyed it they must have been responsible for their abuse. Recollection of the relief of tension that accompanies sexual climax increases their guilt, many victims feeling profound self-hatred for having physically enjoyed what mentally they had hated. They may blame their bodies for betraying them and mutilate themselves as a result. Remember how Jane cut 'whore' into herself, knowing at one level she was innocent of blame but being unable at another level not to brand herself with the insults her grandfather had enjoyed throwing at her. In his workshop at the NSPCC 1990 Conference Hank Giarretto, referring to such self-mutilation said, 'It really tears your heart out. "I had to let the bad blood out," they say. One boy, I'll never forget this, said, "Hank, you know, I'm a total piece of shit. Is there any way I can get rid of this? I can't even approach anybody, they know I'm utterly worthless; not only that, I stink the place up." '

The coping mechanisms which helped children survive their molestations at the time of their happening can cause severe problems if they continue to be used inappropriately in later life. One such is dissociation, when the victim dissociates her/his mind from the body that was being abused, often leading to the numbing of the assaulted part of the body and a blocking or forgetting of the assault. Some victims (we will see later, pp. 151, this happened in Peter's case) imagine themselves physically behind or at some distance away from their actual bodies which are undergoing the abuse. Or they go into an altered state of consciousness, perhaps feigning sleep or pretending that the part of their body which is being violated does not exist. Because so much of their life is blocked out of their mind they probably feel incomplete, lacking confidence and self-esteem. New relationships can be ruined by the numbness of feeling which survivors often report, both of physical and emotional feelings: unable to trust anyone fully they are alarmed by unexpected touches, cannot develop faith in another's genuine concern and remain isolated from people as a whole. Because they learned to repress their feelings in the past, they may now find it very difficult to feel real joy or pleasure, or even deep sadness. Negative and positive feelings are both repressed.

As children victims are likely to learn to be manipulative and devious in order to survive. They may also develop an unbalanced sense of their worth. On the one hand they may be told how much prettier, sexier, more special they are than their siblings or their mother and may be given presents other members of the family are not given, while on the other hand they are already despising themselves for what is happening to them. This picture can then change as the abuser moves from his early corrupting bribery and flattery to the verbal abuse and denigration we have seen in cases like Jane's. Many abusers get a sexual kick out of 'talking dirty', especially if this includes demolishing the self-respect of the person they are abusing. These patterns are internalized by the victim and in adult life the manipulation and/or deviousness adult survivors learned as children, along with a despairing sense of worthlessness, may often be observed.

The need to find someone close whom they can trust sometimes leads to a hasty marriage, often undertaken mainly in order to escape from the home, only too frequently with unhappy results. A victim's capacity for developing long-lasting relationships will in any case most likely have been impaired by the experience of their betrayal by a family member or a known person. Even in potentially good relationships the sudden touch or a particular tone of voice recalling the abuser can bring to the fore a long-forgotten or deliberately put-aside abusive moment or relationship. One victim, who had not at that time told her husband that her father had abused her, explained how sometimes – when she was working in the kitchen, for example – her husband would come up behind her and put his hands on her breasts, which was exactly what her father used to do. Her emotion then was indescribable, she said, a mixture of fear, freezing, pain and anger, and at the same time intense anguish that she could not stop herself from reacting in this way to the perfectly normal action of a man she loved.

Two of the victims – one man, one woman – about whom I wrote earlier, illustrate the difficulties of having successful and happy sex in such marriages. The reader might remember how, in Chapter 3, Brenda said:

It's like whenever I'm with my husband, whatever it is triggers off something, you know, like the breathing in my face.... There is a problem, and I can't get rid of it. I get them both confused, what's actually going on. The treatment's not solved it as yet. ... I still can't talk to my husband. He thinks it'll all go away, he says just relax and forget about it. At times, after we've had intercourse or something, I'll come down and I'll cry. I've never ever climaxed. I can't let go.... I begin to get feelings, but when that happens I have to push him away, and I cry, I sob.... That crying comes from the bottom of my boots, it is totally out of control. Instead of getting a climax I shut it off and cry. It devastates me, it makes me feel suicidal. I can't function as a woman.'

Peter wrote to me about his marriage:

My relationships after school have all been with ladies, and that is a blessing! However, they have all followed a pattern, up to and including my marriage. They all began with courting, and few included sex. When I got married, the same was true. However, after the initial romance matured into affection and respect and love, as opposed to *being in love*, then sex became something a man does to a woman, and not a joint venture. Thus the sex side of the marriage went downhill, about ten years ago. What has sustained the marriage is affection, love and things we do in common. While I am aware that sex is supposed to be a mutual desire, my wires are still crossed in that area. I am aware this is not normal, however, therapy both individual and group have not modified my mind in that area. The choice not to have children was originally economic, then I did and she didn't, she did and I didn't, and now my dislike of sex with my partner dictates no children.

Certain illnesses and physical reactions affect some victims in later life. Difficulties with vaginal entry and reaching orgasm will, not unexpectedly, affect many, as do problems, for example, with their skin, menstruation, vaginal infections and migraine. Forced oral sex often causes pains and irritations in throat, jaw and neck. I remember years ago, early on in my researches, meeting a very fat lady who helped organize regular drugs abuse meetings which had begun originally as a lesbian group. Gradually, as the members came to know each other better, they all discovered they had been sexually abused as children. The lady I was interviewing had no objection to her weight – she accepted it was a partly conscious protest against her mother (who had not protected her from her orally abusing father) to whom elegance of body and dress was all-important – but I noticed she was continuously swallowing and giving little coughs as though clearing her throat. The actions were so automatic to her that mostly she was not conscious of them, although if she had thought about it she would have been aware of their origin.

Eating problems are another symptom that many victims suffer from, anorexia nervosa and bulimia nervosa frequently following c.s.a. These last may be present from early childhood but are likely to become more noticeable in adolescence when sometimes the young girl does not start menstruating at the expected time. These can be ways in which the girl punishes herself because of her perceived guilt and/or attempts to make herself so unattractive she will be safe from sexual abuse. The frequent purging of bulimics is not only a way of cleansing the body but it also allows the victim to feel a sense of power over how their body is treated. Anorexia and bulimia have been written about so frequently that physicians ought by now to be aware of the possibility of c.s.a. being a cause, but many doctors still will not let themselves face the possibility that the too-skinny, non-menstruating 17-year-old in front of them, whose family might have been well known and respected by her/him for many years, may not in fact be slimming out of vanity or a desire to become a model.

Withdrawal and depression are very common ailments for victims, sometimes leading to complete breakdown. In a list by Giarretto of externalized reactions to child abuse (more common in boys than girls, who, he says elsewhere, are more likely to internalize), he includes truancy, mutilation of pets, running away, stealing, vandalism, fire setting, sexual aggression, criminal behaviour, child abuse and homicide. He considers that the self-loathing and guilt victims feel for allowing the abuse to happen is present in varying degrees in all victims of c.s.a., even when adult, increasing over time and leading in extreme cases to 'homicide–suicide inclinations' (Giarretto 1989). Bannister adds to this list the possible presence of psychotic symptoms, delusional and fixed sexualized thinking patterns, and, in the aggressive person, exploitative, antisocial and delinquent behaviour (Bannister 1989).

Some victims, in spite of devoted treatment and care, never do recover from their early trauma. In my discussion with Dr Jane Wynne and Helge Hanks in Leeds they talked about a girl they had treated several years previously: Wynne: 'We had this 13-year-old girl who was being sexually abused and beaten by her single-parent father, who otherwise had looked after her and her younger sister well. The stress was too great, so she flipped, had a major breakdown – her psychiatrist said she had already been predisposed to major psychiatric illnesses. She still hasn't recovered. She's 17 now, and no, she won't recover. Her sister's done extremely well, but no therapy will make the other one all right.' Hanks: 'Once they've gone over the edge like that they're not going to make it, they're not going to recover. If it starts that early it might be that the stress gets so much they hallucinate, get themselves into endless hypnotic states in order to avoid the abuse when it's happening and they can become mentally ill. Something else might happen to them later, and it becomes a way of life – as the years go by these people do not recover, however much they're treated they can't recover. They might go into silence. If they stay out of hospital they might well end up having children, and then it starts all over again.'

We have seen earlier that probably around one-third of victims will themselves sexually abuse, many beginning in very early childhood. They will have been highly eroticized by their premature sexualization which may express itself in excessive masturbation. Linda Jones, talking of some of the problems of her work in Howard House, the residential children's home in London, said, 'The staff here are very keen and in spite of all the difficulties they cope very well. They get sworn at, beaten, kicked, the kids here use words at 6 years old I've never come across at 33 – it's very difficult dealing with this sexualized behaviour. We have to watch what's happening very closely; for instance, we've just found we can't allow two of the little boys here to play together unsupervised any more, not even for a few minutes, because the other day the smallest one was actually talking about "we've been playing fuck-up games".'

Dr Juliet Harper, Senior Lecturer in Psychology at Macquarie University, Sydney, told me about a child she had spent a great deal of time with:

Jenny was very badly abused by her grandfather who had also abused her mother. She was very highly eroticized, especially anally, which was how she masturbated too. If you tried to give her affection or if you picked her up she immediately started masturbating; at night she'd masturbate herself to sleep. A lot of these children act out afterwards: it is a replaying of the trauma over and over. In an unconscious way they're trying to master it, come to terms with it, but of course it doesn't appear like that to other people. At the child-care centre where we put Jenny, to the young boys' amazement she was involving them in sex-play, offering oral sex all around at 4 years old. I think in adolescence there are going to be tremendous difficulties. With the increase in the sexual drive I would think she's likely to do a lot of sexual acting out.

Some of the victims, called sexy bitches, whores, wimps or bum-boys by their abusers, and already subjected to corruption through the gifts or money pressed on them, may as they grow older begin to live out these internalized images, becoming promiscuous and/or selling themselves as prostitutes. Boys, perhaps doubting their sexual identity as a result of their abuse and at 14 or more growing 'a bit long in the tooth' for paedophiles, can find plenty of homosexual customers in the streets of big towns if they run away, as large numbers do. We have seen earlier how pimps look out for such runaways of both sexes at the main stations in big cities, and once the pattern of prostitution has been resorted to it is very difficult to break. Linda Jones again: 'They think, well, what the hell, I might as well make money at it, and they turn it to their own advantage. That's what is happening with a lot of adolescents, intensively in London, they're becoming rent boys and young prostitutes: the only way to survive what has happened to them is to turn to drink or drugs, and one way to afford to do that is to sell your body. So younger and younger people are learning how to get money that way as a means of survival.' But, as Giarretto has said, 'There is no joy in this sex, they are servicing people as they have been taught to do, and there's no joy.'

Even while the molestation is still going on they may have begun to smoke heavily, or sniff solvents, and later they often turn to tranquillizers, prescription drugs, alcohol and various illegal drugs to help relieve their stress and anxiety. The use of such substances can begin or increase the fragmentation or splitting of the personality which may already be present as a result of the abuse, although it is only comparatively recently that child sexual and physical abuse have been widely recognized as precipitants of the dissociative disorder of multiple personality. The abuse in such cases would usually have been severe, lasted a long time and have been committed by family members. At present the symptom of multiple personality is rarely recognized, partly because of the reticence of sufferers who are frightened of being thought crazy, and partly because clinicians believe it is very rare and don't look for it (Coons 1986). Jane was one such who drank and took drugs excessively, we remember. Phil, her partner, was embarrassed to discuss the subject in front of her because, as a social worker, he was aware that in Britain the subject of multiple personality is often scoffed at, and also because he did not want to disturb Jane, but he told me that he was convinced that she had thirty or more different personalities which had been created at different times to deal with her grandfather's abuse. Phil had heard her speak in different voices during her waking sleep and thought much of the resulting disorientation was behind her earlier self-abuse with drugs and alcohol and her self-mutilation.

Peter, whose story we read in Chapter 3, wrote to me:

high drop-out rate: here our problem is the opposite, no one wants to go.'

When I was talking to Ray Wyre he explained to me that they make it clear to their clients that they care about them but they do not trust them.

If a man told me he hadn't done it and I believed him he'd think I was a right wally, and where would he go to get help then, because in a sense I would have taken all hope away. As I said before, we talk about control here, not cure: no one's cured of sexuality. Another important point is that we are the only agency I know who will take a man into assessment who is still denying – but no one has stayed denying after coming here.

The men are much tougher on each other than we are – in groups they won't let anyone get away with anything – but we control what happens carefully, we don't want the sort of confrontation that makes the person who's being attacked withdraw. But in general they are very supportive to each other. They are all very vulnerable and they know it. After all, even the most violent man is only violent for a very small part of his life.

The system seems to be working: not one man who's been through here has been interviewed by a police officer for any offence committed, and that includes the ones who've left. Considering we get the more difficult ones, that's pretty remarkable.

Trevor Price added, 'You cannot run a programme like this without the three elements: of high therapeutic skill, the appropriate programme, and having it operate in the right therapeutic environment. It's not possible to do it properly under the usual circumstances that operate in prison – regrettably most of the programmes you hear about are merely cosmetic.'

In June 1991 the British Home Office proposed that therapy should be offered to imprisoned offenders who were jailed for four years or longer. Although in theory the scheme will be offered to sixty jails, in practice only about twenty jails will be involved, with pilot schemes running at Littlehey and Grendon Underwood prisons where therapeutic schemes have been in progress for some time already. Treatment will mostly be run by prison officers, with a certain amount of input from psychologists and other specialists. It does not seem, however, that any new, specialized training is envisaged for prison officers, and, as I understand it, any follow-up treatment will be put into the hands of already over-worked probation officers.

Tony Heal, to whom I spoke before this scheme was announced, at that time was himself a senior probation officer at Wandsworth prison, London. Out of a prison population there of 1550, about 450 were sex offenders, the largest concentration anywhere. Although Heal would very much have liked to see more done in the way of treatment, he explained that a major problem at Wandsworth was that 'the prisoners here are not long-stay, i.e. they're here for under four years, so conditions are fairly poor, with two to a cell, no proper sanitation, and poor facilities for education and work. Prisoners as a whole should not be staying here for more than a few months at most, but at present Rule 43 prisoners serving up to four years spend their entire sentence here. We never see many of those 450, except perhaps for a brief interview for some welfare reason or other, until they come round for parole. I personally would like to organize some proper group work for them, but until recently we were about one officer to 150 prisoners, although now it's about one to eighty; so you can see there is very little time left for any specialized treatment after the immense amount of routine work is done, even if the facilities were here, which they are not.'

In September 1991 the Home Secretary launched the White Paper which was intended to transform the prison service as a whole, but although its ideas were revolutionary it was immediately severely criticized because it was not backed with extra money or with detailed plans for implementing those proposals. Complaints of lack of government finance are as many as the incessant requests for more cash, but of all the causes to be treated sympathetically by the Government surely the need for child sexual offenders to receive the kind of treatment that on discharge from jail can be slotted into a Gracewell-type system must be amongst the most important. If more money enabling better resources for such a purpose is not given, countless as yet unharmed young children will in future join the ranks of the abused.

Much is already known about what treatment is necessary for offenders who stand a chance of rehabilitation. Putting together a list of programmes from the US, Canada, Australia and Britain, the following would be included in most of them: denial of the abuse to be overcome and responsibility accepted; an empathy with and understanding of the victim's distress and pain developed; facts of sexuality and sex roles taught, together with a changing of wrongful beliefs such as the paedophilic insistence on the value of 'teaching sex' to young children and wrong cognition about rape; work on the individual abuser's cycle of abuse so that he fully understands it; work on behavioural techniques to eliminate abusive arousal patterns; a coming to terms by the client with his own abuse, of whatever kind, as a child; developing an understanding of the use and abuse of power; developing social skills and close relationships with others, be they hetero- or homosexual; assertiveness training; anger control; and, where appropriate, family work. For young child/adolescent offenders any or all of the above would be appropriate, depending on their very varied characters, intelligence, upbringing, etc., but a particular emphasis should always be put on working with their families wherever this is possible.

It has frequently been mentioned before how essential it is that young offenders are found and treated while they are still malleable. By the time they are 10 years old or more the abusive pattern may already be so entrenched it will be extremely difficult, if not impossible, to eradicate it entirely. Dr Eileen Vizard, British Consultant Child and Adolescent Psychiatrist, who has considerable experience of offenders of all ages, commented to me,

> What's very chilling is if you talk to these young boys about what's on their minds and why they actually did hold a younger child down and do something that seems very much like rape, then you hear the same kind of stories from them as you do from older adolescents and adult men because they've been very indoctrinated with patterns of coercing and bullying and sexualizing. I remember one adolescent boy saying that one of the good things about getting hold of young children was that it made you feel clever, made you feel good when they did what you told them exactly down to the last detail, it made you feel strong, grown-up. Yes, that's right, it's power, that's very central to it, particularly so for the young children because they feel so lacking in power when they themselves have been abused.

The treatment cannot be rushed. Psychologist Alan Fugler, SOTAP, South Australia, writing in his paper 'Community treatment of sex offenders then, now, and in the future?' about the programme for adolescents that he was setting up, reported, 'It is expected the initial, intensive treatment process will take eight months, with a lengthy follow up period over a number of years.' And although the Gracewell Clinic tries to insist on treatment lasting a minimum of at least one year, they would much prefer to treat their clients for a further year whenever possible. But, as always, lack of finance is the element which restricts most treatment facilities, so that workers are always aware of how much more could be done if only there were more money and more time.

The National Children's Home recently carried out a survey for the British Department of Health of the treatment facilities available for both abused children and young sexual abusers of children. Looking only at the latter we see that, although half of the non-hospital-based clinic work and 92 per cent of special groups for young sexual abusers of children have been established since 1985, there have been very few new residential facilities. In general, counselling has proved to be the most popular form of treatment (83 per cent), followed by behaviour modification (63 per cent), psychotherapy (58 per cent), skills training (54 per cent) and play therapy (24 per cent), some facilities offering more than one method. In the special projects (widely funded in part by the Home Office), however, behaviour modification is the most common method used. Most of the facilities have clearly been influenced by the cognitive/behavioural methods developed in North America by Finkelhor, Becker and Abel, and by the work of Ray Wyre in England which we have just been examining.

The survey estimated that the majority of the children seen by the various facilities were between 15 and 17, but just under a quarter had reported occasionally seeing boys under 9; virtually no female abusers were seen. Finally, the survey reported that, in spite of the increase in facilities over the last twenty years, 'perhaps the most striking feature .. . is the number of areas in England and Wales with no facilities at all which fall within the survey's definition of treatment' and, of those which do, 'there is a lack of facilities which offer a specialist function. . . . Where treatment work is offered, it takes place within settings which devote much more of their time to other types of work' (NCH 1990).

One form of treatment we have not yet looked at is 'chemical castration'. Actual castration was used for a time in Europe to allow the release from prison of men otherwise thought too dangerous, but although research showed recidivism to be extremely low and some men asked for castration as an alternative to lengthy imprisonment, unwanted side-effects and ethical and moral arguments have meant that it has been replaced by 'chemical castration' with drugs such as anti-androgen and cyproterone acetate, a form of treatment which, at least initially, is not irreversible. These hormone suppressants, although no longer available in British prisons, are sometimes thought useful as a temporary way of bringing sexual impulses under control while other treatments such as psychotherapy are begun (West 1987).

Ray Wyre argues that the use of these drugs appears to turn abuse into a medical problem, which it is not, although he agrees such drugs can be helpful in the early stages of treatment. 'But it's not arousal that's primarily the problem, it's the way the abusers think and fantasize that has to be dealt with. I've had men here masturbating ten times a day to illegal fantasies of children, and we have succeeded in reducing that through behavioural work, without the use of drugs.' Vizard similarly commented to me, 'In our experience it doesn't actually stop the sexual thoughts; they're not there because of physiological arousal but because of power issues, emotional confusion and all other sorts of reasons, so if you damp down the hormones in the hope of getting rid of the sexual behaviour it doesn't succeed. We actually had a man in one of our groups who was being treated by one of the main exponents of so-called chemical castration – he was on anti-androgen – and he came to us because he was complaining of recurrent sexual thoughts and fantasies towards children; the concern was that he was going to repeat the acts. These offenders have been having these thoughts for years, sometimes since early childhood, and the pictures and ideas about children are very pervasive – it's not just sexual arousal they're hooked into.'

Treatment of child sexual abusers is a fast-growing field which has attracted many first-rate workers, all of whom are very aware there is no easy answer to the many problems involved. But the main problem is that we do not know who the abusers are. Comparatively few are discovered, even fewer are convicted, and fewer still are given the kind of treatment which may eventually result in their rehabilitation.

Everything possible must be done to prevent those offenders we know about from re-offending. But it is the child and adolescent offenders who need to be the focus of future work if there is to be even a slight chance that this book with its seemingly endless lists of horrific facts is ever to become merely a sad memorial to an age that cared more for material prosperity than for the welfare of its children.

Time, thought, resources and, above all, care is what must be given in quantity – care for those who have been offended against, care for offenders themselves whose lives are hardly enviable and, above all, care for the children of the future whose innocence has not yet been destroyed.

Bibliography

Abel, G.G., Becker, J.V., Cunningham-Rathner, J., Rouleau, J. and Murphy, (1987) 'Self-reported sex crimes of non-incarcerated paraphiliacs', *Journal of Interpersonal Violence*, 2 (1).

Bannister, A. (1985a) *The Non-Offending Parent in Child Sexual Abuse – Thoughts from U.S.A.*, Manchester: NSPCC.

—— (1985b) 'Monster-man has gone', *Community Care* 28 November.

—— (1986) 'The key is co-operation', *Community Care*, 16 October.

—— (1988a) 'Conclusions from Cleveland', *Social Work Today*, 15 September: 17.

—— (1988b) 'The "child-centred philosophy" in dealing with child sexual abuse', paper at NSPCC national conference, *Treatment Approaches to Child Sexual Abuse*, Manchester: NSPCC & Greater Manchester Authorities Child Sexual Abuse Unit.

—— (1989) 'The effects of child sexual abuse on body and image', paper for Drama-therapy Conference 1989, *Journal of British Assocation for Dramatherapists*, 12 (1).

Bannister, A. and Print, B. (1988) *A Model for Assessment Interviews in Suspected Cases of Child Sexual Abuse*, London: NSPCC.

Becker, J.V., Cunningham-Rathner, J. and Kaplan, M. (1985) *Adolescent Sexual Offenders, Demographics, Criminal and Sexual Histories and Recommendations for Reducing Future Offenses*, New York: New York State Psychiatric Institute.

Becker, J.V., Rathner, J. and Kaplan, M.S. (1987) 'Adolescent sexual offenders: demographics, criminal and sexual histories, and recommendations for reducing future offenses', *Journal of Interpersonal Violence*, 1: 431–45.

Bonner, B.L. (1990) 'Adolescent sex offenders: community-based treatment models', paper presented at the VIIIth International Congress on Child Abuse and Neglect, Hamburg, September.

Brown, H. and Craft, A. (eds) (1989) *Thinking the Unthinkable – Papers on Sexual Abuse and People with Learning Difficulties*, London: FPA Education Unit.

Browne, A. and Finkelhor, D. (1986) 'Impact of child sexual abuse: a review of the research', *Pyschological Bulletin*, 99: 66–77.

Burgess, A.W., Hartman, C.R., Wolbert, W.A. and Grant, C.A. (1987) 'Child molestation: assessing impact in multiple victims (part 1)', *Archives of Psychiatric Nursing*, 1 (1): 33–9.

Burgess, A.W., Hartman, C.R. and Kelley, S.J. (1990) 'Assessing child abuse: the TRIADS checklist', *Journal of Psychosocial Nursing*, 28 (4): 8.

Campbell, B. (1988) *Unofficial Secrets*, London: Virago.

Cavanagh, J.T. (1988) 'Child perpetrators – children who molest other children: preliminary findings', *Child Abuse and Neglect*, 12: 219–29.

Chamberlain, A., Rauh, J., Passer, A., McGrath, M. and Burket, R. (1984) 'Issues in fertility control for mentally retarded female adolescents: I. sexual activity, sexual abuse, and contraception', *Pediatrics* 73 (4): 445–50.

Coons, P.M. (1986) 'Child abuse and multiple personality disorder: review of the literature and suggestions for treatment', *Child Abuse and Neglect*, 10: 455–62.

Craft, A. and Hitching, M. (1989) 'Keeping safe: sex education and assertiveness skills', in H. Brown and A. Craft (eds) *Thinking the Unthinkable – Papers on Sexual Abuse and People with Learning Difficulties*, London: FPA Education Unit.

Davie, R. and Smith, P. (1988) *Child Sexual Abuse: The Way Forward after Cleveland*, London: National Children's Bureau.

Davis, G.E. and Leitenberg, H. (1987) 'Adolescent sex offenders', *Psychological Bulletin*, 101: 417–27.

Department of Health (1991) *Children and Young Persons on Child Protection Registers, Year Ending 31 March 1990 (England)*, London: Department of Health, Personal Social Services, Local Authority Statistics.

Dingwall, R., Eekelaar, J. and Murray, T. (1983) *The Protection of Children, State Intervention and Family Life*, Oxford: Basil Blackwell.

Edgar, D. (1988a) *First Report upon the Inquiry into Strategies to Deal with the Issue of Community Violence*, for the Parliament of Victoria, Australia, Social Development Committee.

—— (1988b) 'Child abuse: social forces and prevention', paper for conference on *Prevention of Child Abuse*, Child, Adolescent and Family Health Service, Adelaide, May.

Fehrenbach, P.A., Smith, W., Monastersky, C. and Deisher, R.W. (1986) 'Adolescent sexual offenders: offender and offense characteristics', *American Journal of Orthopsychiatry*, 56: 225–33

Finkelhor, D. (1978) 'Sexual victimization of children in a normal population', paper given at the 2nd International Congress on Child Abuse and Neglect, London, September.

—— (1979a) 'Social forces in the formulation of the problem of sexual abuse', early version of Ch. 1 in *Sexually Victimized Children*, New York: Free Press.

—— (1979b) *Sexually Victimized Children*, New York: Free Press.

—— (1981a) 'Sexual abuse of boys, the available data', *Family Violence Research Program*, Durham: University of New Hampshire.

—— (1981b) 'Four preconditions of sexual abuse: a model', paper presented to the National Conference of Family Violence Research, Durham, NH, *Family Violence Research Program*, Durham: University of New Hampshire.

—— (1984) *Child Sexual Abuse: New Theory and Research*, New York: Free Press.

—— (1985) 'Sexual abuse and physical abuse: some critical differences', in E.H. Newberger and R. Bourne (eds) *Unhappy Families*, Littleton, MA.: PSG.

—— (ed.) (1986a) *A Sourcebook on Child Sexual Abuse*, Beverly Hills, CA: Sage.

—— (1986b) 'The adolescent sexual perpetrator: a new challenge in the field of sexual abuse', keynote address at *Treating the Juvenile Sexual Abuse Perpetrator*, a national training conference, Bloomington, MN, April.

—— (1988) 'The trauma of child sexual abuse – two models', *Journal of Interpersonal Violence*, 2: 356.

—— (1990) 'New ideas for child sexual abuse prevention', in *Understanding and Managing Child Sexual Abuse*, Australia: Harcourt Brace Jovanovich.

Finkelhor, D. and Russell, D. (1983) 'How much sexual abuse is committed by women', *Family Violence Research Programme*, Durham: University of New Hampshire.

Finkelhor, D., Hotaling, G., Lewis, I.A. and Smith, C. (1990) 'Sexual abuse in a national survey of adult men and women: prevalence, characteristics, and risk factors', *Child Abuse and Neglect*, 14: 19–28.

Fraser, B.G. (1981) 'Sexual child abuse: legislation and law in the US', in P.B. Mrazek and C.H. Kempe (eds) *Sexually Abused Children and Their Families*, Oxford: Pergamon Press.

French, M. (1990) 'Prison intervention programs', proceedings of *Sex Offenders, Management Strategies for the 1990s Conference*, Melbourne.

Freud, A. (1981) 'A psychoanalyst's view of sexual abuse by parents', in P.B. Mrazek and C.H. Kempe (eds) *Sexually Abused Children and Their Families*, Oxford: Pergamon Press.

Furniss, T. (1991) *The Multi-professional Handbook of Child Sexual Abuse*, London: Routledge.

Giarretto, H. (1989) 'Community-based treatment of the incest family', *Psychiatric Clinics of North America*, 12 (2): 351–61.

Glaser, D. and Collins, C. (1989) 'The response of young, non-sexually abused children to anatomically correct dolls', *Journal of Child Psychology and Psychiatry* 30 (4): 547–60.

Goddard, C. and Hiller, P. (1989) 'Tracking child sexual abuse', *Legal Service Bulletin*, 14 (1): 25–8.

Goldman, J. (in press) 'Children's sexual cognition and its implications for children's court testimony in child sexual abuse cases', *Australian Journal of Marriage and Family*.

Goldman, R. and Goldman, J. (1986) 'Australian children's sexual experiences within the family', paper presented at the 6th International Congress of Child Abuse and Neglect, Sydney.

—— (1988a) *Show Me Yours*, Australia: Penguin.

—— (1988b) 'The prevalence and nature of child sexual abuse in Australia', *Australian Journal of Sex, Marriage & Family*, 9 (2): 94–106

Harper, J. (1988) 'Recognizing sexually abused children through their stories, artwork and play', *Australian Journal of Early Childhoold*, 13 (1): 35–8.

Harrison, L. (1990) 'The SAIF Programme: community based prevention of sexual assault in families', paper given at *National Child Protection Conference*, Macquarie University, Sydney.

Hartman, C.R. (1988) 'Information processing of trauma', *Journal of Interpersonal Violence*, 3 (4): 443–57.

Hartman, C.R. and Burgess, A.W. (1987) 'Child molestation: assessing impact in multiple victims, Parts I and II', *Archives of Psychiatric Nursing*, 1 (1): 33–46.

Henderson, D. (1972) 'Incest: a synthesis of data', *Canadian Psychiatric Association Journal*, 17: 299–313.

Hiller, P.C. and Goddard, C.R. (1990) 'Family violence and the sexual and physical abuse of children: some empirical light on theoretical darkness', *Proceedings of the Third Annual Conference of the Victorian Society for the Prevention of Child Abuse and Neglect*, Port Melbourne: VicSPAN.

Hobbs, C.J. and Wynne, J.M. (1989) 'Sexual abuse of English boys and girls: the importance of anal examination', *Child Abuse and Neglect*, 13: 195–210

Hough, M. and Mayhew, P. (1985) *Taking Account of Crime: Key Findings from the 1984 British Crime Survey*, Home Office Research Study 85, London: HM Stationery Office.

Kavoussi, R.J., Kaplan, M. and Becker, J.V. (1988) 'Psychiatric diagnoses in adolescent sexual offenders', *Journal of the American Academy of Child and Adolescent Psychiatry*, 27: 241–3.

Kaye, M. and Winefield, H. (1988) 'Child sexual abuse: a cybernetic description and its implications for professionals', *A.N.Z. Fam. Ther.*, 9 (3): 131–8.

Kempe, R.S. and Kempe, C.H. (1978) *Child Abuse*, London: Fontana.

Law Reform Commission of Victoria (1988) *Report No. 18: Sexual Offences against Children – Research Reports*, Victoria.

Lawrance, K. (1989) *Statement Validity Analysis: Evaluation Report*, Domestic Violence and Child Abuse Unit, West Yorkshire Police, West Yorkshire.

Meiselman, K.C. (1979) *Incest: A Psychological Study of Causes and Effects*, San Francisco: Jossey-Bass.

Morrison, T. (1989) 'Treating the untreatable? Groupwork with intrafamilial sex offenders', *The Treatment of Child Sex Abuse: NSPCC Occasional Papers Series No. 7*, London: NSPCC, pp. 6–13.

Mrazek, P.B., Lynch, M.A. and Bentovim, A. (1983) 'Sexual abuse of children in the United Kingdom', *Child Abuse and Neglect*, 7: 147–53

NCH (National Children's Homes) (1990) *Survey of Treatment Facilities for Abused Children and of Treatment Facilities for Young Sexual Abusers of Children*, London: The Department of Health.

National Deaf Children's Society *You Choose*, Leeds: Keep Deaf Children Safe.

NSPCC (National Society for the Prevention of Cruelty to Children) (1989) *Child Sexual Abuse in Greater Manchester, A Regional Profile of Child Sexual Abuse Registrations*, Manchester: NSPCC.

—— (1990) *Working with the Aftermath of Child Sexual Abuse*, Manchester: NSPCC.

New South Wales Department of Education (1989a) *Child Protection 7–12*, Sydney: NSW Department of Education.

—— (1989b) *Child Protection K6*, Sydney: NSW Department of Education.

—— (1989c) *Child Protection – Students with an Intellectual Disability*, Sydney: NSW Department of Education

Oates, R.K. (ed.) (1990) *Understanding and Managing Child Sexual Abuse*, Australia: Harcourt Brace Jovanovich.

'Pigot Report' (1989) *Report of The Advisory Group on Video Evidence*, London: Home Office.

Prison Reform Trust (1990) *Sex Offenders in Prison*, London: Prison Reform Trust.

Queensland Centre for Prevention of Child Abuse (1989) *Newsletter*, 3: 1.

Renvoize, J. (1978) *Web of Violence – A Study of Family Violence*, London: Routledge & Kegan Paul.

—— (1982) *Incest – A Family Pattern*, London: Routledge & Kegan Paul.

Rose, L. (1991) *The Erosion of Childhood*, London: Routledge.

Russell, D.E.H. (1983) 'The incidence and prevalence of intrafamilial and extrafamilial sexual abuse of female children', *Child Abuse and Neglect*, 7: 133–46.

—— (1984) *Sexual Exploitation: Rape, Child Sexual Abuse and Workplace Harassment*, Beverly Hills, CA: Sage.

—— (1986) *The Secret Trauma: Incest in the Lives of Girls and Women*, New York: Basic Books.

Ryerson, E. (1984) 'Sexual abuse and self-protection education for developmentally disabled youth: a priority need', *SIECUS Report XIII*, 1: 6–7.

Scott, D. (1989) 'Legally enforced treatment of the incestually abusing parent – problems of policy and practice', *Journal of Social Welfare Law*, 4.

Sgroi, S.M. (1977) 'Kids with clap: gonorrhoea as an indicator of child sexual assault', *Victimology*, 11: 251–67.

Spring, J. (1987) *Cry Hard and Swim*, London: Virago.

Steven, I., Castell-McGregor, S., Francis, J. and Winefield, H. (1988) 'Child sexual abuse', *Australian Family Physician*, 17: 427.

Tilelli, J.A., Turek, D. and Jaffe, A.C. (1980) 'Sexual abuse of children: clinical findings and implications for management', *New England Journal of Medicine*, 302: 319–23.

Vinson, T. (1988) 'Why child abuse appears to have increased', *Modern Medicine of Australia*, September: 62–73.

Vizard, E. (1988) 'Child sexual abuse: the child's experience', *British Journal of Psychotherapy*, 5 (1): 77–91.

—— (1989) 'Child sexual abuse and mental handicap: a child psychiatrist's perspective', in H. Brown and A. Craft (eds) *Thinking the Unthinkable – Papers on Sexual Abuse and People with Learning Difficulties*, London: FPA Education Unit.

Walmsley, S. (1989) 'The need for safeguards', in H. Brown and A. Craft (eds) *Thinking the Unthinkable – Papers on Sexual Abuse and People with Learning Difficulties*, London: FPA Education Unit.

Weinburg, S.K. (1955) *Incest Behaviour*, New York: Citadel.

West, D.J. (1985) *Sexual Victimisation*, Aldershot: Gower.

—— (1987) *Sexual Crimes and Confrontations*, Cambridge Studies in Criminology LVII, Aldershot: Gower.

Westcott, H., Davies, G. and Clifford, B. (1989) 'The use of anatomical dolls in child witness interviews', *Adoption and Fostering* 13 (2): 6.

White S., Strom G., Santilli G. and Halpin B. (1986) 'Interviewing young children with anatomically correct dolls', *Child Abuse and Neglect*, 10: 519–29.

Williams, L.M. and Finkelhor, D. (1988) 'The characteristics of incestuous fathers: a review of recent studies', Family Research Laboratory, Durham: University of New Hampshire.

Winefield, H.R. (1987) 'Child sexual abuse cases: facilitating their detection and reporting by general practitioners', *Australian Journal of Social Issues* 22 (3): 28.

—— (1988) 'Psychologists' experiences and views in relation to child sexual abuse', *Australian Psychologist*, 23 (1): 16.

Winefield, H.R. and Castell-McGregor, S.N. (1986) 'Experiences and views of
    general practitioners concerning sexually-abused children', *The Medical
    Journal of Australia*, 145: 312
Woman's Own (1986) 'Report on Rape Survey of 10 May', 23 August.

Index